Cambridge Studies in Social Anthropology

General Editors

M.FORTES, J.R.GOODY, E.R.LEACH, S.J.TAMBIAH

No. 9

ELITE POLITICS IN RURAL INDIA

Political Stratification and Political Alliances
in Western Maharashtra

OTHER TITLES IN THE SERIES

1
The Political Organization of Unyamwezi
R. G. ABRAHAMS

2
Buddhism and the Spirit Cults in North-East Thailand
S. J. TAMBIAH

3
Kalahari Village Politics: An African Democracy
ADAM KUPER

4
The Rope of Moka:
Big-men and Ceremonial Exchange in Mount Hagen, New Guinea
ANDREW STRATHERN

5
The Majangir:
Ecology and Society of a Southwest Ethiopian People
JACK STAUDER

6
Buddhist Monk, Buddhist Layman:
A Study of Urban Monastic Organization in Central Thailand
JANE BUNNAG

7
Contexts of Kinship:
An Essay in the Family Sociology of the Gonja of Northern Ghana
ESTHER N. GOODY

8
Marriage among a Matrilineal Elite
CHRISTINE OPPONG

Elite Politics in Rural India

Political stratification and political alliances in Western Maharashtra

ANTHONY T.CARTER

Department of Anthropology, University of Rochester

CAMBRIDGE
UNIVERSITY PRESS

Published by the Syndics of the Cambridge University Press
Bentley House, 200 Euston Road, London NW1 2DB
American Branch: 32 East 57th Street, New York, N.Y. 10022

First published 1974

Library of Congress Catalogue Card Number: 73–86043

ISBN: 0 521 20366 x

Printed in Great Britain by
William Clowes & Sons, Limited
London, Beccles and Colchester

Contents

List of illustrations vi
Acknowledgements ix

Part 1
Introduction

1 The problem   3
2 The region: Girvi, Phaltan Taluka, and
   Western Maharashtra   15

Part 2
Aspects of political stratification

3 Political arenas and the political class   29
4 Caste status and distribution   49
5 Land, labour, credit, and share capital   59
6 Descent groups and affinal networks   77

Part 3
Political alliances

7   Vertical alliances   101
8   Horizontal alliances   127
9   Alliances and political stratification   147
10 Conclusions   162

Map of main Girvi settlement area 179
Appendix 185
Notes 188
References 195
Index 203

Illustrations

Figures

1   The distribution of offices in Girvi   4
2   Girvi population by caste and settlement   16
3   Girvi registered voters by caste and ward   38
4   Credit and marketing co-operatives   40
5   The distribution of offices in Phaltan Taluka   47
6   Castes in Satara District   52
7   Caste rank in Girvi   54
8   Caste composition of urban and rural areas   56
9   Caste composition of selected villages   57
10 Distribution of occupancy rights in Girvi land,
    1966–7   70
11 Caste affiliation of gəḍis employed by Girvi
    vətəndar Marathas, 1966–7   73
12 Access to agricultural credit in Girvi, 1966–7   74
13 Ownership of shares in area co-operatives   75
14 Marathi kinship terms used by non-Brahmins   78
15 Family composition among Girvi Marathas   90
16 Marriage distances of Vətəndar Marathas in
    Girvi   94
17 Marriage distances of non-vətəndar Marathas in
    Girvi   95
18 Intra-village marriages among Girvi Marathas   96
19 Results of 1966 Girvi Panchayat Election   124
20 Kinship connections linking the Raja of Phaltan
    to some of his allies   140
21 Shriram Sugar Factory election alliances   148

Genealogies

1   *Vərči ali* Kadams   80

Illustrations

2   *Khalči ali* Kadams   82
3   Dhumalvadi Marathas   85
4   Bodkevadi Marathas   85
5   Jadhavvada Marathas   86

Maps
1   Maharashtra State   2
2   Phaltan Taluka   20
3   Main Girvi Settlement Area   179

Acknowledgements

The following work is a revised version of a dissertation submitted for the Ph.D. degree at Cambridge University in 1970. It is based on fieldwork carried out from October 1965 until September 1967. The research was supported by a Fellowship and Research Grant from the National Institute of Mental Health, Bethesda, Maryland, USA. In revising the dissertation I have made no attempt to keep up to date with current Indian politics. The book thus deals with events which took place in 1965–7 or earlier and does not touch on such important later events as the 1969 split in the Congress Party. I do not feel that this constitutes a serious weakness, however, for as far as I know nothing has occurred to alter the patterns of stratification and alliances described here.

I am grateful to my supervisor, Dr E. R. Leach, for much useful advice. His comments, as well as those of my dissertation examiners, S. J. Tambiah and F. G. Bailey, have been very helpful.

The late Professor Mrs Irawati Karve advised me while I was in India. It was she who suggested that I work in Phaltan and I also am indebted to her for sharing with me her vast knowledge of things Indian. Mr and Mrs B. V. Nimbkar, Professor Karve's daughter and son-in-law, kindly took me into their home in Phaltan while I was searching for a suitable village and introduced me to many of Phaltan's leading citizens. Mrs Y. B. Damle taught me Marathi with great patience and thoroughness.

I enjoyed and profited by many stimulating conversations with my colleagues J. P. Parry and Maxine Bernsen both in India and in Cambridge.

Nilakantrao and Tarabai Kamble, with whom I lived in Girvi, gave me a home, a family, and love. They made me feel a part of Maharashtra and I dedicate this book to them.

Department of Anthropology   Anthony Carter
University of Rochester
February 1973

PART 1
INTRODUCTION

Map 1   Maharashtra State

1
The problem

This study is a descriptive analysis of political stratification and political alliances in rural Western Maharashtra. My primary focus is Girvi, a large village on the southern boundary of Phaltan Taluka near the northwest corner of Satara District, but the analysis also deals with more inclusive political arenas: Phaltan Taluka, Maharashtra Legislative Assembly constituencies which overlap with Phaltan Taluka and, to a limited degree, Satara District. I make a few references to political stratification and alliances in Phaltan Municipality as well in order to contrast political activity in a small market town with that in more strictly rural areas.

POLITICAL STRATIFICATION AND UNSTABLE ALLIANCES

It long has been a commonplace among interested participants and observers that one important feature of Indian politics is the fact that power in the countryside is distributed unequally. Thus Mountstuart Elphinstone, Commissioner of the Deccan when the territories which include what is now called Western Maharashtra were annexed by the British in 1818, understood that orderly government could not be maintained without the support of the rural elite and he sought at every step to ally British rule with what he regarded as the rural aristocracy, the hereditary village officers as well as the great and small *jagirdars* (see Elphinstone 1821 and Ballhatchet 1957). Similarly, from studies such as those of Seal (1968) and Broomfield (1966, 1968) we learn to see Indian Independence not simply as the replacement of European imperialism by Indian nationalism and democracy but also as a complex process of elite circulation. Concern with political stratification in the form of elite segments of the population or of dominant castes figures largely, too, in studies of contemporary local, state, and national politics in India and in evaluation of such development programs as the 'green revolution'. In spite of all this attention, however, political stratification has been the subject of few detailed empirical studies, especially above the village level. One purpose of this study is to begin to fill that gap.

An approximate idea of the unequal distribution of power in rural Western Maharashtra, and one which strikes the observer very early, can be

3

obtained from an examination of office-holders in Girvi (see Fig. 1). It must be remembered, however, that the distribution of power and the distribution of office are not completely equivalent. Some office-holders have no power, while some very powerful persons hold no office. Nor are all office-holders equally powerful.

Fig. 1   The distribution of offices in Girvi

	Marathas		Other castes	Total
	vətəndar	non-*vətəndar*		
Share of total population	24.8%	32.1%	43.1%	100%
Number of offices held	20	2	8	30
	(66.7%)	(6.7%)	(26.%)	(100.1%)
No. of individual office-holders	19	2	7	28
	(67.9%)	(7.1%)	(25.0%)	(100%)
No. of joint families with office-holders	15	2	7	24
	(62.5%)	(8.3%)	(29.2%)	(100%)

Leaving aside the Talathi, keeper of land records appointed by the government of Maharashtra, who is an outsider, there are thirty offices in Girvi: thirteen Panchayat (village council) members, nine members of the Managing Committee of the Multi-Purpose Credit Society, five members of the Managing Committee of the Lift-Irrigation Society, secretaries for each of the co-operative societies, and a Police Patil. The two secretaries and the Police Patil are appointed by authorities outside the village, the Patil from among the members of a particular localized patrilineage. All of the other office-holders are elected. In addition, the Panchayat elects from among its own members a chairman and a vice-chairman, and each co-operative society elects a chairman. The chairmen of the three elected bodies are the most influential office-holders.

The thirty offices in Girvi are held by twenty-eight persons. The Secretary of the Lift-Irrigation Society is also a member of the Panchayat and the Police Patil is also a member of the Managing Committee of the Lift-Irrigation Society.

The concentration of office-holding is greater, however, than the analysis of it in terms of individuals indicates. The thirty offices are held by persons who are members of twenty-four joint families. In one case the eldest of six joint brothers is Chairman of the Lift-Irrigation Society and former Chairman of the Panchayat, the fifth brother is a member of the Panchayat, and the youngest brother is a member of the Managing Committee of the Multi-Purpose Credit Society. (The eldest of the six brothers is also Vice-Chairman of the Managing Committee of the Shriram Co-operative

Sugar Factory in Phaltan town.) The brother of the Vice-Chairman of the Panchayat is a member and former Chairman of the Managing Committee of the Multi-Purpose Credit Society. The Police Patil's brother's wife is a member of the Panchayat.

Viewed in terms of caste membership the concentration of office-holding is greater still. Twenty-two of the thirty offices are held by members of the Maratha caste, the dominant caste in rural Maharashtra with roughly fifty-five per cent of the population. Of the eight offices held by non-Marathas, five are the result of special features of the electoral law rather than a reflection of the distribution of power. Two offices are reserved for members of the Scheduled Castes. A few members of other minority castes are able to win election to the Panchayat because candidates stand for election in geographically defined wards in which their castes are numerically significant. Within the Maratha caste an important distinction is made between *vətəndars*, members of patrilineages which traditionally held estates in office and land, and non-*vətəndars* or, as they were formerly called, Kunbis. The Marathas as a whole comprise about fifty-seven per cent of the population of Girvi and the *vətəndars* about twenty-five per cent, but twenty of the thirty offices, and all of the important ones, are held by *vətəndar* Marathas.

It is apparent, then, that power in rural Western Maharashtra is concentrated in the hands of relatively few persons and that a large majority of those who hold power are members of one small section of the population. To borrow terms from the study of political stratification in Occidental countries, there is what C. Wright Mills calls a 'power elite' consisting of a relatively small number of persons who are in a position to influence public decisions (see Mills 1959:3–29). Some sections of the population are represented disproportionately in the power elite and these sections may be termed the 'political class' (see Bottomore 1966). In the rural portions of Western Maharashtra the political class consists almost exclusively of the dominant *vətəndar* Marathas. However, in towns and in those villages where Marathas form a small part of the population the political class includes other groups as well.

Another striking feature of Indian politics is the instability of political alliances at certain levels of the political system. If alliances are examined in terms of the relations between leaders and followers in their roles as members of castes, as patrons, clients, landlords, or tenants there often seems to be considerable stability. However, when one focuses on the political elite their political choices often seem unrelated to their roles as party members, patrons or landlords, or to their positions in the caste and kinship systems, and one finds that alliances among the elite frequently

5

are very unstable. This feature of Indian politics has been well known at least since Weiner's (1957) study of the development of India's multi-party system in the early years of Independence in which he noted the contrast between the relatively stable alliances between leaders and followers within what he called 'factions' and the unstable alliances between faction leaders. Concern with the possibly harmful consequences of unstable alliances may have reached its peak in India in the months following the 1967 General Election when frequent floor crossings led to the fall of the governments of Madhya Pradesh, Haryana, West Bengal, Punjab, and other Indian states. When the Haryana government fell in November 1967 thirty-seven of the seventy-nine Members of the Haryana Legislative Assembly had crossed the floor in the previous eight months and four of them had done so four times (*Manchester Guardian*, 22 November 1967). After the fall of the Madhya Pradesh government in July 1967 Jayaprakash Narayan said that defectors who did not resign and seek fresh mandates from their constituents should be 'gheraoed', confined to their homes by demonstrators (*The Indian Express*, 26 July 1967). Leaders of many parties called for an agreement among the parties to refuse membership to defectors who had not obtained a fresh mandate.

The Maharashtra Congress Ministry has not suffered from such defections, but they are not unknown in the State. Thus in 1957 the Raja of Phaltan, Malojirao Naik Nimbalkar, was the Congress candidate for the Legislative Assembly from the Phaltan–Khandala constituency. He was defeated by Haribhau Nimbalkar, a local labor leader backed by the Samyukta Maharashtra Samiti, a coalition of opposition parties which sought the division of Bombay into linguistic states. In 1967 the Raja and his son, Vijaysingh, resigned from the Congress. Vijaysingh stood for the Legislative Assembly in Phaltan-Khandala as an Independent backed by the Sampoorna Maharashtra Samiti, the successor to the earlier Samyukta Maharashtra Samiti. He was defeated by the Congress candidate, his former ally, K. R. Bhoite. Bhoite was supported by Haribhau Nimbalkar, now a Congressman.

Faced with the fact that in such fluid alliance systems there is no apparent connection between political alliances and such institutions as caste, class, kinship, and community some observers have characterized Indian politics as 'patternless'. Thus Brass writes that

The merging and mixing of regions and peoples in Uttar Pradesh combines with a lack of communication throughout the state among members of ethnic groups to produce a relatively complex politics without clear patterns. The factional character of internal Congress politics in the State also tends to produce patternless politics. (1965:32)

6

The problem

Political coalitions are not based on natural interest groups, but instead are mere factions. It is in this vein that Brass argues that 'a system of factional politics', characterized by a high degree of instability of alliances within and among coalitions,

may develop in any society under certain objective conditions. Three conditions have contributed to the development of the factional system of the Uttar Pradesh Congress: the absence of an external threat, the presence of an internal consensus upon ideological issues, and the absence of authoritative leadership. (1965:232)

In addition to these conditions, however, Brass attributes the instability of alliances in the Uttar Pradesh Congress to the availability of a multiplicity of patronage sources and to the 'status motivations of individual faction members and leaders' (1965:152). Status aspirations lead faction personnel to seek new alliances while the availability of alternative sources of patronage ensures that such changes are possible. Once one man changes his alliances the movement is communicated throughout the factional system according to the principle that 'the enemy of an enemy is a friend' (Brass 1965:151). Thus, although certain objective conditions permit a factional system to develop, the motive forces behind such a development, in this view, are individual status aspirations and irrational personal antagonisms (Brass 1965:168–82; see also Weiner 1957:251). This is what Brass means, I think, when he argues that in a status orientated factional political system such as the Uttar Pradesh Congress 'personal enmity is the primary organizing principle of factional conflict' (1965:328).

Speculations concerning the personality characteristics of Indian politicians are unnecessary, however, for the instability of political alliances in India can be explained much more simply by reference to the elite nature of Indian politics. What is more, such an explanation will account for the areas of stable alliances in the Indian system as well. The second aim of this study, then, is to delineate some of the connections between political stratification and the pattern of political alliances.

To say that Indian politics are dominated by a powerful elite recruited predominantly from a small political class is to argue that there is a discontinuity in the distribution of power. Although the chairman of a district council is much more powerful than the chairman of a village panchayat, both are members of the power elite and have some influence on political decisions, as may members of the political class who have privileged access to official and unofficial positions of influence. Persons who are outside the political class have no such influence. The political system is so structured and managed that even their vote often counts for nothing. It follows that we may distinguish two kinds of political alliances, vertical and horizontal. Vertical alliances are those between elite leaders and

7

members of the political class generally, on the one hand, and their followers outside the political class, on the other. Horizontal alliances are those between one elite leader or political class member and another. As I shall argue, vertical alliances occur primarily within village arenas and are most often based on ties of economic dependence. Horizontal alliances are found in all political arenas. They sometimes are influenced by ties of caste and kinship, but purely tactical considerations are of much greater importance. Vertical alliances are relatively stable, while horizontal alliances are relatively unstable.

SOCIAL STRUCTURE AND SOCIAL ORGANIZATION

Of the two tasks which I have set myself in this essay, the first, to describe the pattern of political stratification in rural Western Maharashtra, is relatively straightforward, but the second, to delineate the relations between political stratification and the pattern of alliances in the region, is extremely complex. I must examine the impact of political stratification on political alliances in all the arenas for which I have data and also on different sorts of occasions. At the same time I must consider the influence on political alliances of caste, class, and kinship, for much of the literature on Indian politics suggests that these are important variables. I attempt to analyse this complex of relationships by using the distinction between social structure and social organization. In particular I regard political alliances as the result of decisions to extend or withhold support or cooperation and, therefore, as an aspect of what Firth calls 'social organization', i.e. 'the systematic ordering of social relations by acts of choice and decision' (Firth 1961:40), and I then attempt to show how these decisions are related to a variety of antecedent structural frameworks which 'serve to define and restrict the alternatives which are offered to each actor' (Barth 1959a:3). Although I consider the role of caste and kinship, I argue that the most important structural frameworks are the pattern of political stratification and the system of governmental and administrative arenas of political action.

In his lectures on *Models of Social Organization* (1966) Barth distinguishes between descriptions of patterns of regularity and explanation of the processes which generate such regularities. In his view,

Explanation is not achieved by a description of the patterns of regularity, no matter how meticulous and adequate, nor by replacing this description by other abstractions congruent with it, but by exhibiting what *makes* the pattern, i.e. certain processes. To study social forms, it is certainly necessary but hardly sufficient to be able to describe them. To give an explanation of social forms, it is sufficient to describe the processes that generate the form. (1966:2)

8

The problem

Most previous accounts of local-level politics in India have been attempts to describe patterns of regularity. The patterns are quite complex, however, and the attempts have met with only limited success; some observers even have felt that there are elements of irrationality and unpredictability in the behavior they attempt to describe (e.g. Brass 1965:238). Barth's studies of Pathan leadership and coalition formation (1959a and 1959b), Bailey's work on confrontations (1968), Mayer's work on action-sets and quasi-groups (1966), and the present analysis of alliances in rural Western Maharashtra, on the other hand, are attempts at explanatory, generative models. All are concerned with social organization, which, as Firth notes, introduces a dynamic element into the anthropologist's analytical framework.

Structural forms set a precedent and provide a limitation to the range of alternatives possible – the arc within which seemingly free choice is exercisable is often very small. But it is the possibility of alternative that makes for variability. A person chooses, consciously or unconsciously, which course he will follow. And his decision will affect the future structural alignment. In the aspect of social structure is to be found the continuity principle of society; in the aspect of organization is to be found the variation or change principle – by allowing evaluation of situations and entry of individual choice. (Firth 1961:40; see also Firth 1954, 1955 and 1964.)

Analyses of social organization in terms of generative models raise a number of important theoretical questions. Barth observes that the value of such models is that they allow us to test our explanations of the relations between structural frameworks and organizational choices by observing the consequences of variations in the frameworks. In order to use generative models in this manner, however, we need to know (1) how structural frameworks are interconnected, (2) how organizational decisions are influenced by structural frameworks, and (3) how organizational decisions, in turn, affect structural frameworks. I must stress that my analysis of political alliances in rural Western Maharashtra is too crude to advance our understanding of these problems very far, but I do want to make a few brief comments in order to put my argument into perspective.

Anthropological understanding of the connections between structural frameworks is well advanced, but we have made little progress on the relations between decisions and frameworks. My own analysis is a case in point. I am able to show how a particular pattern of unstable alliances is reasonable given a certain configuration of structural constraints, but I am unable to deduce the pattern of alliances from the configuration of constraints. Nor has this issue been faced squarely by those who have written most extensively on social organization. Firth writes only that 'structural forms set a precedent and provide a limitation to the range of alternatives

9

Introduction

possible' (1961:40), while Barth argues that structural frameworks 'serve to define and restrict the alternatives which are offered to each actor' (1959a:3). In his later lectures on generative models Barth states that transactional or organizational behavior

takes place with reference to a set of values which serve as generalized incentives and constraints on choice; it also takes place with reference to a pre-established matrix of statuses, seen as a distribution of values on positions in the form of minimal clusters of jurally binding rights. (1966:5)

This is all very well, but Barth's claim to have generated or deduced patterns of regularity from such distributions of values is overstated.

The problem is a very difficult one because, as such diverse scholars as Leach (1954) and Levi (1949) have shown, the system of structural frameworks upon which action is based in any given society is likely to be ambiguous and self-contradictory in at least some respects. Leaving such difficulties aside, however, the problem of generating organization from structure seems to resolve into two major parts. It is a matter of interests and constraints, of carrots and sticks. Some courses of action are prohibited; of those which are not prohibited, some are likely to prove more successful than others in achieving given interests. Our difficulty is less in understanding what actions are prohibited than in understanding why some permitted actions are preferred over others.

Two developments in social theory may provide us with some help in elucidating the relations between organizational decisions and antecedent structural frameworks. As Barth notes (1966:5), the theory of games is a generative model of just the sort he advocates. Given a particular set of rules and a minimax definition of rational behavior, the theory of games allows one rigorously to deduce optimal organizational strategies. But the interests and constraints which are operative in the situations with which anthropologists typically are concerned rarely can be stated with the rigor demanded by the theory of games. Nor do optimal minimax strategies seem to do full justice to the ambiguities of actual behavior. The results of Riker's (1962) attempt to apply games theory to the analysis of political coalitions, for example, are indeterminate; the data neither confirm nor refute the theory.

The work of Fortes on domain theory also is of use in connection with generative models. Fortes nowhere defines what he means by 'domain', 'trusting that its import would show in its usage' (1969:87), but a careful reading of his analyses of the Tallensi and Ashanti social systems (see especially 1945, 1949a, 1949b, 1953a, 1953b, and 1969) reveals that he so far has identified three domains: (1) ritual, (2) politico-jural, and (3) domestic or familial. Each domain consists of a class of ideas or rules concerning social relations distinguished by the manner in which they are sanctioned and the interests which they serve. Thus the domestic domain consists of ideas or rules which are morally sanctioned and serve the interests of individuals. Those ideas and rules concerning social relations which may be ascribed to the politico-jural domain are legally sanctioned and serve the interests of groups within the total society. Those which may be ascribed to the ritual domain are mystically sanctioned and serve the interests of the entire society. The manner in which Fortes defines these three domains is consonant with his understanding of the

functionalist hypothesis that the customs and institutions of any people make up a system of interdependent parts and elements, which work together to maintain the system in a steady state and have value for the realisation of legitimate social and personal goals. (1953b:193)

It should be noted that this view of functional explanation, with its concern for 'the realisation of legitimate social and personal goals', makes room for what Firth calls social organization, and, indeed, properly understood Fortes' analysis of *The Dynamics of Clanship among the Tallensi* (1945) and of households among the Ashanti (1949b) are examples of powerful generative models. The important point here, however, is that the concept of domain enables us to begin weighing the various constraints which enter into organizational decisions. Fortes is quite explicit about this aim and has criticized Malinowski's concept of culture, for example, because it does not provide a means to differentiate aspects of social relations in terms of their contribution to social structure (1953a:20). The problem, he writes, is one of

assigning an order of relative weight to the various factors involved in culture and in social organization, or alternatively of devising methods for describing and analyzing a configuration of factors so as to show precisely how they interact with one another. (1953a:25)

Fortes' notion of domain may serve as a first step in sorting out the relations between organization and structure in generative models because it helps us to identify social relations serving 'different collective interests, which are perhaps connected in some sort of hierarchy' (1953a:29). If nothing else it discourages us from thinking of all the constraints on choice as of equal weight. I shall make use of this concept at several points in my argument, but especially in my discussion of the effects on political choice of caste and kinship. In discussing aspects of political strategy, on the other hand, I shall make some use of concepts borrowed from the theory of games.

As I noted earlier, the third major issue raised by the use of generative models of social organization has to do with the effects of organizational

Introduction

decisions upon the structural frameworks in terms of which they were made. Because my own research covers only a short interval of time I cannot deal with this issue in a satisfactory manner in this study, but in my summary remarks I will indicate several areas in which additional research might prove fruitful.

Finally, it must be emphasized again that the distinction between social structure and organization is an analytic or heuristic device. Structure and organization refer to different abstract qualities of action and not to different kinds of concrete actions (see Parsons 1949:27–41). What in one context may be seen as a structural framework underlying organizational decisions may be viewed in another context as the result of many individual decisions made in terms of still other frameworks. It is possible to regard rules of descent, for example, as a structural antecedent of political decisions, but it is equally possible to analyse some aspects of descent group formation as the outcome of decisions regarding succession, inheritance, and so on made in terms of such antecedent factors as the economic and political systems. Nevertheless, the distinction between structure and organization is not an arbitrary one. On the contrary it parallels the position in which the individual decision-maker finds himself. A politician, for example, is aware that the strategy of other politicians must be taken into account when making his own choices, but there are many other factors that he treats as the permanent structure of the situation in which he must act. And the actor's view of the structure of the situation in which he must act varies with the kind of decision he must make.

THE ARGUMENT

The argument which follows is divided into two parts. Part 2, Chapters 3 through 6, has a dual purpose. Its primary aim is to describe the pattern of political stratification in rural Western Maharashtra, to identify the political class and describe its ramifications in the caste, class, and kinship systems. A secondary aim is to describe the system of governmental and administrative frameworks of political action and also the caste, economic, and kinship systems in sufficient detail that one can discern to what degree and in what manner they influence the pattern of political alliances independently of their role in political stratification.

Chapter 3 deals with the modern administrative and governmental frameworks of political activity. These institutions are the arenas of political action (see Bailey 1963b:224). They determine the nature of the participants in the political system, lay down the actions which are open or forbidden to them, and provide many of the rewards for successful choices of action. Chapter 3 concludes with a brief analysis of the political elite in terms of caste identity and estate (*vatən*) possession. This analysis demonstrates the existence and composition of the political class. Subsequent chapters in Part 2 are concerned with its caste, economic, and kinship characteristics.

Chapter 4 is concerned with the relations between political stratification and caste and also contains an account of the caste hierarchy in Western Maharashtra and of the distribution of castes in the villages and market town of Phaltan Taluka.

In Chapter 5 I analyse the distribution of wealth in Girvi. The politically dominant *vatəndar* Marathas are also the wealthiest class in the village. They own the largest amount of land, much of it irrigated. They are the principal employers in the village and they control the major sources of agricultural credit.

Chapter 6 deals with the differences in the kinship systems of the *vatəndar* and non-*vatəndar* sections of the population. The *vatəndars* place considerable emphasis on patrilineal descent and have large, localized, corporate patrilineages. *Vatəndars* marry others equal in status to themselves, often at a considerable distance and only rarely in their own villages. Non-*vatəndars* also marry persons equal in status to themselves, but they do not have to go to any great distance to find suitable marriage partners. Very often they marry within their own natal villages. Neither the patrilineages of the *vatəndars* nor those of the non-*vatəndars* are segmented into a merging series of sub-lineages. The only distinguishable group within the localized Maharashtrian patrilineage is the 'family' (*kutumb*). The large localized patrilineages and widely dispersed affinal networks of the *vatəndars* are both a reflection of and a means to the maintenance of their dominant position in Maharashtrian society. The number, size, and internal structure of their local patrilineages and the distribution of their affinal ties often influence their choice of political allies.

In Part 3, Chapters 7 through 10, the argument shifts from the structural antecedents of political choice to an examination of the details of political action, from structure to organization. Here the aim is to analyse the pattern of political alliances and to show how it is related to antecedent structural frameworks, especially the pattern of political stratification.

In Chapters 7 and 8 I deal in turn with the two forms of political alliance: vertical and horizontal. As I noted above, the relatively stable vertical alliances occur almost exclusively within village arenas, while the relatively unstable horizontal alliances occur in all arenas. The former are most often based on ties of economic dependence, while the latter, although sometimes influenced by caste and kinship, are generally based on principles of strategy which derive from the nature of the political arenas and the economics of patronage. This distribution of vertical and horizontal alliances results in part from the fact that politicians rarely make appeals directly to the mass of the electorate. Rather they resort to the second type of alliance and appeal to village leaders, lesser members of the political elite, to deliver the support of their villages. Politicians rarely have, and rarely attempt to have, direct relations with the electorate in villages other than their own. Most direct contact between the elite and non-elite occurs between residents of the same village. The distribution of political alliances is a function of occasion as well. Alliances between elite and non-elite occur more frequently during elections, both in villages and in more inclusive political arenas. Most of the time, however, the massing and displaying of support in any form based on vertical political alliances does not occur at all. Even in village arenas politics are dominated by alliances within the elite. The differential impact of caste and kinship on vertical and horizontal alliances is partly a function of the nature of these institutions and also of the manner in which they intersect the system of political arenas.

Chapter 9 is concerned with the relations between vertical and horizontal alliances in a network of such alliances. Although elite leaders have stable alliances with their followers outside the political class, they change their alliances within the elite very frequently. The instability of horizontal alliances is an indication that in some respects choices with regard to the two forms of alliances may be made independently. That is, a leader's choice of followers does not determine his choice of elite allies. Nor does his choice of elite allies determine his choice of followers. The independence of the two forms of political alliance is a consequence of the existence of the political elite. The privileged position of the elite, expressed and perpetuated by the frequent occurrence of uncontested and indirect elections and by the use of consensus decision-making procedures, encourages politicians to seek support primarily from other elite members rather than from the electorate at large and permits them to change their horizontal alliances without incurring adverse responses from their followers. Vertical and horizontal alliances are linked, however, by the economics of political patronage. It is the necessity of providing patronage for their followers which leads politicians to switch their horizontal alliances with surprising frequency, often ignoring considerations of caste or kinship, ideological commitments, party membership or personal loyalty.

2

The region: Girvi, Phaltan Taluka, and Western Maharashtra

The argument which follows may be understood in the context of two issues of general anthropological relevance. It is a contribution to the study of political stratification and also to the analysis of the relationships between social structure and social organization. At the same time the argument bears on issues peculiar to Western Maharashtra as a distinct region of India. The locality of my investigation, Girvi and Phaltan Taluka, is virtually in the center of Western Maharashtra. It may be assumed that the patterns of political stratification and political alliances found there are illustrative of those occurring throughout the region.

THE LOCALITY: GIRVI AND PHALTAN TALUKA

Girvi is located in Satara District just below the steep north slope of the Mahadev hills in the Nira valley. Consisting of several distinct settlements scattered over an area of twenty square miles (see Map 3, p. 179 and Fig. 2), the village lies along the southern boundary of Phaltan Taluka about six miles from Phaltan town, the taluka headquarters. A motorable dirt road links Girvi proper, the main settlement, to Phaltan and two or three times a day buses of the State Transport Corporation travel from Phaltan to Girvi and back, passing through the neighboring village of Nirgudi on the way. The homes of the residents of Girvi proper together with the principal village temples, the offices of the Panchayat and village co-operative societies, and the market yard are clustered on high ground between two branches of a stream which have their origin in the Mahadev hills a mile or two away. Although water as much as two feet deep may run in these streams for a few hours during and after a heavy monsoon rain, they are dry for by far the greatest part of the year. Dhumalvadi, the largest of the secondary settlements, is located about two miles to the east where another stream emerges from the hills, while Bodkevadi and Jadhavvada are located near other streams about a mile west and southwest of the main settlement. The entire area consists of low rocky hills good for little but grazing sheep interspersed with narrow valleys. The rainfall averages only eighteen inches a year and is extremely unreliable, but where the fields

15

Fig. 2 Girvi population by caste and settlement

Caste (alphabetical order)	Settlement										Total (%)
	Girvi proper	Pimpalaca Mala	Bara Biga	Cavarvasti	Dhumal-vadi	Bodke-vadi	Jadhav-vada	Harata Mala	Nava Mala	Other[a]	
Brahmin	39	.	.	.	.	.	.	.	.	.	39 (1.0)
Chambhar	96	.	.	.	.	.	.	.	.	.	96 (2.5)
Dhangar	38	.	.	.	13	.	.	.	.	13	64 (1.7)
Kumbhar	55	.	.	.	.	.	.	.	.	.	55 (1.4)
Mahar	326	.	.	.	.	.	.	.	.	.	326 (8.5)
Mali	123	.	.	.	.	.	.	112	118	22	375 (9.8)
Mang	79	.	.	.	.	.	.	.	.	.	79 (2.1)
Vatandar Maratha[b]											
v.a. Kadam: {p	254	.	.	.	.	.	.	.	.	.	254 (6.6)
a	138	.	.	.	.	.	.	.	.	.	138 (3.6)
k.a. Kadam: {p	285	72	.	.	.	.	.	.	.	.	357 (9.3)
a	39	.	40	126	.	.	.	.	.	.	205 (5.3)
Other Maratha	133	.	11	9	491	379	185	.	.	24	1232 (32.1)
Muslim	82	.	.	.	.	.	.	.	.	.	82 (2.1)
Nhavi	53	.	.	.	.	.	.	.	.	.	53 (1.4)
Ramoshi	242	.	.	.	38	.	.	.	.	102	382 (9.9)
Sutar	28	.	.	.	.	.	.	.	.	.	28 (0.7)
Other castes[c]	71	.	.	.	.	4	.	.	.	1	76 (2.0)
Total	2081	72	51	135	542	383	185	112	118	162	3841 (100)

[a] Other settlements: Shelkevasti (13 Dhangars), Janichivadi (22 Malis), Guradara (61 Ramoshis), Scattered Houses (24 Marathas, 41 Ramoshis, and 1 'Konkonat Maratha').
[b] There are separate entries for *varci ali* (v.a.) and *khalci ali* (k.a.) Kadam lineages. Each lineage has proper (p) and attached (a) members (see Chapter 5).
[c] Other castes: 10 Gadshis, 23 Lohars, 2 Parits, 4 Patruts, 15 Shimpis, 7 Sonars, 7 Vani Lingayats, 7 descendents of inter-caste marriages and 1 'Konkonat Maratha'.

16

can be irrigated from wells good crops can be grown on the rich black soils of the valley bottoms.

Girvi proper is dominated by two Maratha patrilineages (*bhaubunds*) of the Kadam clan (*kul*). These are referred to on the basis of residence as *vərči ali* ('upper street') and *khalči ali* ('lower street'). It also contains the great majority of the non-Maratha castes, including the Mahars, the largest of the ex-Untouchable or Scheduled Castes, who reside just to the east of the village across one of the streams. Dhumalvadi is occupied mainly by a Maratha lineage of the Dhumal clan. The Dhumals are fairly active in village politics, but they feel that they get little benefit from the village council and would rather have an independent council of their own. The two other large hamlets – Jadhavvada, occupied by a Maratha lineage of the Kshirsagar clan, and Bodkevadi, occupied by Marathas of the Dhembre, Bhandvalkar, Yadav, Saste, Chavan and Jadhav clans – have much less to do with village affairs. The total population is 3841. Girvi proper has 2081 inhabitants, Dhumalvadi 542, Bodkevadi 383 and Jadhav-vada 185. There are 650 persons living in other small settlements and isolated houses.

There are nineteen castes in Girvi. The Marathas, with about fifty-seven per cent of the population, are clearly dominant. They are the largest landowners and claim to be the ritual equals of the Brahmins. The Kadams are the largest and richest of the Maratha groups. With their attached families they comprise about one-quarter of the village population. Traditionally, they are the Patils of Girvi and are differentiated from other Marathas by their possession of the Patilship *vətən* (estate).

Each of the main Girvi settlements, Girvi proper, Dhumalvadi, Bodkevadi and Jadhavvada, is ritually an independent unit. Bodkevadi and Dhumalvadi have their own Bhairavnath, Maruti and other temples. They hold independent celebrations of such festivals as the Bhairavnath fair and Bendur.[1] Jadhavvada people attend the festivals at Varugad, an adjacent revenue village in Man Taluka, where they used to live. To a limited extent these settlements are united by the *baluta* system of economic exchange between agricultural and service castes.[2] The Brahmins, Sutars, Nhavis, Kumbhars, Mangs, etc. who live in Girvi do *baluta* work for the residents of all the hamlets. However, the *baluta* system also includes some relations with otherwise completely separate villages.

Girvi as a whole is primarily an administrative unit. Traditionally, all the settlements formed a single village because they were all subject to a single Patil *vətən*. In the past the most important official in a Maharashtrian village was the Patil. Originally the Patils were appointed, but the appointment conferred hereditary rights on the holder and his heirs. The Patil was

Introduction

the representative of the government in the village and also represented the villagers to higher government officials. He collected the land revenue and was responsible for maintaining law and order. The Patil also held part of the village land as a tax-free estate. These rights in land and office were the Patil's *vatən*. Frequently the Patilship was divided into two parts hereditary in different lineages (*bhaubunds*). This was the case in Girvi where the *vərči ali* Kadams held the Revenue Patilship and the *khalči ali* Kadams held the Police Patilship. The position has been changed considerably since Independence. The office and tax-free estate of the Revenue Patil were abolished in 1962. There continues to be a Police Patil, but his powers are severely limited and he no longer has a tax-free estate. Now the institutions that unite all the Girvi settlements are the revenue system and the Panchayat.

When the Satara land revenue was first settled in 1859, Girvi was part of Khatav Taluka, most of which lay to the south, above the Mahadev hills. By the time the settlement was revised in 1890 Girvi was part of Man Taluka, a new unit comprising the eastern villages of Khatav. Although there was a road from Dahivadi, Man Taluka headquarters, to Phaltan, travel between Girvi and Dahivadi was difficult and Girvi people did most of their trading in nearby Phaltan (Government of Bombay 1890). Girvi was transferred to Phaltan Taluka in 1948 when Phaltan State was merged with Bombay.

Phaltan was one of the oldest principalities in the Deccan and the Naik Nimbalkars, the rulers of Phaltan, are one of the most ancient and honorable Maratha families. The principality was founded in 1284 by Nimbraj I. Nimbraj I's original surname was Pawar, but his descendants called themselves Nimbalkar after their village in Phaltan, Nimbalak.[3] In 1327 Nimbraj I's son, Podakhala, was killed in battle while fighting in the army of Muhammad Tughlug, Emperor of Delhi. In appreciation the Emperor gave the hereditary title Naik to Podakhala's son, Nimbraj II. The Phaltan Naik Nimbalkars fought on various sides during the many Deccan wars, but when the British took control of the Peshwa's domains in 1818 the Naik Nimbalkars were feudatories of the Raja of Satara. Phaltan remained subject to Satara until 1848 when Satara was annexed by the British. After 1848 Phaltan was in the charge of the Resident for Kolhapur and the Deccan States at Kolhapur. The present Phaltan Naik Nimbalkar was awarded the hereditary title of Raja in 1936. Phaltan was merged with the Indian Union in 1948.

THE REGION: WESTERN MAHARASHTRA

Phaltan and Girvi are located in the heart of Western Maharashtra. They lie in the rugged countryside from which Maharashtrians emerged to play

18

a major role in Indian history in the seventeenth and eighteenth centuries. The great Maratha hero, Shivaji, was born in 1627 in Shivner Fort near Junnar in Poona District, about 98 miles north of Girvi. Shivaji had his capital at Satara, thirty-five miles southwest of Girvi. His tomb is near the Mahadev Temple at Shingnapur, about sixteen miles east of Girvi.

Maharashtra began to take on its modern form as a distinct cultural and linguistic region in the twelfth and thirteenth centuries under the Yadava dynasty of Devagiri, the modern Daulatabad. The court languages of the earlier dynasties, the Rashtrakutas, the Satavahanas, and the Chalukyas, were Sanskrit, Kannada, and the Prakrit Maharashtri. However, under the Yadavas, who with the Hoysalas emerged as the successors to the Chalukyas in the twelfth century, Marathi developed into a distinct language with a large written literature. The Yadavas also established a relatively stable boundary between their own territory and that of the Kannada-speaking Hoysalas in the Dharwar–Belgaum–Kolhapur region. Although the Yadavas fell under the impact of Muslim invasions from the north in the fourteenth century, Maharashtra remained a distinct region characterized by a common language, by common religious observances and, at least since the days of Shivaji, by a common administrative system (see Deleury 1960: Chapter 2).

Since the 1960 reorganization of Bombay State into linguistic provinces most Marathi speakers are contained within the new state of Maharashtra. However, Marathi is spoken by a substantial minority in neighboring districts. For example, from northeast to southwest, in 1901 Betul District was 39.8% Rajasthani, 28.6% Gondi and 23% Marathi. Chhindwara was 46.6% Hindi, 25.5% Gondi and 19% Marathi. Adilabad was 44% Telugu, 27.8% Marathi and 6.4% Urdu, and Bidar was 35% Kanarese, 33% Marathi, 16% Telugu and 14% Urdu (Johnson 1970: Map 2).

In addition to the linguistic tie, the region of Maharashtra is distinguished by widespread participation in the *bhakti* cult of the god Vithoba whose main temple is at Pandharpur on the Bhima river about sixty-five miles southeast of Phaltan. It is believed that the worship of Vithoba in its present form was begun in the thirteenth century by an outcaste Brahmin named Jnanadev. Jnanadev wrote the *Jnaneshvari*, a Marathi commentary on the *Bhagavadgita* which is still widely read today, as well as many popular *abhangs* in praise of Vithoba. He was born either in his father's village, Apegav, near Devagiri in the Godavari valley or in his mother's father's village, Alandi, a few miles north of Poona. Eventually Jnanadev settled at Alandi with his sister, Muktabai, and his brothers, Nivritti and Sopanadeva, all of whom were also *bhakti* poets. He made frequent pilgrimages to Pandharpur as well as to other holy places and

Introduction

Map 2   Phaltan Taluka

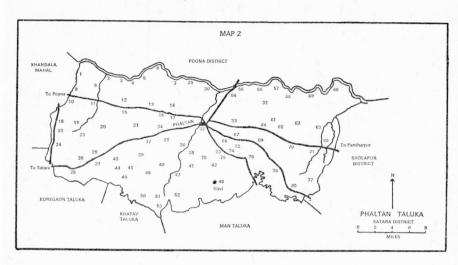

Key to Map 2

No.	Name of village	No.	Name of village	No.	Name of village
1	Padegaon	28	Adarki Kh.	55	Sangvi
2	Ravadi Kh.	29	Khunte	56	Songaon
3	Ravadi Bk.	30	Kambleshwar	57	Sarade
4	Murum	31	Rajale	58	Sathe
5	Khamgaon	32	Phaltan	59	Gokhali
6	Hol (Sakharvadi)	33	Vidni	60	Asu
7	Jinti	34	Mirgaon	61	Takalwade
8	Koregaon	35	Wathar	62	Gunaware
9	Kusur	36	Tawadi	63	Munjavdi
10	Kapadgaon	37	Khadki	64	Pimparad
11	Taradgaon	38	Kuravali Kh.	65	Nimbalak
12	Tadavale	39	Malavadi	66	Rajuri
13	Suravadi	40	Wakhri	67	Sonwadi Kh.
14	Bhilkatti	41	Mandavkhadak	68	Sonwadi Bk.
15	Kalaj	42	Nirgudi	69	Vadale
16	Nimbhore	43	Bibi	70	Barad
17	Vadjal	44	Korale	71	Kuravali Bk.
18	Tambve	45	Vadgaon	72	Tirakwadi
19	Aradgaon	46	Dhaval	73	Bhadali Bk.
20	Saswad	47	Dalavadi	74	Bhadali Kh.
21	Nandal	48	Girvi	75	Dudhebavi
22	Koparde	49	Waghoshi	76	Mirdhe
23	Hingangaon	50	Tathavada	77	Andrud
24	Salpe	51	Tardaf	78	Vinchurni
25	Kapshi	52	Upalve	79	Saskal
26	Adarki Bk.	53	Veloshi	80	Jaoli
27	Aljapur	54	Somanthali		

finally took *samadhi* at Alandi. Jnanadev was the first of a series of poet devotees of Vithoba in Maharashtra of whom the most popular are Namdev, a Shimpi; Cokhamela, a Mahar; Bhanudas, a Deshastha Brahmin; Eknath, Bhanudas' grandson, and Tukaram, an impoverished Kunbi shopkeeper.

Devotees of Vithoba are called *varkaris*. As the name implies, they are expected to make regular pilgrimages to Pandharpur, especially on Ashadh and Kartik *ekadəši*, i.e. the eleventh day of the bright fortnight of Ashadh (June–July) and of Kartik (October–November). The *varkaris* believe that *mokša*, final liberation from the cycle of death and rebirth, may be obtained through the grace of God given in response to the devotee's loving devotion (*bhakti*). They follow this path (*pənth*) to *mokša* rather than that of sacrifice (*puja*), knowledge (*jnanə*), or asceticism (*yoga*). Membership is open to laymen, men and women, and to all castes. A member is not required to give up his family obligations or employment. There is no elaborate rite of initiation.

There are probably several *varkaris* in every village in Maharashtra. When they are not on pilgrimage, and few can afford to go to Pandharpur twice every year, they gather to sing devotional hymns. They are joined in these *bhəjəns*, as such gatherings are called, by many of their non-*varkari* neighbors.

The approximate boundaries of the Maharashtrian region may be seen in the distribution of the semi-annual pilgrimages. The main pilgrimage route is that following the *palkhi* (palanquin) carrying Jnanadeva's *padukas* (footprints) from Alandi to Pandharpur by way of Poona, Sasvad, Jejuri, Lonand and Phaltan. According to Deleury (1960:76–80) there are some forty other *palkhis* originating in all parts of Maharashtra except the Konkon. Three *palkhis* commemorating Muktabai, Jnanadeva's sister, originate in East Khandesh District in the north. A *palkhi* commemorating Eknath comes from Paithan in Aurangabad District near the capital of the Yadavas. From Trimbak, near Nasik, and from Sasvad, south of Poona, come the *palkhis* of Nivritti and Sopanadev, Jnanadeva's brothers. Tukaram's *palkhi* starts from Dehu, his village eighteen miles west of Poona. Other *palkhis* come from Nagpur and Amraoti districts in the northeast; from Sholapur and Osmanabad districts in the east; from Buldana, Aurangabad, Ahmadnagar, Poona and Satara districts, and from Belgaum District, Mysore State, in the extreme south. Except for the last *palkhi*, which comes from a district which is almost equally divided between Kannada and Marathi speakers, all the groups of pilgrims come to Pandharpur from within Maharashtra. All parts of the Maharashtrian Deccan are covered by the network of pilgrimage routes. The only part of the state which is excluded is the Konkon, the coastal region below the Western Ghats. Communication across the Ghats between the Deccan and coastal districts of the state is difficult and the latter have developed a distinct dialect, Konkoni, as well as distinct castes, a distinct pattern of social stratification, and distinct agrarian system. My argument is concerned only with the Deccan districts of Maharashtra and within that region, primarily with the hilly western districts of Kolhapur, Satara, Poona, Ahmadnagar, and Nasik.[4]

The dominant *vatəndar* elite of rural Mahashtra has its origin in certain features of the traditional Maratha administrative system common to the whole of Western Maharashtra. The *vatəndar* position was based on control of the principal village office and on remuneration in tax-free land. It found, and continues to find, expression in high caste status and other ritual perquisites. A completely satisfactory account of these institutions would have to be based on the many Marathi records from the administrations of the Peshwas and the Rajas of Satara preserved by the Inam Commission in Poona, but a useful first approximation can be gained from studying the early British reports on the Deccan by Elphinstone (1821), Coats (1823), and Gooddine (1852). It is to be feared, however, that the accounts in English smooth over many variations and conflicts in the working of Maratha institutions.

Under the Maratha administration, as today, the village was defined as a unit of revenue administration, a *mauja*. According to early British accounts the village population at the beginning of the nineteenth century was divided into the following categories:

1. *Tulkarrees* or *meerasdars*. Cultivators with an hereditary right in the land, including the Patils (village headmen).
   (*a*) *vatəndars*.
   (*b*) non-*vatəndars*.
2. *Ooprees*. Persons cultivating on leases.
3. Brahmins. Including the hereditary village accountant (Kulkarni) and the priest.
4. *Balutedars* or hereditary village servants. Sutar, Lohar, Parit, Nhavi, Kumbhar, Sonar, Gurav, Chambhar, Mang and Mahar.
5. Others. Ramoshi watchmen, Gujar and Marvari shopkeepers, Muslims.

Some of these categories are defined in terms of rights in land while others are defined in terms of caste. They are not mutually exclusive.

Meerasdars and *ooprees* might be of any caste. The distinction between them lay in their rights in land as these existed in the Deccan before British rule. *Meerasdars* had an hereditary right in the land and paid the land revenue regardless of whether or not they actually cultivated their holdings. *Ooprees*, on the other hand, held their land on short term leases even though they might stay in the same village for many generations. *Ooprees* paid the revenue only when their land was actually being cultivated. *Ooprees* might be tenants of *meerasdars* or, and this was apparently more common, they might be tenants on government land. In the latter case they received their contract (*cowl*) from the Patil. The Patil also had the power to convert *oopree* to *meeras* tenure for a fee. The land revenue paid by *ooprees* was generally somewhat lower than that paid by *meerasdars*, but *ooprees* paid a number of special dues to the Patil from which *meerasdars* were exempt.

Meerasdars, hereditary owners of land, were of two kinds. *Vətəndars* were members of the Patil's patrilineage (*bhaubund*) who had a share in the Patil's tax-free estate and who might succeed to the office of Patil. As shares in the Patilship could be sold there were often more than one lineage of *vətəndars* in a village. In addition to their tax-free land *vətəndars* held other *meeras* land which was liable to the land revenue. Non-*vətəndar meerasdars* were those who had no share in the Patilship and all of whose land was liable to the regular land tax. In Loni, a village near Poona studied by Coats in 1820, thirty-five of the fifty *meerasdar* families were *vətəndars*. According to Coats,

They consider themselves higher in rank than the other fifteen Tulkarrees, as being descendents of the Patail; but they have no superior privileges. (1823:241)

The early British sources do not give the caste composition of the first two cultivating categories of village inhabitants. It is likely, however, that the majority were Marathas. Such castes as Dhangars and Malis also were included, the proportions varying from village to village. Persons who are now considered to be Marathas but who never have been *vətəndars* were, until early in the twentieth century, called Kunbis (farmers) (see Chapter 4).

The last three categories of nineteenth-century village inhabitants are occupational castes rather than groups holding various rights in land. Although the hereditary occupation of the castes in these categories, with the possible exception of Muslims, was not agriculture, many of them certainly received a substantial part of their income from cultivating their own land or from agricultural labor. Brahmin Kulkarnis, *balutedars* and Ramoshi watchmen received part of their remuneration in the form of grants of tax-free *vətən* land held on *inam* tenure, but were distinguished from other *vətəndars* by their hereditary occupation, caste status, and/or political power. Persons from any of the last three categories might hold land on ordinary *meeras* or *oopree* tenure as well.

Introduction

According to Elphinstone,

The Patails are the most important functionaries in the villages, and perhaps the most important class in the country. They hold their office by a grant from the government (generally from that of the Moghuls), are entitled in virtue of it to lands and fees, and have little privileges and distinctions of which they are as tenacious as of their land. Their office and emoluments are hereditary, and saleable with the consent of the Government, but are seldom sold except in cases of extreme necessity, though a partner is sometimes admitted with a careful reservation of the superiority of the old possessor. The Patail is head of the Police, and of the administration of justice in his village, but he need only be mentioned here as an officer of revenue. In that capacity he performs on a small scale what a Mamlutdar or a collector does on a large: he allots the land to such cultivators as have no landed property of their own, and fixes the rent which each has to pay: he collects the revenue for Government from all the ryots, conducts all its arrangements with them; and exerts himself to promote the cultivation and prosperity of the village. (1821: 21)

The Patil's powers as a revenue officer were very extensive. It was he who, aided by the Kulkarni, negotiated with the Mamlatdar the amount of revenue to be paid by his village, contracted for the cultivation of vacant land by *ooprees*, and arranged with his fellow *meerasdars* the share of the village revenue to be paid by each after the amount due from the *ooprees* was deducted. Coats describes the process as follows:

The annual settlement with the township for the revenue it is to pay for the ensuing year, takes place a little before the commencement of the rainy season. The Patail and Koolcarnee first assemble all the cultivators, when the Lowgum Jara, or written details of cultivation for the past year, is produced, and an agreement made with each of them for the quantity he is to cultivate in the approaching season. As the Patail's credit with the Government depends on the prosperity of his township, and the state of cultivation, he endeavors to extend this by all the means in his power. He will not allow a Tulkarree to throw up lands he had cultivated the year before; and should any part of his tul be lying waste, he upbraids him and threatens to exact the land-tax for it if he does not bring it under cultivation. He has less hold on the Oopree, who will go where he can get land on the best terms, and is obliged to treat him with great consideration. If the Oopree threaten to throw up his lands, from any cause, he is promised privately better terms and greater indulgence; or if he is in distress for money, to get him advances (tuggee) from the Government, &c. When the Patail and Koolcarnee have made these preliminary agreements, they proceed to the collector, or his agent, and enter into another agreement for the amount of revenue to be paid for the approaching year, subject to remissions on account of asmanee and sultanee, that is, losses from bad season, including crops being destroyed by locusts and other insects and the plunder of armies. (1823:274–5)

The perquisites of the Patil were of several kinds: the *vətən* lands or tax-free estate, *həkkəs* or taxes in kind levied on all the villagers except the *meerasdars*, and *manpan* or ritual marks of dignity and precedence. These are well illustrated by an eighteenth-century deed of sale of a half share in the Patilship of a village in Poona District. Among the perquisites received by the purchaser as his share of the Patilship estate were half of the Patil's tax-free *vǝtǝn* land, half of the old Patil's *meeras* land, half of the village land without either tenants or laborers and over which the Patil had the power of disposal, half of a variety of taxes in kind, half of a well owned by the old Patil and half of his house. In addition the new Patil shared in numerous marks of ritual precedence among which were the following:

1. On the Polse Amauass the Bullocks of both shall set out at the same time, your's on the left, and mine [the old Patil's] on the right, and in this way the one equal with the other they shall be walked in procession around Hanuman: but the Music shall precede my Bullocks home, while your's remain until it returns, when you shall bring your Bullocks home with Music also.

2. On marriages . . . I shall first receive Beera Til (Paun Sopery and a mark on the forehead,) and then you; on like occasion the Candwa (a large round sweet Cake) shall be shared equally by us.

3. On the Dewally, &c. the Pipers shall play at my door first, and then at your's.

4r We shall make the Dussora Pooja together. (Elphinstone 1821: i–vii, Appendix No. 1)

When the British took control of the Peshwa's domain in 1818 the difference between the dominant *vǝtǝndar* political class and the rest of the population involved a number of important social distinctions.[5] The political class controlled the village Patilships, perhaps the most important office in the traditional administrative system. With their control of office went *vǝtǝn* land held on tax-free *inam* tenure, and rights to administer or to tax much of the rest of the village land. Power in office and land was expressed in high caste status. Only *vǝtǝndars* were recognized as proper Marathas with a claim to Kshatriya status. Persons now accepted as Marathas but who do not have *vǝtǝns* were then relegated to inferior Kunbi status. The power of the Maratha *vǝtǝndars* also found expression in village ceremonies. They organized and led the processions at Dassara and Bayl Pola or Bendur and offered sacrifices on behalf of the whole village.

Although the government has abolished Revenue Patilships and severely limited the powers of Police Patils, abolished the tax-free status of the Patils' *vǝtǝn* lands and the taxes in kind paid to Patils, the *vǝtǝndar* Marathas remain a privileged political class. Their dominance continues to be based on their control of important rural offices and of wealth. It continues to be expressed in high caste status and in village ritual. In regional terms, then, this study is an analysis of the modern bases of *vətəndar* Maratha power and of the implications of the position of the former *vətəndars* for their political choices.

PART 2
ASPECTS OF POLITICAL STRATIFICATION

3
Political arenas and the political class

In view of the importance of political stratification and elite circulation for an adequate understanding of contemporary Indian politics and of many aspects of Indian social history as well it is remarkable that so little has been written on the subject. There is a useful body of material on dominant castes, but so far it has been focused mainly on village dominance. Little is known about regional dominance or about dominance in more inclusive, higher level political arenas (see Mayer 1958a). Few of those who have written on dominant castes have broken through the overlay of issues related to caste to deal with the phenomenon of dominance *per se* (see Gardner 1968). Much of what has been written explicitly about dominance and stratification is based on secondary sources (e.g. Bottomore 1967) or upon the most casual sort of fieldwork (e.g. Betéille 1967). Although a number of historical and political studies use the concept of the elite (see Broomfield 1966 and 1968, Stokes 1970, Mukherjee 1970, Dobbin 1970, Rosenthal 1970, and, on Maharashtra, Johnson 1970 and Sirsikar 1970), in most such work

theory has been of minor relevance; the word 'elite' then implies no more than 'the men at the top', whatever the particular context of discussion happens to be. (Leach and Mukherjee 1970:x)

As a result, outside of the literature on village dominance there have been few detailed empirical studies of the social origins of Indian political leaders and of the relations between the mass of the electorate and the groups from which most such leaders seem to be recruited. A major aim of Part 2 of this essay is to fill that gap.

Chapter 3, therefore, begins with an outline of the governmental and administrative arenas of political action in Girvi, Phaltan Taluka, and Satara District. I describe institutions which I knew at first hand, but since their form is determined by laws written in Bombay the account applies to the entire state with only minor exceptions. In the second part of Chapter 3 the personnel who hold office in the governmental and administrative arenas are analysed in terms of two variables: caste identity and estate (*vatэn*) possession. The second part of the chapter thus documents the assertion that the politics of rural Western Maharashtra are dominated by a political elite and indicates the sections of the population from which this elite is recruited, i.e. the dimensions of the political class. The distinguishing characteristics of the political class in terms of caste, economics, and kinship are outlined in the remaining chapters of Part 2.

Settlements

In Western Maharashtra people typically build their houses close together in compact clusters surrounded by the land which they cultivate. Only rarely does one find a family living alone in its fields. Different kinds of settlements are distinguished by their size and complexity.

The term *gav* may be applied to any settlement from a tiny hamlet to a city the size of Poona and to its surrounding land, but it is used most often in the sense of 'village'. Villages range in population from a few hundred to four or five thousand.[1] The population of a village is divided into a number of castes which traditionally performed complementary economic functions within a non-monetary form of economic exchange (*baluta*) confined to a single village. A village is protected by its guardian deity whose wedding the inhabitants celebrate in an annual village fair. Members of a village also co-operate in performing such ceremonies as Bendur or Bayl Pola and Dassara. Several villages in Phaltan Taluka have weekly markets, but such markets as well as village shops draw the bulk of their patronage from within the village. The entire population of a village may live in a single cluster of houses, but in many cases part of the population lives in small hamlets at distances of up to one or two miles from the central village settlement.

A hamlet (*vaḍi, vasti* or *mala*) is a small, named cluster of houses which is part of a larger village unit. The ten hamlets in Girvi may be taken as examples. These range in size from twenty-two to five hundred and forty-two. Most are inhabited by a single caste, although the two largest have a few members of one or two additional castes. Residents of such hamlets generally participate in the *baluta* system of the village of which they are a part. They usually worship the guardian deity of the main village settlement and participate in village-wide ceremonies with the members of the other settlements.

A town or city (*nagar* or *šahar*) is distinguished by its size, by the caste composition of its population, and by the complexity of its economic activities. In 1961 the eight municipalities of Satara District had an average population of 18,828.[2] There are many differences in the caste composition of rural and urban populations (see Chapter 4), but the most distinctively urban elements are trading and commercial castes such as the Marvaris,

30

Gujars, and Vani Lingayats. The markets and shops of the towns are centers of moneylending and wholesale and retail trade which involve residents of villages miles away. Small market towns such as Phaltan are important, too, as centers for the dissemination of all kinds of information.

Revenue administration

Hamlets, villages, and towns are grouped together in a variety of ways for purposes of administration and government. However, the administrative structure of the Revenue Department, which is concerned with the oldest of governmental functions and preserves the highest degree of continuity with the past, serves as the framework on which other institutions such as the *panchayati raj* organs of local self-government and co-operative societies are arranged.

The smallest unit of revenue administration is the 'revenue village' or '*mauja*', 'a statutorily recognized village having a defined boundary and separate land records' (Government of Maharashtra 1963:3). Until the abolition of *vatans* after Independence each revenue village was the estate of two or three *vatandar* lineages which helds its hereditary offices: Patil, in some cases Police Patil, and Kulkarni. A *mauja*, village in the administrative sense, generally is coextensive with a *gav*, village in the social sense, but this is not always so. Although it is unusual for a village (*gav*) to include more than one *mauja*, a *mauja* occasionally may include more than one distinct village. In some instances, too, the social and administrative boundaries of neighboring settlements may come to overlap as a result of population movements. For example, Girvi proper and nine of its ten hamlets make up a village (*gav*) which is also a distinct *mauja*, but *mauja* Girvi also includes a hamlet, Jadhavvada, which is socially part of neighboring Varugad *gav*. The land owned by Jadhavvada people is part of *mauja* Girvi territory, but they consider themselves to be members of the Varugad *gav* from which they moved to Girvi. A few Jadhavvada residents spend part of the year in Varugad and many more visit there for the annual Bhairavnath fair.

The main officer of the Revenue Department at the village level is the Talathi. Successor to the hereditary Brahmin Kulkarni, the Talathi maintains the land records, collects the land revenue, prepares lists of voters, and so on. The Talathi is an appointed official who rarely is a natal member of the village in which he is employed. The Revenue Department also appoints a Police Patil from among the members of a local patri-lineage who have a right to the office by virtue of descent, but nowadays the Police Patil has no real powers.

The next most inclusive unit of revenue administration is the taluka or mahal.[3] It consists of fifty to two hundred villages plus in some cases a town and has a total population of around one hundred and thirty thousand.[4] With the establishment of the rural development scheme in 1953, talukas were deemed to be equivalent to one or more blocks for purposes of administering block development grants.[5] This change in terminology, however, did not involve any change in taluka boundaries. Ten to fifteen talukas form a district. The head of the revenue administration at the district level is the Collector and, at the taluka level, the Mamlatdar. There also are Deputy Collectors or Prant Officers who supervise the Mamlatdars of several talukas and have special responsibility for land reform legislation dealing with tenancies and land ceilings.

Revenue Department officials have extensive powers in the political sphere. They prepare lists of voters, supervise the division of villages and other electoral units into constituencies, and administer elections. In certain circumstances the Collector or a subordinate designated by him may take a direct part in the activities of local councils. The Collector and Mamlatdar also have limited judicial powers, especially in cases concerning rights in land.[6]

Local government

The organs of local government in Maharashtra are panchayats at the village level and in some towns, municipalities in other towns, panchayat samitis for talukas, and zilla parishads for districts. The arrangement of settlements under these institutions is slightly different from that under the revenue administration. A district coincides with a zilla parishad and a taluka with a panchayat samiti, but a panchayat does not necessarily coincide with a revenue village. In Phaltan Taluka nine panchayats include two revenue villages each and one panchayat includes three revenue villages. In addition there are three revenue villages which have been divided into two independent panchayats each. A town may choose to have either a panchayat or a municipal form of government. As far as the revenue administration is concerned municipalities are part of the taluka and district in which they are located, but, although municipalities were included in the old district boards, they have been excluded from the new zilla parishads.

A village panchayat is a corporate body with seven to fifteen members, depending upon the size of the village. For purposes of panchayat elections each village is divided into wards, the number of wards and the number of members to be elected from each to be determined by the Collector. However, two seats always are reserved for women and one or more seats may be reserved for Scheduled Castes and Tribes if the proportion of such groups in a village warrants it. Except for reserved seats, any adult resident of a village panchayat may contest for a seat in any ward of the village. Members of a panchayat elect from among themselves a sarpanch (chairman) and upa-sarpanch (deputy chairman). The panchayat may dismiss its officers by a motion of no confidence passed by at least two-thirds of all members. Both panchayat members and officers are elected for four year terms. The adult population of all the settlements comprising an independent village panchayat constitutes a gram sabha which is to meet at least twice a year to hear reports and make suggestions on the current work of the panchayat.

The Maharashtra Zilla Parishads and Panchayat Samitis Act of 1961 established a panchayat samiti for every taluka or block in the state. Such councils have a variable number of members falling into six categories.

(*a*) Zilla parishad councillors elected from the electoral divisions of the block.

(*b*) Co-opted zilla parishad councillors residing in the block.

(*c*) The chairman of such co-operative society conducting exclusively the business of purchase and sale of agricultural products in the Block, as the State Government may by order specify in this behalf (to be an associate member).

(*d*) The chairman of a co-operative society conducting business relating to agriculture not being a society falling under clause (*c*) in the Block co-opted by the *Panchayat Samiti* (to be an associate member).

(*e*) (i) If no members under categories (*a*) and (*f*) are women, then one woman co-opted by the panchayat samiti; (ii) if no members in categories (a) and (*f*) belong to the Scheduled Castes or Scheduled Tribes, then a person from one of these communities residing in the block is co-opted by the panchayat samiti.

(*f*) Two panchayat members from each electoral division of the block elected by the members of the panchayats in the electoral division.[7]

Elected panchayat samiti members (categories *a* and *f*) elect from among themselves a chairman and choose the co-opted members (categories *d* and *e*; *b* is co-opted by the zilla parishad). All full members of the panchayat samiti (categories *a*, *b*, *e* and *f*) then elect a deputy chairman from amongst themselves. The chairman and deputy chairman may be dismissed by a vote of no confidence carried by a two-thirds majority of all panchayat samiti members other than associates. Both members and officers are elected for five year terms.

The district council or zilla parishad consists of:

(*a*) Councillors chosen by direct election from electoral divisions in the District being not more than sixty in number and not less than forty as may, by notification in the *Official Gazette*, be determined by the State Government so however that there is one councillor as far as is reasonably practicable for not more than every thirty-five thousand of the population;

(*b*) (i) if the elected Councillors do not include a woman, then two women, each residing in different Blocks in the District, and
(ii) if the elected Councillors include one woman, then one more woman residing in a Block in the District (other than the Block in which the woman elected is resident), co-opted by the Councillors elected under clause (*a*);

(*c*) the Chairman of all *Panchayat Samitis* in the District, *ex-officio*; and

(*d*) the Chairman of such five federal co-operative societies (being societies which as far as practicable conduct business or activities in the District in relation to (i) credit, (ii) land development, (iii) marketing, (iv) industrial co-operatives, (v) co-operative training or education), as the State Government may by notification in the Official Gazette, specify in this behalf (to be called 'associate Councillors').

If the caste composition of the population warrants it the State Government may reserve one or more seats in a zilla parishad for members of the Scheduled Castes and Scheduled Tribes. Elected councillors (category *a*) choose a president and vice-president from among their own number. However, no councillor may hold either office for more than two consecutive terms nor may a member hold the office of chairman or deputy chairman of a panchayat samiti simultaneously with that of president or vice-president of the zilla parishad. The president and vice-president of the zilla parishad may be removed from office by a simple majority of all councillors other than associates (category *d*). Members and officers are elected for five year terms.

Every zilla parishad has a standing committee and the following subject committees: finance, works, agriculture, co-operatives, education, and health. The standing committee is composed of the zilla parishad president as *ex officio* chairman, the chairmen of the subject committees, seven councillors, and as many as two outside experts co-opted by the zilla parishad. The co-operative committee consists of five councillors and the five associate councillors, all with voting rights. The education committee includes seven councillors, not more than two outside experts as associate members, and two presidents of municipalities which make annual payments to the zilla parishad for primary education within their boundaries, also as associate members. Each of the other subject committees consists of seven councillors and as many as two outside experts as associate members. No Councillor may be elected to more than two committees, nor is any panchayat samiti chairman or deputy chairman eligible for zilla parishad committee membership. The vice-president is automatically chairman of such two subject committees as the council may decide. The zilla parishad also chooses from among its councillors who are subject committee members two persons to be chairman of such two committees as the council may decide. Committee membership and offices are held for five year terms coterminous with that of the zilla parishad.

Panchayat samiti and zilla parishad officers are expected to be full-time public officials. They are paid salaries and such benefits as housing and travel allowances. A zilla parishad president receives a salary of Rs. 500 monthly; a vice-president, subject committee chairman and panchayat samiti chairman receive Rs. 300 monthly, and a panchayat samiti deputy chairman receives Rs. 150 monthly.

A zilla parishad is supposed to meet at least once every three months. Zilla parishad committees, panchayat samitis and panchayats should meet at least once a month. Decision-making procedures in all bodies follow the same pattern. Formally, all questions except no confidence motions are decided by a simple majority of those present and voting. The presiding authority has a second vote in case of a tie. One-third of the members constitute a quorum. In the absence of a quorum the presiding officer adjourns the meeting to some future date. The questions which would have been placed before the original meeting, had there been a quorum present, may be decided by the adjourned meeting with or without a quorum. Although all councils are careful to carry out the requirements of the law, informal procedures are generally quite different (see Chapter 9).

The purpose of the linked hierarchy of local government councils in Maharashtra, panchayats, panchayat samitis, and zilla parishads, is to increase the amount and pace of rural development. Councils at each level are empowered to engage within the limits imposed by local resources in activities relating to agriculture and animal husbandry, minor irrigation works, community development, public health, education, public works, and co-operation. In addition, zilla parishads and panchayat samitis are empowered to supervise the administration of and grant financial aid to councils immediately below them in the hierarchy. Although village panchayats have been granted fairly extensive powers, they have very limited resources and rarely take the initiative in development projects. Instead they serve as a channel through which local leadership and resources can be drawn into projects initiated by taluka and district level councils.

The powers of local government over primary education provide an illustration of the way authority is distributed within the hierarchy. The Maharashtra Zilla Parishads and Panchayat Samitis Act of 1961 gave extensive control over primary education in urban as well as rural areas, including the power to appoint teachers in public schools, to the zilla parishad and subordinate taluka and village councils. The educational activities of local government which have the greatest political significance are teacher patronage and school construction. Teachers are hired by the zilla parishad education committee but school construction involves the entire hierarchy. Most of the funds for school construction come from the zilla parishad which allocates them to panchayat samitis, often without specifying that they be spent for school construction. Panchayat samitis, however, have some funds of their own which may be used for this purpose. The decision to appropriate money for a school with a particular number of rooms in a particular village is made by the panchayat samiti formally in consultation with village panchayats. But, although panchayats sometimes express their wishes in the form of resolutions directed to the panchayat samiti, most such consultation is assumed to follow from the presence of panchayat members on the taluka council. Appropriations for school construction, as for other purposes, are often made in the form of matching grants. Panchayats are expected to contribute to the total cost of construction by appropriating resources or by raising public contributions.

The resources of councils on each level of the local government system come from local fund cesses and grants from higher authorities. Panchayat samitis and zilla parishads share a cess of between twenty and one hundred per cent on the land revenue and nineteen per cent on the water rate collected by the State Government within their territories. Panchayats receive a cess of thirty per cent of the land revenue collected on the land within their jurisdictions. Councils may request the State Government to raise the rate of the local fund cess for specified purposes during specified periods. In addition, local government councils receive grants from the State government and from higher level councils. A majority of grants are tied to provide for particular development schemes or council expenses.

The powers of councils at each level of local government are limited by their dependence on a higher level for money. For example, the 1965–6 budget of the Satara Zilla Parishad amounted to Rs. 40,247,500 of which Rs. 36,425,400 were received in the form of grants from the State Government for projects decided upon entirely by the State Government.

Panchayats, panchayat samitis, and zilla parishads are required to prepare annual budget estimates of income and expenditure for the following financial year. Panchayat budgets are subject to review by panchayat samitis and panchayat samiti budgets are subject to review by zilla parishads. The State Government exercises financial control over the zilla parishads.

Each local government council has its own executive staff. The State Government appoints a chief executive officer (CEO), deputy CEO and department heads for each zilla parishad and a block development officer (BDO) responsible to the CEO for each panchayat samiti. The CEO is a member of the All India Services equivalent in rank to a Collector. The deputy CEO, department heads, and BDOs are members of the State

Services. In each district lower offices are filled by members of the district services appointed by divisional and district selection boards or by the CEO. The gram sevak, who serves as village panchayat secretary and is the main channel of communication between panchayat and panchayat samiti, is a member of the district services responsible to the BDO.

In the view of the CEO of the Satara Zilla Parishad the zilla parishad system in Maharashtra is intended to provide a meeting point between executive machinery and local leadership. Delays in decision-making are avoided because development decisions now can be taken at the local level within the framework of a state-wide plan. The involvement of local leaders insures that planning is adjusted to local needs and resources and that local savings are mobilized for planned development. Co-ordination within the system is assured by the overlap of zilla parishad and panchayat membership on the panchayat samiti and by the centralization of the executive staff under the authority of the CEO. Co-ordination with the State Government is achieved by making the CEO and other senior zilla parishad officials responsible to the State Government as well as to their own councils. Since its establishment in 1961 the zilla parishad system has become a focus of political interest and local politicians agree that as far as patronage (*vikas*) is concerned the chairman of a panchayat samiti is far more important than a member of the Legislative Assembly.

The Girvi Panchayat, founded in 1952, has thirteen members elected from five wards. The geographical distribution and caste composition of the wards are shown in Map 3 and Figure 3. Janubai and Hanuman wards elect two members each while Vitthal, Shriram and Lakshmi wards elect three members each. One seat in Lakshmi ward is reserved for Scheduled Castes. Vitthal and Shiram wards each have one seat reserved for women.

The 1962–7 Phaltan Panchayat Samiti had fifteen members: eight from category (*f*); four from category (*a*), and one each from categories (*c*), (*d*), and (*e*). The new Phaltan Panchayat Samiti elected in 1967 also had eight members from category (*f*) and four from category (*a*), but the co-opted members had not yet been chosen when my fieldwork ended. Phaltan sends four councillors (category (*a*) panchayat samiti members) and the Panchayat Samiti Chairman to the sixty-four member Satara Zilla Parishad. The Nimbalak electoral division, a general seat in 1967, was reserved for Scheduled Castes in the 1962 local government elections.

The Phaltan Municipal Council was established in 1868. Following the 1948 merger of Phaltan State it was governed by the Bombay District Municipal Act of 1901. The Maharashtra Municipalities Act of 1965 took effect on 27 June 1966.

Fig. 3   Girvi registered voters by caste and ward

Caste (alphabetical order)	Vitthal	Janubai	Lakshmi	Shriram	Hanuman	Total
Brahmin	.	.	.	.	14	14
Chambhar	.	.	.	29	.	29
Dhangar	4	5	6	.	12	27
Kumbhar	.	.	.	.	23	23
Mahar	.	.	105	.	.	105
Mali	.	5	.	124	24	153
Mang	.	.	.	32	.	32
Vətəndar Maratha						
v.a. Kadam: $\{$ p	115	5	.	.	4	124
$\phantom{\text{v.a. Kadam: }\{}$ a	39	27	.	.	7	73
k.a. Kadam: $\{$ p	.	.	.	105	61	166
$\phantom{\text{k.a. Kadam: }\{}$ a	.	.	.	.	80	80
Other Maratha	19	275	230	13	29	566
Muslim	11	.	.	.	15	26
Nhavi	.	.	.	.	17	17
Ramoshi	152[a]	50[a]	15	.	6	223
Sutar	18	.	.	.	.	18
Other castes[b]	4	12	8	2	7	33
Unknown[c]	81[a]	42[a]	33	35	46	237
Total	443	421	397	340	345	1946

[a] 56 Ramoshis, known and unknown, are registered in the list of voters (*mətədaranči yadi*) twice: once in Vitthal ward again in Janubai ward.
[b] Other castes: 4 Gadshis, 11 Lohars, 2 Parits, 1 Patrut, 6 Shimpis, 3 Sonars, 4 Vani Lingayats, and 2 descendents of an inter-caste marriage.
[c] Unknown: Includes all registered voters who cannot be identified in the village census as well as those who can be identified but are known to be deceased or permanently absent, e.g. married daughters of Girvi men.

During the period of my fieldwork the Phaltan Municipal Council had sixteen members elected for four year terms from five wards, one ward with four seats and four with three seats. Two seats were reserved for women and two for Scheduled Castes.

The Council had a Standing Committee and two subject committees: (a) Sanitation, Medical and Public Health and (b) Water supply and Drainage. The Standing Committee managed all Council business in the intervals between full Council meetings and also took responsibility for Phaltan's markets. Members elected from among themselves a President, who was also Chairman of the Standing Committee, and a Vice-President for four year terms. The Council also elected chairmen and members of committees for one year terms. Municipal Council officers could be removed by a vote of three-fourths of the members.

Political arenas and the political class

The Municipal Council was reconstituted on 27 June 1966 under the Maharashtra Municipalities Act of 1965. The old Council was continued in office, but new officers were elected. Under the new act officers can be removed by a vote of no confidence supported by a simple majority of council members. New municipal elections were to be held no later than 31 December 1967. For the new elections the town was divided into nineteen single seat wards of which two were reserved for women and one was reserved for Scheduled Castes.[8]

Co-operative societies

Co-operative societies are an important source of political power in Western Maharashtra. A large part of the economic activity of the region is channeled through co-operatives and they control patronage in the form of jobs, credit, access to valuable equipment, and marketing contracts. The structure of the credit and marketing co-operatives in Girvi, Phaltan and Satara is shown in Figure 4. There are other co-operatives engaged in processing agricultural products, in regulating markets, in lift-irrigation projects, and so on. Many of the societies are linked together by their economic activities and by overlapping membership. All have similar structures.

The Satara District Land Development Bank provides credit for periods greater than eighteen months to agriculturalists for land improvement, construction of wells, purchase of equipment, payment of debts under the Bombay Agricultural Debtors Relief Act of 1947, and for the purchase of land by agriculturalists or tenants under the Bombay Tenancy and Agricultural Lands Act of 1948. Loans are secured by mortgages on land. The Satara District Land Development Bank is managed and its loans are sanctioned by its Board of Directors and Chairman. It has a branch office in Phaltan to which the Revenue Department has assigned a Mamlatdar to help the bank investigate loan applications. The bank's capital comes from membership fees, sale of shares, deposits, and loans from the Maharashtra State Land Development Bank.

A member of the Girvi Multi-Purpose Credit Society must pay an entrance fee of Re. 1.00 and purchase at least one share for Rs. 5.00. In 1967 the society had 505 members. The society makes short term loans to cultivators in the following amounts per acre: Rs. 1250 to Rs. 2250 for sugar-cane; Rs. 1500 to Rs. 4000 for grapes; Rs. 350 for cotton, and Rs. 100 to Rs. 150 for *jawar* or *bajri*, the staple millets of the area. Applications for loans must first be approved by the Managing Committee and Chairman of the Girvi Credit Society. The Credit Society sends them to the

Fig. 4   Credit and marketing co-operatives

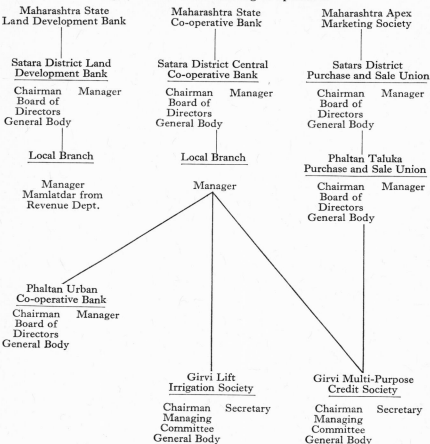

Board of Directors of the Satara District Central Co-operative Bank which provides about two-thirds of the Girvi Society's capital.

Village societies, of which there are sixty-eight in Phaltan Taluka, lend to farmers at nine per cent interest. Village societies borrow from district central co-operative banks at six per cent and the latter borrow from the Maharashtra State Co-operative Bank at four per cent.

In addition to its credit activities, the Girvi Multi-Purpose Credit Society is involved in marketing. Members may purchase hybrid seeds, fertilizers, and pesticides and sell their crops through the co-operative. The society has three small ration shops which sell food grains and, most importantly, sugar. It also owns several pump sets which members may use.

The Phaltan Urban Co-operative Bank performs banking and credit functions in Phaltan. Most of the bank's capital comes from deposits and the sale of shares, but it also borrows from the Satara District Central Co-operative Bank.

Marketing and credit societies meet in the marketing activities of the village multi-purpose societies. Taluka and district purchase and sale unions perform on a larger scale the same sort of marketing activities performed by the Girvi Multi-Purpose Credit Society. For instance, the Phaltan Taluka Purchase and Sale Union operates in markets regulated by the Phaltan–Lonand Agricultural Produce Market Committee in Phaltan and Lonand, the railroad station in neighboring Khandala Mahal. The Union acts as commission agent for its members on trading in cotton, groundnuts, onions, and other crops. It sells hybrid seeds, fertilizers, and pesticides both directly to individuals and to village co-operatives. The Union owns and manages two ration shops in Phaltan, a stationery shop, a machinery shop, and a new co-operative consumers' store.

There are two important processing co-operatives in Phaltan. The Shriram Co-operative Sugar Factory was registered in 1954 and began working in October 1957. The Factory has members in sixty-four villages in Phaltan plus two in Malshiras Taluka. It has an authorized share capital of Rs. 7,450,000 and 3015 members. The Factory provides a large number of seasonal jobs for cane harvesters as well as factory workers and in the year ending 30 June 1965 paid Rs. 969,852.98 in salaries and wages and Rs. 2,094,832.35 for harvesting cane and transporting it to the Factory.

The Society has three classes of members. Producer members must hold land as owners or tenants and grow at least half an acre of cane, own at least one share of stock, and pay an entrance fee of Rs. 5.00. Ordinary members must own at least one share and pay the entrance fee, while nominal members are required only to pay the entrance fee. Nominal members do not have the right to vote.

Each producer member agrees to supply one-half acre of sugar-cane for every share he owns. If he produces more than the required amount of cane for sale to the Factory the Board of Directors may require him to purchase additional shares. The Factory undertakes to purchase all the cane a member produces not in excess of twenty-five acres and, after giving advance notice, it may require members to supply their entire cane crop to the Factory.

The Board of Directors arranges and pays for the harvesting of cane produced by Society members and for its transport to the Factory. The Society contracts with one man in each village who, in return for Rs. 0.25 per ton of cane delivered, takes responsibility for managing the cane harvest and transport in his area. Such a contract carries considerable political potential. Cane harvesting is an important source of employment for agricultural laborers and the timing of the harvest and the quality of the cutting are important variables in the producer's profit. If his cane is allowed to dry before it is cut or if it is not cut close to the ground it will weigh less when delivered to the Factory. The price per ton which the Society pays for cane, as well as the dividends on shares and employees' bonuses, are determined by the Board of Directors after completion of the crushing season.

The sugar market has been subject to control since 1963. Before control was established the Sugar Factory could sell sugar to any licensed dealer in amounts and at prices agreed to by the Factory and the dealer. Under control prices and buyers are set by the government. The Factory is licensed by the Union Government to sell sugar to specified prices for various grades. It may sell to private traders, to institutions and to purchase and sale unions which in turn sell sugar to village co-operatives and to ration shops. The buyers and the amount to be sold to each are determined by the Maharashtra Food and Agricultural Department.

In addition to its processing and marketing activities, the Shriram Co-operative Sugar Factory owns diesel pump sets, bulldozers for leveling fields, tractors, and a tube-well boring machine which it rents to members. Members may repair their own machinery in the Factory workshops. Housing and a kindergarten have been built for permanent employees. The Factory is repairing old agricultural approach roads and building new ones in the area of its operation and has been given a government subsidy for this work.

The other processing co-operative in Phaltan is the Phaltan Cotton Ginning and Pressing Society. The Ginning and Pressing Society began work in 1963 and engages in activities similar to those of the Shriram Co-operative Sugar Factory, but on a much smaller scale.

Other co-operative societies in Phaltan are of much less political interest. The Phaltan-Lonand Agricultural Produce Market Committee supervises market yards in Phaltan, Lonand and Nimbalak. There are three lift-irrigation societies in Phaltan, one of which is located in Girvi. The Girvi Lift-Irrigation Society, which includes Nirgudi in its area of operation, has purchased three pump sets for the use of its members. Its resources include a government subsidy as well as share capital and loans from the Satara District Central Co-operative Bank, but the Society is in poor financial condition. There are also thirteen industrial societies in the Taluka: seven contract labor societies, two rope making societies, two weaving societies, a pottery making society, and an oil pressing society.

The last six societies, as well as a backward classes housing society and a handloom weavers' society, draw their members from particular castes.

The broad features of co-operative society government are laid down by the Maharashtra Co-operative Societies Act of 1960. Final authority in a co-operative rests in the general body of shareholders, each of whom has one vote. Management is vested in a committee elected by the general body and a chairman elected by the committee. For example, the Board of Directors of the Shriram Co-operative Sugar Factory consists of sixteen to nineteen members: twelve elected by producer members, two elected by ordinary members including one representing society shareholders and one representing traders, the Managing Director *ex officio*, a nominee of the Maharashtra State Co-operative Bank, not more than two nominees of the Industrial Finance Corporation of India, and not more than one expert co-opted by the Board. Neither the Managing Director nor the co-opted expert may vote when the Board elects its officers. Previously there were ten producer members elected in rotation in groups of three, three and four; ordinary members were elected annually. New by-laws passed in 1966 call for the entire Board to be elected every three years. There must be a general meeting of all shareholders every year in the quarter ending 30 September and one-fifth of the shareholders may call for a special meeting. General meetings hear and approve reports on the management of the Society, approve changes in the by-laws, and elect the Board of Directors.

Shares may be purchased and membership in a society may be acquired by institutions, including other co-operatives, as well as by individuals. When one society invests in another the former may choose one of its members to vote as its representative in the latter. This provision of the law has two important consequences: it leads to overlapping membership on managing committees and allows politicians to achieve high office in the co-operative system by indirect election.

Area co-operatives are supervised by the Deputy Registrar of Co-operatives in Satara, an official of the Maharashtra Department of Co-operation. Village multi-purpose societies, industrial societies, backward class housing societies, and the Phaltan-Lonand Market Yard Committee are supervised by the Satara Zilla Parishad Department of Industries and Co-operation as well. Representatives of some categories of co-operatives are co-opted on to the Panchayat Samiti and Zilla Parishad. The Phaltan Taluka Co-operative Supervising Union also has supervisory powers over multi-purpose credit societies. The Supervising Union is a non-official body composed of representatives of member credit societies, but its secretary is responsible to the State Department of Co-operation.[9]

Education societies

There are two education societies in Phaltan. The Phaltan Education Society was founded in 1951. It now manages Mudhoji College, Mudhoji High School, three primary schools, and a hostel in Phaltan town as well as high schools in Sakharvadi and Asu in Phaltan Taluka, and in Mhasvad and Gondavale Bk. in Man Taluka. The Shriram Education Society, established in 1959, manages high schools in Girvi, Sasvad, Taradgaon and Wakhri, and several boarding schools in Phaltan.

Education societies are charitable institutions. Since they get their funds from contributions rather than from the sale of shares they are not eligible to borrow from co-operative banks. They may receive grants from the government, however.

Each member of the Phaltan Education Society falls into one of several categories depending upon his contribution. Patrons are those who have given Rs. 3000 or more; Fellows, Rs. 1000 or more; Benefactors, Rs. 500 or more; Ordinary Members, Rs. 100 or more, and Sympathizers, Rs. 50 or more. A Life Member is a qualified teacher who has undertaken to serve the Society for at least twenty years. Applicants are elected into the Society by the Governing Council.

Shrimant Malojirao Naik Nimbalkar, Rajasaheb of Phaltan, is the Permanent President of the Phaltan Education Society with power to preside over meetings of the General Body, to call special meetings of the General Body, and to cast a second vote in case of ties.

Final authority in the Society vests in the General Body made up of all members. The General Body is empowered to elect up to three Vice-Presidents, to elect the Governing Council, to consider and approve the annual report and accounts of the Society, to make and alter by-laws, and to decide proposals to start new educational institutions.

The Governing Council of the Phaltan Education Society consists of fifteen members elected for three year terms: two Patrons, three Fellows, three Benefactors, five Ordinary Members, and two Sympathizers. The Council elects a Chairman, Vice-Chairman, Secretary and Treasurer from among its own members, also for three year terms. The Governing Council is responsible for the management of the Society's educational institutions, including the appointment of staff. For each of its institutions the Council appoints a supervisory committee consisting of the head of the institution, members of the Governing Council, and members of the institution's staff.

The investments of the Society are managed by a Board of Trustees consisting of one nominee of the President, two nominees of the Governing

Council who are not themselves Council members, one nominee of the General Body, and the Treasurer of the Governing Council as Secretary.

The Shriram Education Society has a similar constitution. Its members fall into different categories depending upon their contributions, but it has no equivalent of the Life Membership of the Phaltan Education Society. The General Body of the Shriram Education Society meets anually to hear a report of the activities of the Society. Every third year the General Body elects a Governing Council consisting of a President, up to three Vice-Presidents and seventeen representatives of the various classes of members. The Governing Council is empowered to elect new members, adopt annual reports, make and amend by-laws, administer the assets of the Society, and to appoint and dismiss staff. The Governing Council of the Shriram Education Society elects a Secretary, a Managing Committee responsible for over-all administration, a Board of Trustees responsible for investments, and an educational committee for each of its schools.

All secondary education in Phaltan Taluka is provided by one or the other of the two education societies. In both societies the governing bodies and officers have a good deal of influence on staff appointments and student admissions.

Legislative assembly and parliamentary constituencies

Phaltan Taluka used to be the core of a two-seat Legislative Assembly constituency with one general seat and one seat reserved for Scheduled Castes. In 1952 the constituency also included Man Taluka. Khandala Mahal was added in 1957. The Phaltan–Man–Khandala constituency was split in 1961 when double member constituencies were abolished. In 1962 and 1967 the eastern half of Phaltan was joined with Man Taluka in a reserved constituency and the western half of Phaltan, including Phaltan town, was combined with Khandala Mahal in a general seat. Since Independence Phaltan has been part of the North Satara Parliamentary constituency.

Labor unions

There are two pairs of competing labor unions active in Phaltan Taluka. One pair of unions, the Municipal Kamgar Union of municipal employees and the Phaltan Taluka Shriram Sakhar Kamgar Union of sugar workers, is affiliated with the Congress Party's Indian National Trade Union Congress (INTUC). The other pair of unions, the Phaltannagar Palika Kamgar Union of municipal employees and the Phaltan Taluka Sakhar

45

Kamgar Union, was affiliated with the 'Communist' led All India Trade Union Congress (AITUC) until the 1962 conflict with China. It is now independent. The Phaltan Taluka Sakhar Kamgar Union has most of its members in the privately owned Phaltan Sugar Works Ltd. in Sakharvadi while most employees of the Shriram Co-operative Sugar Factory belong to the Phaltan Taluka Shriram Sakhar Kamgar Union. However, the former union is active in both factories because it is recognized as the 'representative union' in the sugar industry in Phaltan under the Bombay Industrial Relations Act of 1946. Only the representative union has the right to represent workers in its industry and local area before the Industrial Tribunal.

THE POLITICAL CLASS IN WESTERN MAHARASHTRA

The analysis of the distribution of offices in Girvi (Chapter 1) suggested that the political class in rural Western Maharashtra is composed largely of *vətəndar* Marathas. The analysis of office-holding at more inclusive levels of government confirms and extends this hypothesis. Maratha *vətəndars* continue to dominate in larger population units, but variations in the distribution of castes lead to the inclusion of other elements in the political class.

During much of 1966, before the general and local government elections of 1967, one hundred and forty-four municipal, taluka, district and state offices were held by people connected with Phaltan Taluka. There were sixteen members of the Municipal Council, fifteen members of the Panchayat Samiti (eight in category *f*, including the Chairman; one each in categories *c*, *d*, and *e*; four in category *a*, i.e. members of the Zilla Parishad), six members of the Zilla Parishad (four in category *a*, i.e. Panchayat Samiti members; the Panchayat Samiti Chairman; one in category *d*), fifty-one offices in taluka co-operative societies, forty-two in education societies, seven labor union offices, five offices in district co-operative societies, one office in a state co-operative, and one Member of the Legislative Assembly. Some of these offices, for example those in state and district co-operatives, are not restricted to Phaltan residents and are included only because they happened to be held by Phaltan people in 1966. Other offices are open only to Phaltan residents. The most important office in each of these institutions is that of the chairman.

In this wider sphere of political activity *vətəndar* Marathas remain the predominant element in the political elite. Although *vətəndar* Marathas comprise little more than ten per cent of the population (see Chapter 4, Fig. 6) they hold fifty-nine, or forty-one per cent, of the one hundred and forty-four offices, including ten of the fourteen most important.[10] At this level, as in Girvi, a few Mahars and Chambhars hold office as a result of the reservation of seats for Scheduled Castes. Non-*vətəndar* Marathas continue to be under represented.

In other respects, however, there are significant differences between the distribution of offices in Phaltan and in Girvi. In the wider sphere new elements are introduced into the political elite. Brahmins, with about four per cent of the population, hold more than ten per cent of the offices. Jains, with less than two per cent of the population, hold eight per cent of the offices. Malis, with more than five per cent of the offices, and Dhangars, with more than four per cent of the offices, also appear in the political elite.

Fig. 5   The distribution of offices in Phaltan Taluka

Caste (alphabetical order)	Approximate share of population[a] (%)	No. of office-holders	No. of offices held		
			Rural and general[b]	Urban[c]	Total
Brahmin	4.2	14 (13.6%)	3 (3.2%)	12 (24.5%)	15 (10.4%)
Dhangar	5.0	5 (4.9%)	5 (5.3%)	1 (2.0%)	6 (4.2%)
Jain	1.7	10 (9.7%)	3 (3.2%)	9 (18.4%)	12 (8.3%)
Mali	2.8	7 (6.8%)	6 (6.3%)	2 (4.1%)	8 (5.6%)
Maratha					
vətəndars	10.3	38 (36.9%)	46 (48.2%)	13 (26.5%)	59 (41.0%)
non-*vətəndars*	45.1	13 (12.6%)	21 (22.1%)	5 (10.2%)	26 (18.1%)
Other[d]	30.8	16 (15.5%)	11 (11.6%)	7 (14.2%)	18 (12.5%)
Total	99.9	103 (100.0%)	95 (99.9%)	49 (99.9%)	144 (100.1%)

[a] See Chapter 4 and Fig. 6.
[b] Zilla Parishad, Panchayat Samiti, Legislative Assembly, Maharashtra Apex Marketing Society, Satara District Land Development Bank, Satara District Central Co-operative Bank, Satara District Purchase and Sale Union. Phaltan Taluka Purchase and Sale Union, Shriram Co-operative Sugar Factory, Phaltan Cotton Ginning and Pressing Society, Phaltan Taluka Supervising Union, Shriram Education Society, unions of sugar workers.
[c] Phaltan Municipal Council, Phaltan Urban Co-operative Bank, Phaltan Education Society, unions of municipal employees.
[d] Beldar 1, Chambhar 1, Kasar 1, Koshti 1, Buddhist Mahar 2, Muslim 1, Shimpi 1, Vani Lingayat 2, Unknown 2, Ramoshi 1.

47

Aspects of political stratification

The factors underlying the inclusion of these new elements in the political elite are partially revealed by a closer analysis of the institutions in which each caste holds office. Institutions fall into two classes with regard to the constituencies from which their officers are elected. The Phaltan Municipal Council, the Phaltan Urban Co-operative Bank, and the two unions of municipal employees are based on urban constituencies. The Phaltan Education Society also has an urban base, although in this case the connection is *de facto* rather than *de jure*. Eighteen of the twenty-one officers of the Phaltan Education Society live in Phaltan town. Other institutions are restricted to rural constituencies or are open to persons in both rural and urban areas.

When office-holding is examined in these terms it is found that the offices held by Brahmins and Jains are concentrated in urban institutions. Offices held by *vatandar* and non-*vatandar* Marathas as well as by Dhangars and Malis are concentrated in rural or general institutions. These features of the distribution of office are in accord with the analysis of caste distribution presented in Chapter 4 (see Fig. 8).

The institutions of local and state government, co-operative societies concerned with economic and educational activities, and, to a lesser extent, labor unions provide the arenas within which politicians form alliances. The legislation and conventions relating to these institutions

regulate political conflict by laying down who is eligible to compete, what are the prizes for the winner, and what the competitors may do and what they must not do in their efforts to gain the prizes. (Bailey 1963b:224)

The analysis of the personnel holding office in these institutions discloses that the largest elements in the political elite of Western Maharashtra are the *vatandar* Marathas followed by the non-*vatandar* Marathas, the Brahmins, the Jain Gujars, the Malis, and the Dhangars. It may be assumed that the *vatandar* Marathas, Brahmins and Jains, all of whom have achieved representation in the political elite far out of proportion to their share of the population, comprise the great majority of the political class and have privileged access to political power. Similarly, it may be assumed that those groups, such as non-*vatandar* Marathas, which are under represented on the political elite and those groups, such as Malis and Dhangars, whose control of office is roughly proportional to their share of the population fall outside the political class. It remains to see how the political class may be distinguished from the rest of the population in terms of caste, land tenure, and kinship.

4

Caste status and distribution

As I noted in the previous chapter, much of the literature on political stratification in India centers on the notion of the 'dominant caste'. According to Srinivas, the author of this concept,

A caste may be said to be 'dominant' when it preponderates numerically over the other castes, and when it also wields preponderant economic and political power. A large and powerful caste group can more easily be dominant if its position in the local caste hierarchy is not too low. (1955:18)

Mayer (1958a) observes that Srinivas's definition is concerned with aspects of dominance at the level of a single village, but that more inclusive levels of dominance also may be distinguished. Thus a caste is dominant in a region when it is dominant in a substantial majority of the villages of that region. A caste is dominant in the government of the district or state when it provides a substantial majority of the influential participants in institutions such as district councils, state cabinets, and so on. In some cases, as in Dewas Senior, there may be no regionally dominant caste. It is also possible for a caste to be dominant at a higher level of government without being dominant in the region. For example, in nineteenth-century Guntur District Deshastha (Maratha) Brahmins dominated the highest offices of district administration, while the British monopolized the Presidency administration, including Collectorships, but both groups were foreign to Madras and were without dominance at the village or regional levels (see Frykenberg 1965). Dumont, while accepting that

The notion of dominance, or rather of the dominant caste, represents the most solid and useful acquisition of the studies of social anthropology in India (1970: 158),

throws doubt upon several of Srinivas's criteria. Numerical preponderance, he argues, is more likely a result of dominance than a condition (Dumont 1970:161–2). More importantly, Dumont insists that ritual status derived from the principle of hierarchy, the opposition of the pure and impure, be distinguished clearly from dominance (1970:162) and he notes that dominance *per se* results from control of the land (1970:153).

Neither Mayer's extension of Srinivas's notion nor Dumont's sharpening of it challenges the association of dominance with caste groups. Others, however, have suggested that these are quite separate phenomena. Dube (1968), following up and adding to the evidence suggesting that castes containing powerful persons may be riven by factional conflict, argues that only when a caste meeting all the criteria of village dominance also acts in a united fashion may it be said to wield dominance *as a caste*. All the evidence suggests that such united action is extremely uncommon and suspect even when it does occur. In a study of politics in Dewas District, Madhya Pradesh, for example, Mayer (1967a:124–5) observes that in a given political arena there may be a single dominant caste, two castes competing for dominance, or several landed castes with more or less equal power. In the first case the principal political cleavages are likely to be vertical. They probably will be horizontal in the second case and a mixture of vertical and horizontal in the third case. In the second case it may appear that united caste groups are competing, but, as Mayer points out, it often is hard to tell whether allies have joined together because they are caste mates, because they are lineage mates, or because they have made some sort of agreement regarding their personal political interests.

In Western Maharashtra, too, the evidence suggests that castes do not act politically in a united fashion and that it is better to separate caste from dominance and to speak of dominant groups as comprising a political class. Thus, one may say, as a first approximation, that the Maratha caste is dominant in Girvi and in the region of Western Maharashtra as a whole, but it is clear that one section of the caste has dominance while the other does not. Persons who belong to *vatəndar* lineages have privileged access to office and belong to the political class while non-*vatəndar* Marathas do not. Furthermore, at the regional level the *vatəndar* Marathas are joined in the political class by other elements of the population, notably Brahmins and Jains. At all levels the political class cross-cuts caste. No one caste has a monopoly of power nor are all sections of any powerful caste included within the political class.

One may go further, however, and suggest that caste and dominance are distinct in principle as well as in practice. In *Homo Hierarchicus* (1970), his authoritative study of the caste system, Dumont conclusively demonstrates that one essential element of caste is a principle of hierarchy, the opposition of pure and impure. In Fortesian terms this principle emanates from the ritual domain; that is, it is mystically sanctioned and serves the supreme religious values and most imperative non-utilitarian interests of the society as a whole. Dominance, on the other hand, is related to rulership and control of land (for the connection between these see Neale 1969). At higher levels of the political community it traditionally had to do with kingship (see Dumont 1962) while today it has to do with elective office, but at the local level the traditional notion of landed patron who protects his clients and settles their disputes is almost as strong today as it was in the past. In Fortesian terms, again, the principle of dominance emanates from the politico-jural domain. The position may be changing in contemporary India with its attempt to build a secular state, but, as Dumont notes, in traditional Hindu thought the political-jural domain has only relative autonomy and is encompassed by hierarchy. The important point, here, however, is that neither in the traditional nor the modern system is there any suggestion that offices and land are held by caste groups. Rather, they are held by descent groups of some sort or, especially today, by individuals (see also Gardner 1968).

If we admit that dominance is not a property of hierarchically arranged status bearing units and that the political class and caste are best treated separately we still must ask how each of these phenomena influences the other. In the present context two points should be noted. In the first place, castes are distributed unevenly over the ground. Some of the smaller castes are concentrated in particular settlements and it is here that they are likely to find access to the political class and political elite. In the second place, while ritual caste status is not a prerequisite for office, it is very useful as a kind of asset which in some circumstances may be exchanged for political support. It is with these two aspects of caste, status and distribution, that I am concerned in the present chapter.

In Figure 6 the major castes of Satara District are listed in alphabetical order. On the basis of rank and traditional occupation most of these castes may be grouped into the following rough categories comprising around eighty per cent of the 1901 population of the District: (1) Brahmins; (2) Marathas and Kunbis; (3) other agricultural castes, Dhangars and Malis; (4) service castes, of which the Nhavis, Sutars, and Kumbhars are the largest, and (5) Scheduled Castes, Chambhars, Mahars, and Mangs.

Maharashtrian Brahmins are divided into a number of endogamous castes of which the largest are the Deshasthas, Chitpavans, Sarasvats, and Karhadas. The most important in Western Maharashtra are the Deshasthas and Chitpavans. Until early in the twentieth century most of the hereditary village accountants (Kulkarnis) in the Deccan were Deshasthas (Enthoven 1920:245). Around that time the British began to replace the Brahmin Kulkarnis with appointed Maratha Talathis in an attempt to win Maratha support against the Brahmin-led Independence Movement. Traditionally, the Deshasthas were found mainly in the villages, but in the past fifty years they have been moving to the towns in increasing numbers.

51

Fig. 6   Castes in Satara District[a]

Caste	Traditional occupation	Population	Per cent
Brahmin	Priest and Kulkarni	50,498	4.2
Deshastha 34,911			
Chitpavan 8,733			
Other 6,814			
Chambhar	Leather worker	18,675	1.6
Dhangar	Shepherd	59,547	5.0
Jain		19,649	1.7
Kumbhar	Potter	12,811	1.1
Lingayat castes		34,440	2.7
Vani 4,957			
Other 27,483			
Mahar	Scavenger and watchman	100,427	8.4
Mali	Gardener	33,156	2.8
Mang	Rope maker	19,232	1.6
Maratha		662,922	55.7
Proper 122,607	10.3%		
Kunbi[b] 536,922	45.1%		
Konkoni 3,393	0.3%		
Muslim		45,006	3.8
Nhavi	Barber	15,889	1.3
Ramoshi	Watchman	25,950	2.2
Sutar	Carpenter	12,165	1.0
Other castes[c]		81,407	6.8
		1,189,774	99.8

[a] From *Census of India*, 1901. Vol. IX-B, Table XIII. The data are intended to indicate the caste composition of the population of the region around Girvi. It may be assumed that the percentages are roughly accurate, but in other respects the data are misrepresentative of the contemporary situation. I use the 1901 census because it contains the most complete caste analysis of the population. The figures are a combination of the entries for Satara District and Satara Agency. The former includes three talukas (Khanapur, pop. 82,328; Tasgaon, pop. 79,795; Valva, pop. 128,505) which are not part of modern Satara District. Satara Agency comprised several small native states, including Phaltan, which are now merged in Satara District. There is a separate entry, in alphabetical order, for each caste with one per cent or more of the population.

[b] The census makes an unexplained distinction between, and contains separate entries for, Kunbis and Maratha Kunbis. I have combined the two under the single heading 'Kunbi'.

[c] Other castes include Parit (Washerman): 8192; Gurav (Temple Priest): 9952; Koshti (Weaver): 9223; Lohar (Blacksmith): 5423; Shimpi (Tailor): 10,577; Sonar (Goldsmith): 8337; Teli (Oilman): 6029; Vani (merchant): 6029.

The Chitpavans originated in the Konkon but moved up into the Deccan in large numbers during the rule of the Chitpavan Peshwas in Poona when many of them were employed in government and were rewarded with grants of land. Unlike the Deshasthas, the Chitpavan Brahmins of the Deccan were concentrated in towns. Almost 80 per cent of those living in Poona district lived in the sub-division containing Poona city, and the same pattern of settlement occurs throughout the Desh. (Johnson 1970:99–100)

The Marathas are by far the largest caste in the region. Professor Karve estimates (1961:20) that they comprise forty per cent of the population of Western Maharashtra and in 1901 they made up about fifty-five per cent of the population of Satara District. Most Marathas are agriculturalists, but they also provide the great majority of the Patils (hereditary village headmen) of the area. Since before the days of their great hero, Shivaji, some Marathas have been rulers and soldiers. Many claim Kshatriya status.

Until about 1911 a distinction was made between Marathas and Kunbis. The distinction was one of class rather than caste. Marathas were traditionally landlords and chiefs while Kunbis were cultivators, but hypergamous marriages did occur between them (Enthoven 1922b:8–9). Enthoven reports that,

...if a Poona Brahman were asked the distinction between a Maratha and a Kunbi he would say '*Kunbi majla Maratha jhala*' i.e. when a Kunbi attains to prosperity he becomes a Maratha, i.e. by prohibiting widow remarriage, putting on a sacred thread and enforcing the *purda*. Instances are not wanting, in which Kunbi families, owing to a fortunate turn in their circumstances, have formed connections with poor Maratha families and ultimately became absorbed into the general Maratha community. (1922a:286)

Around 1911 the Kunbi category disappeared into the inclusive Maratha caste, probably because of competition between Marathas and Brahmins for political power in the early years of the twentieth century (see Kumar 1968 and Latthe 1924). In Maharashtra today no one admits to being a Kunbi and it would be insulting to suggest that a Maratha was of Kunbi origin. It is likely, however, that the distinction which I draw between *vǝtǝndar* and non-*vǝtǝndar* Marathas parallels the earlier distinction between Marathas and Kunbis.

The Mahars are the second largest caste in Maharashtra and the largest Scheduled Caste. Traditionally they were employed as village watchmen, messengers and scavengers, but they now refuse to perform such degrading duties. Since 1956 many Mahars have converted to Buddhism in protest against their oppressed status (see Zelliot 1966). In the villages Mahars generally live in separate hamlets to the east of the main settlement (see Map 3).

Few of the other castes require comment here. People say that the traditional occupation of the Ramoshis was thievery, but they also were employed as hereditary village watchmen. Today some of them are owner-cultivators of their own farms. Many more work as agricultural laborers.

53

Some are distillers of illicit liquor. Ramoshis are very poor and are included among the Backward Classes.

Most Jains, Lingayats and Muslims are found in the towns where many of them are merchants.

CASTE RANK

As a rule Girvi people are little concerned with ritual caste rank. There are not, for example, the many restrictions on caste interdining that Mayer (1960) reports for Malwa. However, on the basis of infrequent interdining restrictions and a variety of other ritual observances Girvi castes might be roughly ranked as in Figure 7.

Fig. 7 Caste rank in Girvi[a]

Clean castes

Brahmin   Maratha
Dhangar   Mali
Sutar, Nhavi, Kumbhar, Shimpi
Muslim
Ramoshi

Polluting castes

Chambhar
Mahar   Mang

[a] I have excluded those smaller castes whose members did not play a large role in village social life.

Although it should not be assumed that everyone in Girvi would agree with the ranking of castes in Figure 7, the broad outlines are confirmed by rituals in which status is publicly asserted. For example, in the annual Bendur festival the larger castes decorate their bullocks and take them in procession around the Maruti temple in the village bazaar. The Marathas lead the procession followed by the Malis, Sutars, Ramoshis and, finally, the Mahars.

I am not suggesting that caste rank elsewhere in Maharashtra is exactly the same as it is in Girvi. However, two points of importance for the analysis of the role of caste in politics can be made with confidence. Of the larger castes Marathas and Brahmins are of unambiguously high status while Mahars are of unambiguously low status.

Nevertheless, there is a surprising degree of equality among clean castes. This equality is expressed by widespread interdining. I have, for example, witnessed Brahmins, Marathas, Nhavis, Kumbhars, and Shimpis eating together at a meal prepared by Dhangars. On another occasion Marathas, Dhangars, Nhavis, Shimpis, and Muslims ate together at a meal prepared by Kumbhars. Brahmins and Malis will not take food from Ramoshis, but Marathas and Dhangars will.

54

Furthermore, caste equality is expressed by the tendency to call all clean castes Marathas. The response of the *vətəndar* Maratha President of the Phaltan Municipal Council to an inquiry about the composition of the Council was typical. He distinguished three categories of Councillors: (1) Buddhists, formerly Mahars; (2) people from outside Maharashtra such as Jains and Lingayats; (3) Marathas. Only when pressed for details did he divide the latter into subcastes (*potjat*) such as Maratha Brahmin Maratha Shimpi, Maratha Dhangar, and Maratha Ramoshi.

The relative lack of concern with caste hierarchy is consistent with the *bhakti* beliefs of the devotees of Vithoba in Maharashtra (see Chapter 2). Of course, it is consistent, too, with a desire on the part of Marathas to avoid calling attention to the dominant position of their own caste and with attempts to stress regional identity against outsiders from other linguistic regions.

CASTE DISTRIBUTION

Although Marathas are dominant in Girvi and in the region as a whole they are not dominant in every settlement. Variations in dominance are in part a function of variations in caste distribution. The distribution of castes varies along two axes: a town versus village axis and a village versus village axis. Differences in the caste composition of village populations seem to be random. The differences in the composition of urban and rural populations, on the other hand, probably are related systematically to the different functions of the two kinds of settlements.

Figure 8 contains an analysis of the caste composition of Phaltan town, a small market center, and part of its surrounding rural area. It is based on a survey by Karve and Ranadive of Phaltan town and twenty-three villages in Phaltan Taluka within seven miles of the town (Karve and Ranadive 1965:9–10). Unfortunately it is impossible to include the Maratha/Kunbi or *vətəndar* Maratha/non-*vətəndar* Maratha distinction in this analysis. Although I can identify *vətəndar* and non-*vətəndar* Marathas in Phaltan and in villages with which I am personally acquainted, after 1901 there are no data on the proportions of these two categories in the population as a whole.

Large agricultural castes such as Marathas, Dhangars, and Malis are concentrated in the villages. On the other hand, Brahmins, merchant castes such as Jains and Lingayats, and service castes such as Koshtis, Kumbhars, Lohars, Nhavis, Shimpis, Sonars, Sutars, and Telis tend to be concentrated in the towns. Brahmins, who comprise 13.8 per cent of the urban population versus 1.4 per cent of the rural population, are probably attracted to the towns by opportunities for education and white-collar

Fig. 8   Caste composition of urban and rural areas

Caste	Phaltan Town		Twenty-three villages	
	No. of families	Per cent	No. of families	Per cent
Bhatake	17	2.4	4	0.7
Brahmin	98	13.8	8	1.4
Chambhar	6	0.8	17	3.0
Dhangar	20	2.8	70	12.5
Jain	45	6.4	4	0.7
Koshti	20	2.8	1	0.2
Kumbhar	10	1.4	1	0.2
Lingayat	20	2.8	1	0.2
Lohar	10	1.4	0	0.0
Mahar	64	9.0	69	12.3
Mali	25	3.5	94	16.7
Mang	12	1.7	12	2.1
Maratha	170	24.0	201	35.8
Muslim	48	6.8	14	2.5
Nhavi	10	1.4	8	1.4
Rajput	2	0.3	8	1.4
Ramoshi	22	3.1	32	5.7
Shimpi	22	3.1	1	0.2
Sonar	10	1.4	2	0.4
Sutar	12	1.7	3	0.5
Teli	10	1.4	0	0.0
Wadar	19	2.7	2	0.4
Other Castes	36	5.1	10	1.8
	708	99.8	562	100.1

Source: Karve and Ranadive 1965:9–10.

employment. Merchant and service castes, who comprise altogether 14.6 per cent of the urban population but 2.9 per cent of the rural population, are drawn to the towns by the markets for their products and services. All enjoy the political strength which results from their concentration in a few urban communities.

Although comparable data are not available for other Maharashtrian towns, it may be assumed that a high proportion of Brahmins, merchant castes, and service castes is characteristic of urban populations in Western Maharashtra.

Within the rural population one finds that, although no single caste is dominant in every village, local numerical dominance is confined to four of the five largest rural agricultural castes: Marathas, Dhangars, Malis, and Ramoshis. Only the low caste Mahars, the fourth largest rural group, are excluded from local numerical dominance. I have analysed twenty-one of the villages in the Karve–Ranadive survey for which sufficient data are available in Professor Karve's notes. Marathas are the largest single caste in fourteen of the twenty-one villages. They comprise a majority in nine villages. Dhangars, the third largest caste in the region and the third largest agricultural caste, are the largest caste in five villages. In four of the

Fig. 9   Caste composition of selected villages (per cent)

I. Villages near Phaltan[a]

	Maratha	Mahar	Dhangar	Muslim	Mali	Ramoshi	Other
Mandhav-khadak	30.2	9.8			24.6	32.8	1.6
Kuravli Kh.	42.2	9.3	7.2		31.1		10.2
Tawadi	66.8				5.2	17.5	10.5
Sonwadi Bk.	44.8			7.6	26.3	6.7	21.3
Tirakwadi			33.1	10.0	22.7	9.5	24.7
Girvi	56.9	8.5	1.7	2.1	9.8	9.9	11.1

II. A village near Baramuti, Poona District[b]

	Maratha	Mahar	Sagar Rajput	Mang	Other
Gaon	32.6	8.4	23.4	10.4	25.2

III. Two villages in Man Taluka, Satara District[c]

	Maratha	Mahar	Dhangar	Mang	Ramoshi	Other
Divad	54.1	3.2	25.4	5.4		11.9
Palsavade	24.3	12.1	42.7		15.9	5.0

[a] Data kindly provided by Professor I. Karve from that used in Karve and Ranadive (1965). I have used only those villages for which the population given in the Karve and Ranadive survey agrees with that given in the 1961 census. Where the population figures for a village are not in agreement there is a chance that single caste hamlets were excluded from the Karve and Ranadive survey, thus altering the apparent caste composition.
[b] From Orenstein (1965:26 and 28). Sagar Rajputs are Dhangars who changed their caste name early in the present century (Orenstein 1965:111, 120, 145).
[c] From Valunjkar (1966:2).

villages they constitute a majority of the population. In addition, Malis form a majority in one village and Ramoshis are the largest single caste in another. Figure 9, which confirms the above pattern, gives a more detailed analysis of the caste composition of Girvi, five of the villages in the Karve–Ranadive survey, and three other villages described in the literature.

SUMMARY

In general, given an economic position which permits independent political action and given institutions based on universal adult suffrage, the political influence of a caste is a function of three interdependent variables: (1) its own size and solidarity, (2) the size and solidarity of other castes, and (3) its ability to control the votes of other castes. It is abundantly clear that caste solidarity is a weak vessel, but politicians often profess to believe and act as if they do believe that given a choice people will vote for their caste mate and voters not infrequently explain their own behavior in this manner. It is important, therefore, that, although on the regional level Western Maharashtra is dominated by *vətəndar* Marathas, there remain some wards, towns, and villages in which non-Maratha groups are numerically preponderant. The settlements in which Marathas are few in numbers serve as channels through which members of minority castes may gain access to the political arena. It is important, too, that the *vətəndar* Marathas possess high caste status which in the recent past has not been shared by while yet being accessible to their non-*vətəndar* caste mates. As I shall show, this caste status has been a valuable political asset for the *vətəndar* Marathas in a variety of contexts.

5
Land, labor, credit, and share capital

The fundamental structural framework antecedent to political choice in Western Maharashtra is the division of the population into two categories: a dominant political class, consisting mainly of *vətəndar* Marathas, and the non-*vətəndar* masses. The elite position of the *vətəndar* Marathas has its origin in certain features of the traditional Maratha administrative system. Their continuing dominance is supported by their numerical predominance in the countryside and is reflected in as well as in part based upon their high ritual caste status. *Vətəndar* Maratha dominance is also based on their control of wealth. They are a privileged economic class as well as a dominant political class.

Chapter 5 is an account of the distribution of wealth in Girvi. It is divided into four sections. In the first section I describe the land tenure system in Girvi and the distribution of rights in land among the various groups in the village. In the second section I describe the relations between agricultural laborers and their employers. The third section deals with the main sources of credit available to the villagers. The distribution of shares in co-operative societies is described in the fourth section.

In Girvi the *vətəndar* Marathas control the largest share of village land and the best quality land, as well. They also have privileged access to agricultural credit. They are the major employers of agricultural labor and they own a controlling share of village co-operatives. The system of land tenure and the credit institutions in Girvi are the same as those in other villages of Western Maharashtra. One may assume that Girvi is typical of the great majority of villages in the region with regard to *vətəndar* Maratha economic dominance, also.

RIGHTS IN LAND

The following analysis of the distribution of rights in land in Girvi is based on data contained in the Record of Rights maintained by the village Talathi. The Record of Rights, which purports to be an exhaustive account of rights in land, is divided into columns containing information under the following heads:

59

1. Survey Number and Name of Field.

2. Subdivision Number.

3. Area: (*a*) Cultivable, (*b*) Uncultivable, (*c*) Gross.

4. Land Revenue: (*a*) Assessment, (*b*) Special Assessment, (*c*) Water Share.

5. Occupant and Mutations Register Reference Number.

6. Other Rights or Encumbrances and Holders Thereof; Mutations Register Reference Number.

7. Form of Cultivation or Tenancy.

8. Crops; Whether Irrigated or Non-irrigated.

The Subdivision Number of a mapped Survey Number is the unit of land revenue assessment and the minimal unit in which rights in land can be held. Many Subdivision Numbers are so small that they are classified as fragments (*tukǝḍa*) under the Bombay Prevention of Fragmentation and Consolidation of Holdings Act of 1947. Such fragments cannot be further subdivided even among the heirs of the present holders and can be transferred only to neighboring holders. Although the Subdivision is the smallest unit in terms of which rights in land are recorded, more than one person may have rights in the same Subdivision.

The quantity and quality of land in each Subdivision Number is recorded in columns 3 and 8. The total area of Girvi is 12,672 acres of which 6466.65 are cultivable. The Forestry Department controls 4167.68 acres of land in the Mahadev hills which are used only for grazing. A small tank under the control of the Department of Public Works occupies 130.5 acres in Dhumalvadi. The remaining 1907.17 acres are privately owned uncultivable land, house sites, stream beds, roads, etc.

Villagers recognize two main categories of cultivable land, irrigated (*bagayat*) and non-irrigated (*jirayat*), the incidence of which is recorded in column 8 of the Record of Rights. Highly profitable cash crops such as sugar-cane, cotton, bananas, grapes, and oranges are grown only on irrigated land. The difference in the value of the two kinds of land is reflected both in the price of land and in ceiling legislation. In 1966 informants estimated that non-irrigated land cost from Rs. 500 to Rs. 2000 per acre while irrigated land cost from Rs. 4000 to Rs. 8000 per acre. For the purposes of the Bombay Tenancy and Agricultural Lands Act of 1948 one acre of perennially irrigated land is held to be equal to four acres of non-irrigated land. Irrigation in the southern half of Phaltan Taluka is exclusively from privately owned wells. Where, as in Dhumalvadi, tanks have been constructed their purpose is to raise the water table so that more water can be taken from the wells below the tank. Of the 6466.65 acres of cultivable land in Girvi 1055.33 are irrigated and 5411.32 are non-irrigated.

The rights which are held in each Subdivision Number and the holders of those rights are listed in columns 5, 6, and 7 of the Record of Rights. These include the rights of the government, the rights and duties of occupants or owners, rights of tenants, rights arising from credit transactions, and so on.

As Girvi consists of 19.8 square miles of land divided into 523 Survey Numbers many of which are further divided into tens of Subdivision Numbers, I did not find it possible to check systematically the Record of Rights against the statements of informants. The greatest difficulties arise from the fact that the Record of Rights is not always up to date even though all mutations are supposed to be promptly reported to the Talathi by the parties concerned. However, since I am interested more in the distribution of rights between castes than in the rights held by particular individuals, the errors which the Record of Rights may contain do not present any serious difficulties. Most errors arise from the fact that changes due to death and inheritance are not recorded promptly, but such changes do not alter the caste distribution of rights.

I have checked the names of all right holders listed in the Record of Rights against a complete village census and all available genealogical information, but it still has not been possible to identify all of them. In most cases it is reasonably certain that unidentifiable right holders fall into one of two categories: (*a*) residents of neighboring villages or (*b*) persons who were residents of Girvi but who have since left and of whom present residents have little or no knowledge. There is only one person who might be considered an absentee landlord and that is Vijaysingh Naik Nimbalkar, the Raja of Phaltan's son.

Kinds of rights in land

The rights in land listed in columns 5, 6, and 7 of the Record of Rights are defined by legislation passed by the Bombay and Maharashtra State Governments. The system of land tenure which is actually practiced in the village is virtually the same as that established by the State Government. Villagers are aware of the provisions of the law and are careful to inform themselves of any changes which are made. When, for example, in 1966 new legislation was passed dealing with a cultivator's right to construct irrigation channels across his neighbor's land, the newspaper accounts of the new law were passed around the village and widely discussed for several weeks. The Talathi, the government official in charge of the land records, is required to live in the village where he is employed and he is intimately involved in the affairs of the villagers.

Occupancy or ownership rights. Under the traditional Maratha administration (see Chapter 2) there were three kinds of occupancy rights in land: *vətən meeras*, ordinary *meeras*, and *oopree*. *Meeras* tenure was hereditable. *Vətən meeras* was tax-free while ordinary *meeras* was taxable. *Oopree* tenure was short term, non-hereditable, and taxable.

Upon assuming control of the Deccan in 1818, the British sought to introduce the ryotwari system of revenue settlement which had been originated in Madras Presidency by Read and Munro. The attempt was unsuccessful, however, so long as they depended upon officials and records taken over from the administration of the Peshwas. For some time the British continued to employ the traditional Maratha system of settling the revenue for each village as a whole. In his 1822 instructions for revenue officials Chaplin, the second Commissioner of the Deccan, prescribed two alternative methods:

(i) the old system, according to which the village was to be settled for in bulk and the total arrived at distributed over the individual holdings, and (ii) by which the individual settlements were to be made first and added together to make the village total. The employment of this second method, however, is deprecated on account of the interminable quarrels and delay which is stated to be the inevitable result of all attempts to settle with the rayats individually. Hence the former method is recommended for general adoption. This system was that of the Marathas with the added precaution that the Sub-Divisional Officer and the Mamlatdars were supposed, after settling the village total, to fix the contributions of the rayats also. (Gordon 1959:15)

It was only with the development of survey and assessment procedures which could be applied to each field that a ryotwari system of land revenue settlement and administration could be established. This was attempted by Pringle in 1827 and finally carried out successfully by Goldsmid and Wingate in 1836. As Gordon notes, a major consequence of the new survey and assessment procedures was the abolition of the distinction between *meeras* and *oopree* tenure.

By basing the land assessment upon the value of the land itself and not as, heretofore, upon the status of the holder and by guaranteeing the rates for a long period, Mr Pringle to all intents and purposes did away with all the old distinctions between the two and so prepared the groundwork for the more definite 'survey tenure' which was to come with the new system. (1959:18)

The ryotwari land revenue system reached its fullest development in 1913. In that year the Record of Rights system was introduced and the

Land, labor, credit, and share capital

Subdivision of the Survey Number was established as the unit of land-holding and assessment.

Inam or *vatən* tenures are those in which the government has alienated or relinquished its claim to all or part of the revenue in favor of some individual, group or institution. The Inam Commission, established in 1852 as the successor of the Inam Committee of 1843, divided *inam* tenures into the following classes:

1. Personal *inams*. Lands alienated to individuals.

2. *Devasthan inams*. Land alienated for the support of mosques, temples, and other similar institutions.

3. Hereditary service *inams*.

> By a 'Service Inam' is meant a holding of land or a right to receive cash payments or to levy customary fees or perquisites in return for the performance of certain duties either to Government or the community. The holders of Service Inams, or Vatans as they are called in the Deccan, are divided into the following classes:
>
> (1) District Officers [Desais, Deshmukhs, Deshpandes, and so on].
> (2) Village Officers.
>   (a) useful to Government [Patil and Kulkarni],
>   (b) useful to the Village Community [*balutedars*],
>   (c) useless both to Government and the Community [Potdar and Chaugula].
>   (Gordon 1959:162)

4. Political *inams*.

> ... a grant by the State for the performance of the civil or military duties, or for the maintenance of the personal dignity of nobles and high officials. (Gordon 1959:164)

The British rejected or phased out many claims to *inams*, particularly personal *inams*, but until Independence no attack was made on the principle of alienation. However, since Independence, with the passage of the Bombay Personal Inams Abolition Act of 1952, the Bombay Service Inams (Useful to Community) Abolition Act of 1953, the Bombay Inferior Village Vatans Abolition Act of 1958, and the Maharashtra Revenue Patels (Abolition of Office) Act of 1962, etc., alienations have been attacked in principle and the incidence of *inam* tenures greatly reduced. In Girvi the only remaining alienations are *devasthan inams*.

The 1952 legislation abolishing personal *inams* granted the lands concerned to the cultivator in actual possession on unrestricted Ordinary Survey Tenure. However, in abolishing other categories of *inams* the government resumed the land and made provision for re-granting it to the original holder under Restricted Survey Tenure with limits on the occupant's rights of transfer.

Under the Bombay Land Revenue Code (Act v of 1879) the owner or occupant of a Subdivision Number held on Survey Tenure is a

holder in actual possession of unalienated land other than a tenant: provided that where the holder in actual possession is a tenant, the landlord or superior landlord as the case may be, shall be deemed to be the occupant. (Quoted in Gordon 1959: 148)

The occupant of land held in Ordinary Survey Tenure has rights of inheritance, transfer, and resignation, that is, in favor of the government which may then regrant the land. The assessment of his land is guaranteed for thirty years. The occupant may construct farm buildings or wells and make any manner of improvement for agricultural purposes. Furthermore, he has the right to the full enjoyment of all improvements, that is, they do not affect revisions of his assessment. The occupant also has the right to trees on his land. He has the right to alluvial formations less than an acre in extent, the right of first refusal of the occupancy of alluvial formations greater than a acre in extent, and the right to remission of assessment in the event of losses by diluvion not less than half an acre in extent. In return the occupant is obliged to pay the annual assessment and any cesses which the government may levy. He is required

to attend and give information to Survey Officers,...to furnish flagholders for Survey purposes,...to construct boundary marks and keep them in repair,... [and] to report acquisition of rights. (Quoted and explained in Gordon 1959:152–5)

Restricted Survey Tenure was introduced into the Land Revenue Code by Bombay Acts vi of 1901 and iv of 1913, but at that time it had little application in the Deccan Districts of Western Maharashtra (see Gordon 1959:155–8). However, with the extensive abolition of *inam* tenures since Independence and the regranting of former *inam* lands to the original holders with restrictions on the right of transfer this form of tenure has become more common.

The three varieties of ownership rights in land found in Western Maharashtra at the beginning of British rule, *vǝtǝn meeras*, ordinary *meeras* and *oopree*, thus have been replaced largely by ordinary and restricted Survey Tenure. *Oopree* tenure has disappeared. With the exception of *devasthan* lands, *inam* tenures have been converted to one or the other variety of Survey Tenure. Ordinary *meeras* tenure has been transformed into ordinary Survey Tenure without any marked discontinuities.

The right of ownership in a Subdivision Number may be held by one person or by a group, as is also the case with other categories of rights. Rights of ownership shared by a group, most often composed of close agnates, may be allocated in several ways. If the co-occupants of a field divide it into plots and grow separate crops, then each has a separate share (*hissa*) which may, if the field is large enough, be converted into a separately registered and assessed Subdivision Number. If they raise a single crop and divide the produce or if they let to a single tenant and divide the rent, then they are holders-in-common. If they produce a single crop and consume it undivided or if they let the land and use the rent to support their undivided household, then they are joint holders.

Inferior rights. The person who is obliged to pay the assessment on a piece of land has rights of occupancy. The person who cultivates the land with his own labor or that of members of his family or with hired labor under his personal supervision has rights of possession. Usually the occupant of land also has possession of it, but occupancy and possession rights may be held separately. Tenancy contracts, management (*vǝhivaṭṭat*) agreements and some mortgages confer rights of possession in land on persons other than the occupant. Mortgages and other credit transactions are discussed in the third part of this chapter. I am concerned here with the relations between occupant and possessor which are created by tenancy and management agreements.

The landmarks of tenancy regulation in Maharashtra are the Bombay Tenancy Act of 1939, the Bombay Tenancy (Amendment) Act of 1946, the Bombay Tenancy and Agricultural Lands Act of 1948, and the Bombay Tenancy and Agricultural Lands (Amendment) Act of 1956. The earlier legislation created a special category of protected tenants who were defended from eviction and unreasonable rents, but it left the land tenancy system essentially unchanged. The Amending Act of 1956, however, had the more radical purpose of overturning the tenancy system. By providing for the automatic purchase of their land by all but a few tenants from all but a few landlords the Act sought to abolish nearly all tenancy contracts and to greatly increase personal owner cultivation.

From Independence until 1957 tenancy contracts in Satara District were governed by the Bombay Tenancy and Agricultural Lands Act of 1948. The legislation controlled rents, the duration of tenancies, and the circumstances under which a non-cultivating occupant could resume possession or a tenant could acquire rights of occupancy.

A tenant is a person who lawfully cultivates and is in possession of land in which he does not have occupancy rights. Persons who possess land occupied by a member of their family and persons who possess land by virtue of a mortgage are not tenants.

The law recognizes three kinds of tenants. The Bombay Land Revenue

Code of 1879 held that any tenant the commencement or duration of whose tenancy was lost in antiquity was a 'permanent' tenant (*kayəm kuḷ*). The Bombay Tenancy Act of 1939 as amended in 1946 created a new category of 'protected' tenants (*sənrəkšət kuḷ*), that is, any tenant who had cultivated the same piece of land continuously for six years immediately preceding the first day of 1945. In disputed cases the burden of proof was placed upon the landlord. Every tenant was deemed to be a protected tenant from 8 November 1947, and his rights were to be so recorded in the Record of Rights, unless he was a permanent tenant or unless prior to that date a competent authority, acting on an application of the landlord, declared the tenant not to be protected.[1] Tenancies created after 8 November were ordinary (*sadhe*) tenancies.

Under the 1948 Bombay Tenancy and Agricultural Lands Act protected tenancies, like permanent tenancies, were perpetual. A tenant's rights of possession passed to his heir or heirs at his death. Although a landlord could resume his land for personal cultivation or for any non-agricultural purpose of his own, he could not otherwise terminate a tenancy unless the tenant violated his contract by failing to pay the rent, by sub-letting the land, by injuring the land, or by using it for non-agricultural purposes. The landlord's right of resumption could be exercised only if it did not result in there being more than fifty acres under his personal cultivation, but no minimum was placed on the amount to be left in the possession of the tenant.[2] A tenant was allowed to purchase land in his possession if it did not reduce the landlord's holding to less than fifty acres or raise the tenant's holding to above fifty acres.

Ordinary tenancies were to be for ten years. They were to be renewed automatically at the end of each ten-year period unless the landlord requested that they be terminated. Although ordinary tenancies were not perpetual, ordinary tenants did have complete protection from resumption by the landlord during the ten-year period of their contracts.

Rents were regulated in terms of crop share, although they could be paid either in cash or in kind. The rent for land cultivated by a tenant was to be that agreed upon by the tenant and the landlord but was not to exceed one-quarter of the crop on irrigated land or one-third of the crop on dry land. Whenever the land revenue on a Subdivision Number was wholly or partially suspended the rent also was to be suspended in proportion.

The Amending Act of 1956 requires that all rents be paid annually and in cash. The maximum rent is not to exceed five times the assessment or Rs. 20 per acre, whichever is less. The minimum rent is to be twice the assessment or Rs. 20 per acre, whichever is greater. A tenant also is required to pay the land revenue, irrigation cess and local government fund cesses due on the land possessed by him as tenant. However, if in any year the total of the rent and taxes payable by a tenant on land held by him as tenant exceeds one-sixth of the value of the produce of the land then he is entitled to deduct the excess from the rent.

Most importantly, the Bombay Tenancy and Agricultural Lands (Amendment) Act of 1956 provided for the automatic purchase of land by tenants in possession. On 1 April 1957 every tenant who was personally cultivating was deemed to have purchased the land in his possession provided that he paid the purchase price and that the landlord did not successfully apply to have his tenancy terminated. However, a tenant's rights of purchase can be exercised only so long as the land held by him as occupant does not exceed forty-eight acres of dry land, twelve acres of irrigated land or an equivalent combination of both. Tenants are prevented, too, from purchasing land occupied by a widow, minor, member of the armed forces or other 'disabled' landlord until the disability ends or the disabled landlord is succeeded by a competent adult. With regard to tenancies created after 1 April 1957, tenants may, within the above limits, purchase land held by them as tenants within one year from the beginning of the tenancy contract.

The price of land purchased under the Bombay Tenancy and Agricultural Lands (Amendment) Act of 1956 varies with the status of the tenant. Permanent tenants who are cultivating personally must pay six times the rent of the land. Other tenants are to pay an amount determined by an Agricultural Lands Tribunal attached to the Revenue Department. However, the price is to be not less than twenty times and not more than two hundred times the assessment.

If a permanent tenant has sublet his land, the subtenant, whether protected or ordinary, is deemed to be the purchaser of the land held by him as subtenant. Out of the purchase price of such land, the subtenant is to pay six times the rent to the occupant and the balance to the permanent tenant.

Management agreements (*vahivaṭṭat*) also confer rights of possession on inferior holders who cultivate land personally but do not occupy it. Management agreements, however, do not fall under the provisions of the Bombay Tenancy and Agricultural Lands Act of 1948 or the Amending Act of 1956. They must be renewed annually and the terms are those agreed to by the persons concerned. Rents are not controlled and the contract creates no rights of purchase for the cultivator in possession.

Distribution of rights in land in Girvi, 1966–7

In what follows I am primarily concerned with land occupied by Girvi residents. I distinguish between rights of occupancy, rights of possession

67

arising from tenancies, and rights of possession arising from management agreements (*vəhivaṭtat*). Since permanent, protected, and ordinary tenants in possession now have the same rent obligations, the same rights of purchase, and the same protection against eviction, it is not necessary to distinguish between them. Only permanent tenants have the right to sublet land held by them as tenants. Little land in Girvi is held by permanent tenants and few of them have sublet. For convenience of analysis I ignore the few permanent tenants who have sublet their land. In such cases I take into account only the subtenant in possession and the occupant.

There are 1055.33 acres of irrigated cultivable land in Girvi. Of this, 18.88 acres are occupied by unidentifiable persons or by persons who are residents of other communities. Unidentifiable occupants are in personal possession of 6.78 acres of irrigated land. The remaining 12.10 acres of land occupied by unidentifiable or non-resident occupants are possessed by tenants resident in Girvi: 4.40 acres by *vətəndar* Marathas, 3.60 acres by non-*vətəndar* Marathas, 2.00 acres by Kumbhars and 2.10 acres by Malis.

There are 5411.32 acres of non-irrigated cultivable land in Girvi. Of this amount, 333.85 acres are occupied by unidentifiable persons or by persons who are residents of other communities. Unidentifiable or non-resident occupants are in possession of 91.73 acres of dry land. They have conferred rights of possession in 222.82 acres on tenants who reside in Girvi: 17.90 acres to Chambhars, 27.83 acres to Malis, 4.88 acres to *vətəndar* Marathas, 158.03 acres to non-*vətəndar* Marathas, and 14.18 acres to Ramoshis. Unknown or nonresident occupants have conferred rights of possession in 19.30 acres on unknown tenants.[3]

Occupancy rights in 95.50 acres of cultivable dry land in Girvi are held on *devasthan inam* tenure by temples. Possession rights in all of this land are held by tenants resident in Girvi. Muslims are permanent tenants on 12.95 acres belonging to the Shri Malhari Dev in Jejuri, Poona District. *Vətəndar* Marathas are protected tenants on 21.54 acres of land belonging to the Vithoba Temple. Ramoshis are protected tenants on 16.90 acres belonging to the Maruti Temple and 6.70 acres belonging to the Bhairavnath Temple. In addition, Malis possess 12.00 acres, Chambhars 12.03 acres, and Ghadshis 13.38 acres of land belonging to the Bhairavnath Temple.

The remaining 1036.45 acres of irrigated land and 4981.97 acres of non-irrigated cultivable land in Girvi are occupied by persons resident in the village.

Rights of possession arising from tenancy and management contracts have little effect on the caste distribution of land occupied by Girvi residents. Only 88.65 acres (8.6%) of wet land owned by village residents are

68

cultivated by tenants. Of this, 69.70 acres are cultivated by tenants who belong to the same caste, or to the same section of the Maratha caste, as the owner. Only 18.95 acres (1.8%) of wet land are cultivated by tenants who do not belong to the same caste, or to the same section of the Maratha caste, as their landlord. Only 11.35 acres of wet land (1.1%) are cultivated on a *vəhivaṭṭat* basis. In all cases the cultivator is of the same caste, or division of the Maratha caste, as the occupant. Therefore, as far as caste is concerned tenancy and management contracts affect the control of only 1.8 per cent of the wet land owned by village residents.

Of the 4981.97 acres of dry land occupied by Girvi residents only 287.65 (5.8%) are cultivated by tenants. Of this amount, only 97.20 acres (2.0% of the total) are cultivated by tenants whose caste or status group is different from that of the occupant. Persons cultivating on a *vəhivaṭṭat* basis possess 62.35 acres (1.3%) of the dry land owned by village residents. Of this, 18.00 acres (0.4% of the total) are cultivated by managers who belong to a caste or to a section of the Maratha caste different from that of the occupant. As far as caste, and *vətəndar* and non-*vətəndar* Maratha status, is concerned, therefore, tenancy and *vəhivaṭṭat* agreements alter the distribution of rights in only 2.4 per cent of the non-irrigated land owned by village residents.

The caste distribution of occupancy rights in irrigated and non-irrigated land owned by Girvi residents is shown in Figure 10. *Vətəndar* Marathas own a disproportionately large share of village land. With only 24.8 per cent of the population they own 57.4 per cent of the irrigated land and 28.8 per cent of the dry land. Non-*vətəndar* Marathas and members of other castes comprise 75.2 per cent of the population, but they own only 42.6 per cent of the wet land and 71.2 per cent of the dry land occupied by village residents.

Brahmins, Lohars, Sonars, and Sutars have per capita holdings equal to or greater than those of the *vətəndar* Marathas. However, these groups are so small that their wealth does not constitute a significant share of village owned landed assets: less than ten per cent of the irrigated land and less than three per cent of the dry land.

The large groups in the village other than the *vətəndar* Marathas have disproportionately small shares of village resources. The per capita shares of wet and dry land occupied by Malis and Mahars are well below the average. The two castes comprise 18.3 per cent of the village population, but occupy only 9.2 per cent of the wet land and 8.2 per cent of the dry land occupied by village residents. Non-*vətəndar* Marathas and Ramoshis have above average per capita holdings of dry land, but their per capita holdings of wet land are very low, 0.14 and 0.05 acres respectively.

Fig. 10   Distribution of occupancy rights in Girvi land, 1966–7

Caste	Pop.	% of Pop.	Wet land (acres)	Acres of wet land per head	% of wet land	Dry land (acres)	Acres of dry land per head	% of dry land
Brahmin	39	1.0	46.13	1.18	4.5	90.43	2.32	1.8
Chambhar	96	2.5	22.00	0.23	2.1	33.50	0.35	0.7
Dhangar	64	1.7	8.13	0.13	0.8	88.80	1.39	1.8
Ghadshi	10	0.3	0.00	0.00	0.0	10.23	1.02	0.2
Kumbhar	55	1.4	1.93	0.04	0.2	8.43	0.15	0.2
Lohar	23	0.6	17.73	0.77	1.7	7.10	0.31	0.1
Mahar	326	8.5	14.48	0.04	1.4	221.08	0.68	4.4
Mali	375	9.8	80.48	0.21	7.8	188.03	0.50	3.8
Maratha (*vətəndar*)	954	24.8	594.35	0.62	57.4	1,432.83	1.50	28.8
Maratha (non-*vətəndar*)	1,232	32.1	176.73	0.14	17.1	2,172.85	1.76	43.6
Muslim	82	2.1	16.05	0.20	1.5	80.78	0.99	1.6
Nhavi	53	1.4	9.88	0.19	1.0	36.48	0.69	0.7
Ramoshi	382	9.9	17.53	0.05	1.7	565.75	1.48	11.4
Sonar	7	0.2	13.28	1.90	1.3	0.00	0.00	0.0
Sutar	28	0.7	17.75	0.62	1.7	45.68	1.63	0.9
Landless castes (Mang, Shimpi, Vani Lingayat, Patrut, Parit, etc.)	115	3.0	0.00	0.00	0.0	0.00	0.00	0.0
Total	3,841	100.0	1,036.45	0.27	100.2	4,981.97	1.30	100.0

Land, labor, credit, and share capital

As a group the *vǝtǝndar* Marathas in Girvi own great landed wealth, especially in the form of valuable irrigated land. It is important to note, however, that most occupants cultivate their land personally. When occupants do have their land cultivated by tenants or by *vǝhivaṭtat* managers, the cultivator is most often a member of the occupant's caste or status group. Girvi *vǝtǝndar* Marathas own 62.28 acres of irrigated land cultivated by tenants and 11.05 acres cultivated by *vǝhivaṭtat* managers. However, on all but 3.13 acres the cultivator in possession is also a *vǝtǝndar* Maratha. Similarly, Girvi *vǝtǝndar* Marathas own 64.45 acres of dry land cultivated by tenants and 7.73 acres cultivated by managers, but on all but 0.25 acres the cultivator in possession is also a *vǝtǝndar* Maratha. As a result *vǝtǝndar* Marathas are unable to use tenancy and management contracts to exert economic control over non-*vǝtǝndar* Marathas and members of other castes. The *vǝtǝndar* Marathas are wealthier than the great majority of their fellow villagers, but the relationship between the *vǝtǝndar* Marathas and poorer groups in the village is not that of landlord and tenant.

AGRICULTURAL LABOR

It is as employers of agricultural labor that *vǝtǝndar* Marathas use their wealth to exercise economic control over their fellow villagers. *Vǝtǝndar* Marathas employ agricultural labor while the poorer castes, especially Ramoshis and Mahars, provide it. In fact, the area around the Ramoshi street, in the south end of the village, serves as Girvi's main labor exchange.

Vǝtǝndar Marathas hire agricultural labor on both a short term and a long term basis. Short term labor is either *bhaḍyane* or *mǝjurine*. 'Bhaḍyane' has the sense of 'rent' and refers to the hire of a man's bullocks as well as the wages of his labor. *Bhaḍyane* is always paid daily in cash and earns two to three times as much as *mǝjurine* labor. *Mejurine* labor is paid in cash on either a daily or a piece-rate (*ukta*) basis. Men are paid Rs. 3 per day and women Re. 1. Alternatively a group of men may agree to perform a particular agricultural operation for an agreed amount. Such piece-rate agreements normally bring laborers a slightly better wage.

Long term agricultural laborers are called *gǝḍis*. They are hired on a monthly or yearly basis. As the length of their employment increases, their average daily wage decreases. Most are paid entirely in cash. Others are paid partly in cash and partly in food and clothing. People are now increasingly reluctant to work as *gǝḍis*. Since irrigation has made the demand for labor increasingly constant throughout the year, the higher wages of short term employment now tend to outweigh the security of long term employment.

71

A cultivator may hire long term labor on a sharecrop (*vaṭyaṇe*) basis. This is done only rarely and reluctantly, however, by those who find it difficult to actively supervise the cultivation of their land. It is hard to get rid of laborers paid on a sharecrop basis and it is felt that they are almost certain to steal part of the crop before it is divided.

Vətəndar Marathas enter into reciprocal agreements (*varguḷa*) with one another to exchange bullocks and the services of their *gəḍis*. They do not themselves, however, work for one another in this manner.

I do not have complete statistics on short term agricultural labor in Girvi, but the following cases indicate the main features of the labor market.

In July 1966 Sarjerao Kadam (Genealogy *2d*, *J*10) hired six Ramoshi men for three days on a *məjuriṇe* basis to plant one acre of sugar-cane. He paid each man Rs. 3 per day.

Also in July 1966 Ramkrishna Kadam (Genealogy *1a*, *M*7) hired two Kadam men, two Lohar men, two Mang men, one Kadam woman, one Mang woman and four Muslim women on a *məjuriṇe* basis to plant three acres of sugar-cane. He expected that the job would take three days and he paid the men Rs. 3 per day and the women Re. 1 per day. In October Ramkrishna hired nine women for several days to weed his cane. The weeding party was made up of one Dhangar, one Muslim, five Ramoshis, one Mahar and one Lohar.

At the same time Ramkrishna had another part of his holding plowed. The work was done by three men using six bullocks. Two of the bullocks were Ramkrishna's own and one of the workers was Ramkrishna's *gəḍi*, a Mahar. Vitthalrao Yeshvantrao Kadam (Genealogy *1a*, *L*15), with whom Ramkrishna had a *varguḷa* agreement, provided two more bullocks and his *gəḍi*, a Ramoshi from neighboring Varugad. Ramkrishna also hired (*bhaḍyaṇe*) a Muslim and the Muslim's bullock and a bullock alone from a Mahar. The Muslim was paid Rs. 7 per day and the Mahar Rs. 5.

Girvi *vətəndar* Marathas employ sixty-four *gəḍis*. Twenty are men who have come from other villages to Girvi in search of work. The remainder, thirty-one men, twelve women and one boy, are Girvi residents. No other caste or status group in Girvi employs labor on a long term basis.

The caste membership of *gəḍis* employed by Girvi Marathas is shown in Figure 11.

All of the women are paid Rs. 360 per year. The one boy earns Rs. 150 per year as a shepherd. Twenty-two men are paid in cash on a yearly basis; they earn an average of slightly more than Rs. 650 per year each. Eight men are paid in cash and food on a yearly basis and six are paid in cash, food and clothing on a yearly basis. The average cash earnings of the

Land, labor, credit, and share capital

Fig. 11 Caste affiliation of *Gəḍis* employed by Girvi *vətəndar*
Marathas, 1966–7

| Caste | Girvi residents | | | Non-resident adult males | Total |
	Adult males	Adult females	Boy		
Dhangar	0	0	0	1	1
Ghadshi	2	0	0	0	2
Holar	0	0	0	1	1
Mahar	8	3	0	2	13
Mali	0	0	0	1	1
Mang	3	0	0	1	4
Maratha (*vətəndar*)	2	0	0	0	2
Maratha (non-*vətəndar*)	5	1	0	7	13
Muslim	1	0	0	3	4
Ramoshi	10	8	1	4	23
					64

former are a little more than Rs. 245 per year. The latter average about Rs. 211 per year. Fifteen men work on a monthly basis. Ten earn an average of Rs. 68 per month in cash alone. Two earn an average of Rs. 22.50 per month plus food and three earn an average of Rs. 16.67 per month plus food and clothing.

Although I do not know the extent of agricultural employment in Girvi, the direction of labor relations is clear. The wealthy *vətəndar* Marathas are the principal employers. The employees are the poor Ramoshis, Mahars, non-*vətəndar* Marathas, Mangs and Muslims.

CREDIT IN GIRVI

Agricultural credit is available from both private and public sources. Private sources include traders in Phaltan and money lenders in Girvi. Most of the former are Jain Gujars. The latter are *vətəndar* Marathas. Public sources of credit include the Revenue Department, which makes small loans called *tagai*, the Satara District Land Development Bank, and the Girvi Multi-Purpose Credit Society.

Data on borrowing from private sources are difficult to obtain.[4] There is no public record of such loans and informants are reluctant to discuss the subject. It is agreed, however, that the most important money lenders are two *vətəndar* Marathas, members of the *vərči ali* Kadam *bhaubund*: Ramrao Bapusaheb Kadam (Genealogy 1a, K27) and Govindrao Madhavrao Kadam (Genealogy 1a, K13).[5]

73

Aspects of political stratification

Mortgages obtained from public sources of agricultural credit are entered in Columns 5, 6, and 7 of the Record of Rights. It is possible to use the land records, therefore, to determine the access to public credit of the various groups in Girvi.

Fig. 12   Access to agricultural credit in Girvi, 1966–7

Caste	Acres of wet land owned	Per cent of wet land mortgaged			Acres of dry land owned	Per cent of dry land mortgaged		
		CS	LDB	CS & LDB		CS	LDB	CS & LDB
Brahmin	46.13	42.7	12.1	5.1	90.43	.	.	.
Chambhar	22.00	100.0	.	.	33.50	34.2	.	.
Dhangar	8.13	87.9	.	.	88.80	67.0	.	.
Ghadshi	.	.	.	.	10.23	.	.	.
Kumbhar	1.93	.	.	.	8.43	91.9	.	.
Lohar	17.73	12.4	.	.	7.10	99.0	.	.
Mahar	14.48	9.9	.	.	221.08	12.3	.	.
Mali	80.48	18.1	5.6	14.0	188.03	21.9	9.8	1.0
Maratha (vətəndar)	594.35	48.7	15.8	6.2	1,432.83	26.6	7.3	0.5
Maratha (non-vətəndar)	176.73	21.6	1.3	4.6	2,172.85	14.5	2.7	0.4
Muslim	16.05	43.0	.	.	80.78	.	16.0	.
Nhavi	9.88	85.8	.	.	36.48	54.0	.	.
Ramoshi	17.53	48.8	19.3	.	565.75	25.3	8.8	.
Sonar	13.28	.	.	.	.	.	.	.
Sutar	17.75	13.8	.	.	45.68	.	.	.
Maratha (vətəndar)	594.35	48.7	15.8	6.2	1,432.83	26.6	7.3	0.5
All other land-owning castes	442.10	29.7	3.6	4.9	3,549.14	17.8	3.8	0.3

Note: Land may be mortgaged to the Girvi Multi-Purpose Credit Society (CS), to the Satara District Land Development Bank (LDB) or to both at once (LDB & CS).

Figure 12 shows the amounts of wet and dry land which Girvi land-owners have mortgaged to the Girvi Multi-Purpose Credit Society, to the Satara District Land Development Bank, or to both. *Vətəndar* Marathas have obtained mortgages on 70.7 per cent of their irrigated land and 34.4 per cent of their dry land. Many of the small castes in the village, Chambhars, Dhangars, Kumbhars, Lohars and Nhavis, have had little trouble obtaining loans. However, the access to credit of three of the other large agricultural castes, Mahars, Malis, and non-*vətəndar* Marathas, is severely limited. Of the large agricultural castes, only the Ramoshis have been able to obtain credit on a scale comparable to that of the *vətəndar* Marathas. Ramoshis have obtained mortgages on 68.1 per cent of their wet land and 34.1 per cent of their dry land. On the whole, however, landowners who do not belong to one or the other of the two *vətəndar* Maratha patrilineages have comparatively restricted access to sources of public credit. They have obtained mortgages from the Credit Society or the Land Development Bank on only 38.2 per cent of their wet land and 21.9 per cent of their dry land.

If one considers the total amount of credit obtained the privileged position of the *vətəndar* Marathas is even clearer. For example, between 4 January 1967 and 29 June 1967 the Girvi Credit Society lent Rs. 629,465 to Girvi cultivators of which the *vətəndar* Marathas received Rs. 473,655 or 75.2 per cent.

OWNERSHIP OF SHARES IN CO-OPERATIVES

The relative ease with which *vətəndar* Marathas obtain credit from public sources is connected with the fact that they own most of the shares and hence control most of the votes in the area's co-operative societies (see

Fig. 13 Ownership of shares in area co-operatives

Caste	Shriram Co-operative Sugar Factory (Girvi shareholders)		Girvi Credit Society (shareholders)		Lift-irrigation Society (shareholders)	
	No.	Per cent	No.	Per cent	No.	Per cent
Brahmin	4	4.6	7	1.4	6	9.7
Chambhar	1	1.1	7	1.4	.	.
Dhangar	2	2.3	9	1.8	5	8.1
Kumbhar	.	.	6	1.2	.	.
Lohar	1	1.1	2	0.4	.	.
Mahar	1	1.1	42	8.3	.	.
Mali	3	3.4	36	7.2	.	.
Maratha (*vətəndar*)	64	73.6	195	38.8	33	53.2
Maratha (non-*vətəndar*)	7	8.0	101	20.1	15	24.2
Muslim	1	1.1	8	1.6	.	.
Nhavi	1	1.1	7	1.4	.	.
Ramoshi	1	1.1	78	15.5	.	.
Sutar	1	1.1	2	0.4	.	.
Other	.	.	3	0.6	3	4.8
Total	87	99.6	503	100.1	62	100.0

Fig. 13). *Vətəndar* Marathas comprise 38.8 per cent of the shareholders of the Girvi Multi-Purpose Credit Society, which operates in Girvi alone. The Girvi Lift-Irrigation Society operates in neighboring Nirgudi as well as in Girvi. Over half of its shareholders are *vətəndar* Marathas; 38.7 per cent are Kadams from Girvi (owning 49.8 per cent of the shares) and 14.5 per cent are *vətəndar* Maratha Sastes from Nirgudi (owning 11.9 per cent of the shares). Of the eighty-seven shareholders of the Shriram Co-operative Sugar Factory who live in Girvi, sixty-four are *vətəndar* Marathas.

SUMMARY

Although the *vətəndar* Maratha Kadams of Girvi comprise little more than a quarter of the village population, they control more than half of its resources. They own more than half of the valuable wet land occupied by village residents and nearly thirty per cent of the dry land. They are the largest employers of agricultural labor. They constitute nearly three-quarters of the Girvi investors in the Shriram Co-operative Sugar Factory, over half of the investors in the Girvi Lift-Irrigation Society, and almost forty per cent of the investors in the Girvi Credit Society. They are able to borrow on a larger portion of their landed resources than other groups of comparable size and have obtained more than three-quarters of the credit available from the Girvi Credit Society. It is this great economic strength which enables the Kadams of Girvi to dominate the politics of their village. As I shall show in Part 3, it is the dominance of such *vətəndar* Maratha lineages throughout the region which underlies the most striking characteristics of political alliances.

6
Descent groups and affinal networks

It remains to demonstrate in what manner ties of kinship enter into political stratification. *Vətəndar* Marathas, the predominant element of the political class of rural Western Maharashtra, are linked to the non-*vətəndar* Marathas, the largest section of the population falling outside the political class, by common Maratha caste identity. In principle, therefore, there is no reason why the two sections of the Maratha caste cannot be related also by ties of kinship and marriage which might either permit *vətəndars* to call upon their non-*vətəndar* relatives for support or permit the latter to make claims upon the former for patronage. In fact, however, ties of kinship and marriage link *vətəndar* and non-*vətəndar* Marathas infrequently and in only a few characteristic forms. Furthermore, *vətəndars* may be distinguished from the rest of the Maratha caste by their large corporate descent groups and far flung affinal networks and both of these features of *vətəndar* Maratha kinship are a support for their dominant position as well as a product of it. An analysis of political stratification and alliances, therefore, must take into account the networks of kinship ties which are available to elite politicians and also the ways in which such networks are linked to but different from those found among other sections of the population.

Relatives in the most inclusive sense are called *natləg* or *natevaik* in Marathi. *Natevaik* are of two kinds, *bhauki* and *soyre*. These two categories are mutually exclusive and exhaust the universe of relatives. According to informants *bhauki* are blood (*rəktə*) relatives, while *soyre* are relatives by marriage (*ləgnə*). The two categories have no exact equivalents in English, but an idea of their meaning which is adequate for present purposes can be gotten by an inspection of Marathi non-Brahmin kinship terminology (see Fig. 14). Although the language of Maharashtra is Indo-European, the structure of the kinship terminology is Dravidian. *Bhauki* thus includes those relatives which are variously considered to be 'consanguineal' or parallel while *soyre* includes those which are considered 'affinal' or cross (see Dumont 1950, 1953, 1957, 1961; Leach 1961:125–8; Rivers 1968: 67–8; Radcliffe-Brown 1953; Scheffler 1971; Yalman 1967:209–21, 357–9). The rest of Chapter 6 is concerned with those aspects of Maratha

77

Fig. 14   Marathi kinship terms used by non-Brahmins

G^{+2} *ajoba*   FF, MF, FFB, MFB, FMB, MMB
            aji   FM, MM, FMZ, MMZ, FFZ, MFZ

		BHAUKI		SOYRE
G^{+1}	*vədil*	F	*sasəra*	♂WF, ♀HF
	ai	M	*sasu*	♂WM, ♀HM
	culta⎫ *kaka*⎭	FB, FFBS, FMZS, MZH	*mama*⎫ *mavla*⎭	MB, MFBS, MMZS, FZH
	culti	FBW	(*mama*	♂WF, ♀HF – vocative)
	mavši	MZ, MFBD, MMZD	*kaki* ⎫ *mavleṇ*⎭	FZ, FFBD, FMZD
			mavleṇ⎫ *mami* ⎭	MBW
G^{0}	*bhau*	B, FBS, MZS, FZDH, MBDH, ♂WZH, ♀HZH	*mehuṇa*	MBS, FZS, ♂WB, ♂ZH, ♂BWB
	saɖu	FZDH, MBDH, ♂WZH	*mehuṇi*	MBD, FZD, ♂WZ
	bəhin	Z, FBD, MZD, ♂WBW	*nəṇənda*	♀HZH
	bauje	♂BW	*nəṇənd*	♀HZ
	dir	♀HB	*vyahi*	SWF, DHF
	jav	♀HBW	*vyahin*	SWM, DHM
	navra	♀H		
	baiko	♂W		
G^{-1}	*mulga*	S, ♂WZS, ♀ZS	*bhača*	♂ZS, ♂FBDS, ♂MZDS, ♂WBS, ♀BS, ♀HZS
	mulgi	D, ♂WZD, ♀ZD	*bhači*	♂ZD, ♂FBDD, ♂MZDD, ♂WBD, ♀BD, ♀HZD
	putəṇya	♂BS, ♂FBSS, ♂MZSS, ♀HBS	*javi*	DH, ♂BDH, ♀HBDH
	putəṇi	♂BD, ♂FBSD, ♂MZSD, ♀HBD		
	sun	SW, ♂BSW, ♀HBSW		
G^{-2}	*natu*	SS, DS, BSS, BDS, ZSS, ZDS, ♂WBSS, ♂WBDS, ♂WZSS, ♂WZDS, ♀HBSS, ♀HBDS, ♀HZSS, ♀HZDS		
	nat	SD, DD, BSD, BDD, ZSD, ZDD, ♂WBSD, ♂WBDD, ♂WZSD, ♂WZDD, ♀HBSD, ♀HBDD, ♀HZSD, ♀HZDD		

Note: Although the four kinship terms which denote male and female kin-types of the second ascending and second descending generations do not distinguish between kin-types in the *bhauki* and *soyre* categories, the kin-types are so distinguishable. Paternal grandparents are *bhauki*, while maternal grandparents are *soyre*. The children of one's *mulga*, *putəṇya*, and *bhači* are *bhauki*. The children of one's *mulgi*, *putəṇi*, and *bhača* are *soyre*.

kinship which are relevant to an understanding of political stratification and political alliances.

MARATHA 'CONSANGUINEAL' KINSHIP: *Bhauki*

In Maharashtra the category *bhauki* includes several sorts of relatives. In the first place, the term refers to agnates in the widest sense, i.e. among Marathas, every one with the same patronymic. '*Bhauki*' and its synonym '*bhaubund*' may be used in a narrower sense to refer to a localized patrilineage. All of one's matrilateral parallel relatives are *bhauki*, too, as are the *soyre* of one's own *soyre*.

Maratha agnatic descent: the 'kuḷ'

Descent in Maharashtra is patrilineal. The largest group based on patrilineal descent is the *kuḷ* (pl. *kuḷi*) or clan. There is a vague belief that the members of a *kuḷ* are descended from a single common ancestor. Its members share a common surname (*ədnav*), e.g. Kadam, Dhumal, Dhembre, a common *devət* (god or goddess), and a common *devək* (totem). For example, the *devət* of the Kadam clan is Bhavani or Ambabai, a goddess whose principal temple is in Tuljapur, Sholapur District, about one hundred and ten miles east of Girvi. Girvi Kadams say that their *devek* is *kəḷəmb* (*Nauclea cadamba* or *Anthocephalus cadamba*), a small shrub.[1] Several clans may share the same *devək* and a person must marry someone with a different *devək* as well as a different surname. However, aside from their functions in marriage, clans and *devəks* are of little significance. The members of a clan are generally spread over a very large area and they do not constitute a corporate group. Marathas sometimes claim to have ninety-six clans, but, as Professor Karve notes, 'the actual lists given by Maratha writers however generally contain more than ninety-six names' (Karve 1965:177).

Maratha agnatic descent: the 'bhaubund'

Within the widely dispersed Maratha clan the next most inclusive descent group is the *bhaubund* or *bhauki*, a localized patrilineage. *Bhaubunds* vary greatly in size and genealogical depth. Large *bhaubunds*, found among *vətəndar* Marathas, tend to contain several attached groups as well as a core of proper members. Members of large *vətəndar* lineages often keep written genealogies and put considerable stress on genealogical connections. Smaller *bhaubunds*, found among non-*vətəndar* Marathas, are generally less than half the size of the larger *vətəndar* groups. Members of the smaller lineages keep no genealogical records. Their genealogical

Genealogy 1 Vərči ali Kadams

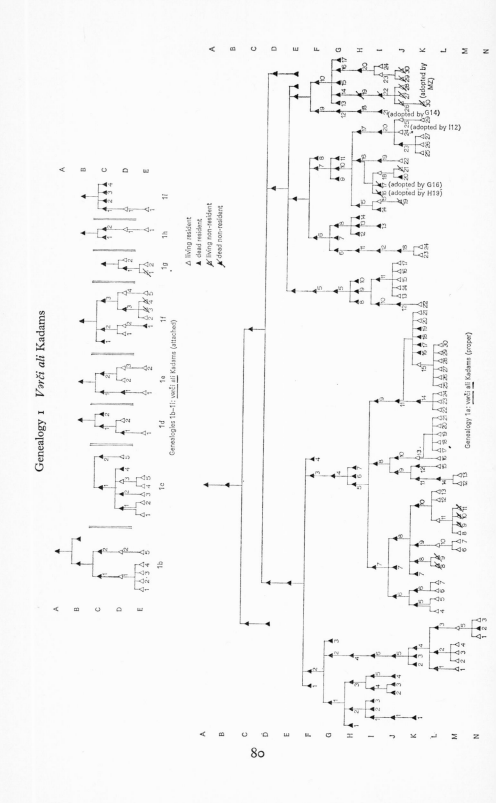

Genealogies 1b–1f: varči ali Kadams (attached)

Genealogy 1a: varči ali Kadams (proper)

△ living resident
▲ dead resident
⧸△ living non-resident
⧸▲ dead non-resident

(adopted by MZ)
(adopted by G14)
(adopted by I12)
(adopted by G16)
(adopted by H19)

80

knowledge is shallower and less complete than that of the members of the larger groups.

'*Bhaubunds*' *in Girvi*. There are two Maratha *bhaubunds* in the main Girvi settlement area. Both are of the Kadam *kul*. They are not named, but are referred to on the basis of residence as *vərči ali* (upper street) and *khalči ali* (lower street). The Kadams are the *vətəndars* of the village. Until the office was abolished the *vərči ali bhaubund*, the senior group, held the Revenue Patilship. The *khalči ali* Kadams have the Police Patilship. The two lineages deny that there is any connection between them except membership in the same clan.

Both Kadam lineages contain, in addition to a core of proper members, a number of attached groups. Attached groups are those whose claims to lineage membership are in some sense incomplete. Here I simply note which groups are attached and which are proper members of each lineage. In succeeding sections I shall discuss, the ritual functions of lineages, which unite all members, and, the political functions of lineages also, which distinguish proper from attached members.

A. The *vərči ali* Kadam *bhaubund* (Genealogies 1a–1i): Except for two families, all the members of this lineage live together in the south half of the village residential area.

 1. The *bhaubund* proper (Genealogy 1a): Several families have copies of a written genealogy, obtained from the Mamlatdar's office, which shows how all the proper members of the lineage are descended through males from a single founding ancestor, Nagoji Kadam. Reckoning from Nagoji to children now living there have been fifteen generations of *vərči ali* Kadams in Girvi. Including wives and unmarried women the lineage proper now includes 254 persons living in Girvi and 38 persons who have left the village to work in Phaltan, Poona or some other town.
 2. Attached lines: None of these groups are named and none have written genealogies.

(*a*) Branch *A* (Genealogy 1*b*): 35 resident members.

(*b*) Branch *B* (Genealogy 1*c*): 27 resident members.

(*c*) Branch *C* (Genealogy 1*d*): 7 resident members.

(*d*) Branch *D* (Genealogy 1*e*): 18 resident members.

Proper members of the *vərči ali* Kadam lineage agree that branches *A* through *D* are really Kadams, but asert that they are not proper members of the lineage. Among other things they point to the fact that these attached groups are not included in their written genealogy. The members of the attached branches themselves say they are members of the *vərči ali* lineage and that they and their ancestors have always lived in Girvi.

(*e*) Branch *E* (Genealogy 1*f*): 24 resident members and 7 non-residents. Recently the surname of these people was Kotval. However, they claim to have acquired the name when an unknown ancestor worked as *kotval* (clerk and messenger) in Girvi. They now call themselves Kadam, which they say is their true surname. Proper lineage members accept these claims in public. In private, however, they recall that this group used to be called Kotval and suggest that the Kotvals are *dašiputrə*, descendants of a Kadam man's illicit union.

(*f*) Branch *F* (Genealogy 1*g*): 15 resident members. The original surname of this group was Punde, but they are now called Kadam. They came to Girvi from neighboring Varugad, Man Talaka.

(*g*) Branch *G* (Genealogy 1*h*): 8 resident members.

(*h*) Branch *H* (Genealogy 1*i*): 4 resident members.

These people are said to be *dašiputrə* too. The last four attached groups do not base their claims to membership in the *vərči ali* Kadam lineage on specific genealogical connections. Their argument seems to be that

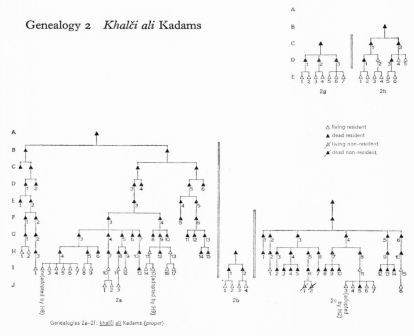

Genealogy 2   *Khalči ali* Kadams

Genealogies 2a–2f: *khalči ali* Kadams (proper)

82

they must be members since they are Kadams and live in the same area as the rest of the lineage.

Including both proper and attached members, there are 392 members of the *vərči ali* Kadam *bhaubund* resident in Girvi.

B. The *khalči ali* Kadam *bhaubund* (Genealogies 2a–2i): Most members of the *khalči ali* lineage live together in the north half of the main residential area. Three groups, however, live in hamlets on the east side of the village. Including both attached and proper groups the lineage has 562 resident members.

1. The *bhaubund* proper: The main part of the lineage is divided into four branches (sing. *šakha*). Three of the branches have written genealogies obtained from the Mamlatdar's office. The fourth branch has no genealogy. The connections between the four branches are unknown, but no one doubts that they are part of a single lineage.

(*a*) Branch 1 (Genealogy 2a): 108 resident members. It is agreed that Branch 1 is the senior branch of the lineage, that it is descended from the unknown founding ancestor through eldest sons. Reckoning from Subhanji, the branch's *mulpuruš* (founding ancestor), to children now living there have been eleven generations of *khalči ali* Kadams in Branch 1.

Genealogies 2g–2i: khalci ali Kadams (attached)

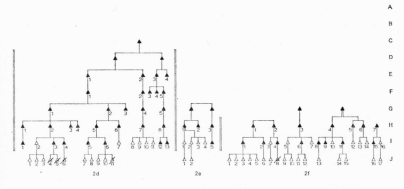

Genealogies 2a–2f: khalči ali Kadams (proper)

83

(*b*) Branch 1*a* (Genealogy 2*b*): Although the exact origin of this branch is unknown, all my informants agree in giving it full membership in Branch 1. 28 resident members.

(*c*) Branch 2 (Genealogy 2*c*): 25 resident members. Seven generations of Branch 2 *khalči ali* Kadams have lived in Girvi.

(*d*) Branch 3 (Genealogy 2*d*): 66 resident members. Nine generations of Branch 3 *khalči ali* Kadams have lived in Girvi.

(*e*) Branch 3*a* (Genealogy 2*e*): 24 resident members. The exact origin of the branch is unknown, but no one denies it full membership in Branch 3.

(*f*) Branch 4 (Genealogy 2*f*): 106 resident members. This branch has no written genealogy. It is impossible to specify all the connections among the constituent families of the branch or between the branch and the rest of the lineage. However, informants both within Branch 4 and in other branches of the lineage agree that Branch 4 is a proper part of the *khalči ali* lineage. Many members of Branch 4 live in Pimpalaca Mala, a hamlet about half a mile east of the main settlement.

2. Attached groups:

(*a*) Branch 5 (Genealogy 2*g*): 39 resident members. It is whispered that these people are *dašiputre*, descendants of a *khalči ali* Kadam man's illicit union. They claim to be members of the *khalči ali* lineage but are unwilling to discuss the details of the connection.

(*b*) Branch 6, Bara Bigha Kadams (Genealogy 2*h*): 40 resident members. This group lives in Bara Bigha hamlet, about a mile east of the main settlement. They say that they are *khalči ali* Kadams, but they have no written genealogy and cannot trace their ties to the proper branches.

(*c*) Branch 7, 'Kokates' (Genealogy 2*i*): 126 resident members. The surname of these people used to be Kokate, but they changed it to Kadam about two years ago. They point out that they have the Kadam *devət* and *devək* and argue that one of their ancestors must have made a mistake; they ought to be called Kadam. They say they are members of the *khalči ali* lineage. The rest of the Kadams have accepted this claim and are careful not to use their old surname in public. The branch has no written genealogy. Most of the Kokate-Kadams now live in Cavarvasti, a hamlet in the northeast corner of the village territory.

Bhaubunds of non-*vətəndar* Marathas are found in Bodkevadi, Dhumalvadi and Jadhavvada. These non-*vətəndar* lineages are smaller than those of the *vətəndar* Kadams and contain no attached groups. Since non-

vətəndars do not have written genealogies, their genealogical knowledge is much less extensive than that of the *vətəndars*. A description of groups in Bodkevadi will serve as an example of non-*vətəndar* lineages.

C. The Dhembre *bhaubund* (Genealogy 4*a*): 171 resident members. The largest group in Bodkevadi is a lineage belonging to the Dhembre clan. The Dhembres claim to be the original settlers in Bodkevadi. They

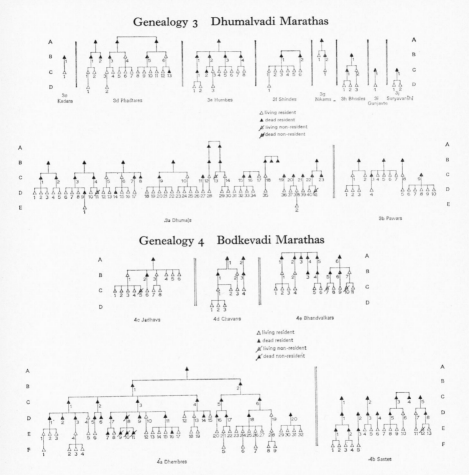

Genealogy 3 Dhumalvadi Marathas

Genealogy 4 Bodkevadi Marathas

do not have a written genealogy, but many men can remember the names of their ancestors and a number of collaterals as far back as Bayaji, four generations before most of the adult men. Bayaji, they say, was the first Dhembre to settle in Bodkevadi. In the case of only one family is it impossible to state the connection between it and the rest of the lineage.

Genealogy 5   Jadhavvada Marathas

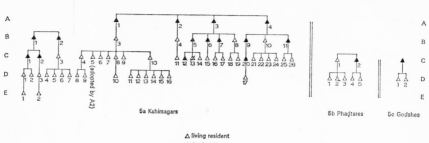

△ living resident
▲ dead resident
◩ living non-resident
◪ dead non-resident

5a Kshirsagars   5b Phaḍtares   5c Godshes

D. The Saste *bhaubund* (Genealogy 4*b*): 71 resident members. The Saste lineage consists of six groups which came to Bodkevadi from neighboring Nirgudi. Some of the families are recent arrivals and in no case have more than four generations of Sastes lived in Girvi. Informants do not know the connections between the six groups of families.

E. The Jadhav *bhaubund* (Genealogy 4*d*): 50 resident members.

F. The Chavan *bhaubund* (Genealogy 4*c*): 31 resident members.

G. The Bhandvalkar *bhaubund* (Genealogy 4*e*): 55 members.

Although some *bhaubunds* have attached groups whose claims to membership are incomplete or fictive the *bhaubund*, nevertheless, may be defined as a localized lineage in which membership is based on a rule of patrilineal descent. As the map of Girvi shows, the *bhaubund* is also a largely co-residential group (see Map 3). In addition, the Maharashtrian *bhaubund* may be defined by its ritual functions and by its relation to estates in political office and land. The ritual functions of the *bhaubund* are common to both the large and small varieties, while the political functions of the *bhaubund* differentiate between them.

Ritual functions of 'bhaubunds'. Each *bhaubund* has a leader called *mukəddəm*. Originally, '*mukəddəm*' and '*paṭil*' both meant 'village headman' (see Molesworth and Candy 1857:501, 654). However, their meanings later diverged, probably during British rule. Traditionally, the Patil was the eldest son of the eldest son, etc., of the *bhaubund*'s founding ancestor. The Patil, or *mukəddəm*, had both governmental and ritual duties and prerogatives. The British, however, did not accept the rule of seniority. They claimed the right to choose any man from the *bhaubund*, including genealogical juniors, to perform the duties required by government.

'*Paṭil*' then came to be applied to the government officer while '*muk-kəddəm*' retained the old meaning in terms of genealogical seniority. The duties and prerogatives of the *mukəddəm* remained wholly ritual. He commands the first respect (*man*) of his lineage and leads its ritual activities. The *mukəddəm* of a *vətəndar* lineage is also a ritual leader of his village.

Under the leadership of its *mukəddəm*, each *bhaubund* participates as a separate unit in some stages of Bendur and Dassara, two of the major village festivals. Dassara, for example, is an eleven-day festival after the autumn harvest in Ashvin month (September/October). The tenth day of Dassara is called *simollənghən* ('the passage of the boundaries'). On the evening of this day each of the Kadam *bhaubunds* in Girvi makes a kind of symbolic raid which the participants believe to be reminiscent of the times when they spent the winter season engaged in warfare. Led by its *mukəd-dəm*, each lineage marches in a group out beyond the edges of the settlement area where there is a big scramble for the leaves of a shrub brought along by the *mukəddəm* and said to represent spoils captured in war. Each lineage then returns to the village where the men spend the rest of the evening visiting the houses of other members of their *bhaubund*. When two men meet they exchange 'loot' and each stoops to touch the other's feet and then his own chest in a gesture of respect. Women honor their guests by seating them on a *pat* and performing *ovaḷne*, a ceremony in which a tray containing a lighted lamp is waved before an image of a god or before an honored person.

The visiting and exchanges of mock spoils are said to promote friendly relations. Like the 'raid' which precedes it, this behavior is confined to one's own *bhaubund* and occasionally a few other close friends. No distinction is made between proper and attached members of a *bhaubund*; all are included.

Funerals and weddings are primarily the concern of individual families, but some of the ritual actions involved serve to state *bhaubund* identity. For example, when a person dies all of his relatives must observe impurity or mourning (*sutək*) for varying lengths of time. All the people in the dead man's house (*ghər*) are prohibited from cooking for three days. The deceased's lineage mates are prohibited from shaving, having guests, and eating 'sweet' foods for ten days. Affines must observe *sutək* for three days.

When a death occurs members of the deceased's *bhaubund* gather to aid the bereaved family in performing the cremation. For example, when Mansingh Bajirao, a proper member of the *vərči ali* Kadam lineage, died four proper members of his *bhaubund* carried the corpse to the cremation ground while a fifth led the procession out of the village. Other members of the lineage helped to build the funeral pyre and stayed with the dead man's son until the cremation was completed.

On the third day after death members of the lineage return to the cremation ground to help the close agnates of the deceased gather the ashes and worship the soul of the dead man in a ceremony called *savədne*. On the tenth day members of the lineage plus the dead man's close affines (*soyre*) gather again at the cremation ground to worship the soul of the deceased in a final ceremony called *dəhava* or *dəspind*. Up to that time the soul has been hovering about the cremation ground, but it is hoped that on the tenth day it will be released to join its ancestors in 'heaven' (*pərmešvər*).

Observance of *sutək* does not separate the proper members of a lineage from the attached members. Rather it seems to divide the prosperous members of the lineage from the poor. It is true, for example, that when one of the Kotval-Kadams died only the members of his own attached group (Genealogy 1*f*) observed the mourning prohibitions or helped in his cremation. However, members of attached groups *A* and *B* (Genealogies 1*b* and 1*c*) observed *sutək* for Mansingh Bajirao, a proper lineage member, and attended each of the cermonies connected with his cremation.

Political functions of 'bhaubunds'. Traditionally, the lineages of Maratha *vətəndars* also had functions in the politico-jural sphere, some of which remain today. I have already described the powers and privileges of the Patil, the traditional hereditary village headman (see Chapter 2). The office of Patil and the tax-free land associated with it were the estate (*vətən*) of corporate *vətəndar* lineages. In Girvi the *vərči ali* Kadam lineage held the Revenue Patilship and the *khalči ali* Kadams continue to hold the Police Patilship. No person who is not a member of the correct lineage may hold a Patilship. In 1947, for example, a member of the *vərči ali bhaubund* (Genealogy 1*a*, *M*6) entered himself as a candidate for the Police Patilship to succeed Eknath Sahebrao Kadam (Genealogy 2*c*, *I*11) but was refused by the government on the grounds that he was not a member of the '*vətən* family' (the official term for the lineage which holds the office). Only one person at a time could act as Patil, but every lineage member had a share in the tax-free *vətən* land. Great prestige is still attached to title in *vətən* land even though it has lost its tax-free status.[2]

The political functions of Maratha lineages differentiate between large lineages with attached members and written genealogies, on the one hand, and small lineages without attached members and without extensive genealogical knowledge, on the other. They also differentiate between proper and attached members of large lineages.

The two Kadam lineages are *vətəndar* lineages. Each had a prestigious corporate estate. The *bhaubunds* of Marathas living in Bodkevadi and the other Girvi hamlets were not *vətəndars*. One consequence of this difference is the greater size of the Kadam lineages. There are, in the first place, more proper members of the Kadam lineages than there are of the other lineages. The Kadams have a valuable estate which holds them in Girvi while the non-*vətəndar* Marathas have a greater tendency to move from village to village. The membership of *vətəndar* lineages stays in one place and grows while that of non-*vətəndar* lineages disperses. The Kadam lineages are made still larger ·by their attached members, persons drawn to them by the prestige of their *vətəns*.

However, while the attached groups are attracted to the Kadam lineages by the prestige of their *vətəns*, the estates also provide the motive for differentiating between proper and attached members. The proper members of the Kadam lineages keep their genealogies and their records of *vətən* land so that they can distinguish between themselves and the attached members and so that they can prevent the attached members from usurping their perquisites. Proper *vərči ali* Kadams observe death pollution with attached groups *A* and *B*, but they remember that the attached groups are not on their genealogy and own no *vətən* land.

Internal structure of 'bhaubunds'. Although one occasionally hears of both *vətəndar* and *balutedar* (serving caste) lineages which have divided the rights and duties of their offices among lineage branches (*šakha*, pl. *šakhe*) or which practice a system of rotation, this has not occurred in the Kadam lineages of Girvi. The division of the *khalči ali* lineage into four branches may be an example of such a partition in its early stages, but opinion on this point is conflicting. Most informants consider that all the *khalči ali* Kadams belong to a single lineage. They say that Shankar Appasaheb Kadam (Genealogy 2a, *H*1), a member of Branch 1, is the *mukəddəm* of the entire lineage and that each branch has a one-quarter share in the Police Patil estate. Four of the last five Police Patils have belonged to Branch 2, but there also has been one Patil from Branch 1. Although the genealogical connections linking the four branches are unknown, several members have documents listing the shares in *vətən* land held by all the proper members. Mourning (*sutək*) and other ritual obligations are accepted by most members of the lineage. One member of Branch 1, however, claimed that the *khalči ali bhaubund* had split into four new lineages (*tutək jhala*). The ceremonial obligations of *bhaubund* members are not always observed and some informants point this out with the comment that the *khalči ali* Kadams are no longer a united lineage. Although the present Police Patil, a member of Branch 2, recognizes the seniority of Branch 1, he insists that only members of Branch 2 have any right to the Patilship. He argues that the previous Police Patil was chosen from Branch 1 only because there was no one from Branch 2 available when the selection was made. Partition of the *khalči ali* Patilship presumably would result in partition of the lineage, as well, but this is unlikely in the present political system.[3]

In most cases, therefore, the only important group within the localized Maratha patrilineage is the domestic group or *kutumb*. The *kutumb* is made up of one or more nuclear families consisting of a man and his wife and their children or, occasionally, of a widow and her children. It is based on agnatic descent in that the male heads of its component nuclear families are related agnatically and are expected to co-operate under the jural authority of their genealogically senior member. The *kutumb* also is a commensal unit, a unit of land use, and a *de facto* if not *de jure* unit of land ownership. Domestic group members live together in a single dwelling, but the residential group (*ghər*, 'house') may include more than one *kutumb*.

Figure 15 gives the size and composition of Maratha *kutumbs* in Girvi. There are no differences between proper and attached Kadams or between

Fig. 15   Family composition among Girvi Marathas

Family type	No. of families	Pop.	Average size	Per cent of families	Per cent of population
I	150	804	5.4	54.7	36.7
II	73	835	11.4	26.6	38.1
III	36	450	12.5	13.1	20.6
IV	4	45	11.3	1.5	2.1
V	1	13	13.0	0.4	1.1
VI	1	25	25.0	0.4	1.1
VII	9	20	2.2	3.3	0.9
Simple families (Types I & VII)	159	924	5.2	58.0	37.6
Joint families (Types II–VI)	115	1,368	11.9	42.0	62.4
Total	274	2,192	8.0	100.0	100.1

Families have been classified according to the number of their married male members and the relations between them:
Type I: one married man;
Type II: two or more married men, father and son(s);
Type III: two or more married men, brothers;
Type IV: three or more married men, father, son(s) and grandson(s);
Type V: three or more married men, brothers and son(s);
Type VI: three married men, father, son and brother's son; and
Type VII: no married man; widow living alone or with unmarried children.
Simple families include Types I and VII.
Joint families include Types II–VI.

vətəndars and non-*vətəndars* in these respects, so the figures for all these groups have been combined. Families have been classified according to the number of their married male members and the relations between them. In addition, families may include the wives of male members, their children, their unmarried sisters, and their widowed mothers. Married sisters and daughters are *soyre* (classificatory 'affines') and members of their marital domestic groups, but in some cases widowed sisters and daughters live with their natal families. In the same position, that of guests rather than proper members, are father's widowed sister, wife's mother, and mother's brother, of each of which one instance is found in Girvi Maratha households.

The important point here is that the jural authority of the father tends to hold the domestic group together in village as well as in household affairs for as long as he lives. Writing of customary law of the nineteenth-century Bombay Deccan, Steele reports that 'the son has no right to demand partition from his father, so long as he conducts himself properly in the management of the family property...' (1868:216). In modern Hindu law, according to Derrett, '...the son may be prevented from separating by his father's veto' (1963:319). Brothers may continue to live in a joint household after their father has died, but as they begin to have children of their own they are likely to quarrel over the unequal demands which their conjugal families make on their joint estate. It is not unknown for such quarrels to become extremely heated and to be brought into the political arena, but once partition has been effected it is more common for the obligations of amity and solidarity arising from co-filiation to re-assert themselves.[4]

Maratha non-agnatic 'consanguineal' kinship

The clan (*kuḷ*) and its subdivisions, the localized patrilineage and the domestic group, exhaust the agnatic category of 'blood' relatives. However, there are other *bhauki*, matrilateral parallel relatives and the 'affines' of one's 'affines', who are like agnates in some ways, but different in others. Non-agnatic *bhauki* are like agnates in that marriage with them is prohibited. Moreover, in some circumstances a non-agnatic *bhauki* may substitute for an absent agnate. However, one's non-agnatic *bhauki* resemble one's 'affines' (*soyre*) in that they generally live in a village other than one's own.

MARATHA 'AFFINAL' KINSHIP: *Soyre*

Relations between 'affines' are characterized by easy equality and co-operation. In this, as in other respects, 'affinity' and descent are complementary opposites. Members of a lineage are supposed to be equal, but villagers are acutely aware that the relationship is fraught with competition and potential hostility. The competition arises partly from the fact that the *bhaubund* is the primary reference group against which status is measured. One gains status with respect to and at the expense of other members of one's lineage. The tension inherent in the assertion of equality within the *bhaubund* is expressed clearly in feelings about money-lending between agnates. It is felt to be very awkward to ask for a loan from a member of one's lineage. To ask is an admission of inferiority; to give is an assertion of superiority, and to refuse to give is an insult (*əpman*). It is better not to ask and, in fact, money is seldom lent within the *bhaubund*. Tension arising from competitive equality is not a problem in relations between 'affines'. It is felt to be easy and natural to ask an 'affine' for a loan and *soyre* do give one another a great deal of help, rarely, as far as I know, charging interest. It is said that one's *mehuṇa* is a closer relative than anyone in one's own lineage except one's brother and father's brother's son and 'affines' frequently are called upon for help in struggles with lineage mates. It is important to determine, therefore, the manner in which networks of 'affinal' (*soyre*) links, deriving ultimately from marriage, are related to the division of the population into a political class and the masses and to the system of political arenas.

Marriage rules

When asked to explain their marriage rules and the criteria they have in mind when seeking spouses for their children informants in Girvi generally mention two factors. In the first place, one must marry a member of one's own caste who belongs to a different clan (*kul*) and who has a different *devət* and *devək*. More broadly, one must marry a caste member who is not a 'blood' relative, thus excluding non-agnatic 'consanguines' as well as agnates. The second set of factors with which informants are concerned in arranging marriages are extraneous to kinship. One wants to establish marriage connections with a family whose social position and wealth are comparable to one's own and one wants to find a marriage partner who has a good character and a good education.

Although the marriage rules are stated simply in terms of endogamy and exogamy, informants explain that they prefer to marry someone who is already related to them in the marriageable category of relatives, i.e. a *soyre*. In many cases it is less risky and more convenient to marry an old 'affine' than it is to find a new relative. One's *soyre*, near or distant, is more likely to be a suitable marriage partner in terms of social position and wealth than some unrelated person. Considerations of wealth and position, however, can cut both ways; informants feel no compulsion to make a new marriage with an 'affine' whose fortunes have declined. It also is felt to be easier to get an accurate notion of the personal qualities of an old 'affine' than of an unrelated person. A very important consideration is that less needs to be spent on a new marriage with an old 'affine' than on a marriage with an unrelated person.

In Girvi both matrilateral and patrilateral cross-cousin marriage are permitted and considered desirable but are not required. Enthoven reports a usage among Kunbis which might be taken to indicate an obligation to marry one's cross-cousin:

> If the child's aunt [father's sister] is present at the time of delivery, she cowdungs the threshold of the room, places a packet of betelnuts and leaves near it and says, looking toward the child, 'This child is to be my son's wife.' The mother smiles and if she has a son says, 'When you get a daughter she will become my daughter-in-law.' (1922:289)

Informants in Girvi, however, state that there is no obligation to marry a cross-cousin. Neither must a man who marries a non-relative compensate his bride's or his own cross-cousins in any way.

Two sisters may marry two brothers and two men may exchange their sisters. However, there are restrictions on the latter practice. Maharashtrians use the term *saṭeloṭe* for those exchanges of sisters in which both marriages are performed at the same time in the same marriage booth. Arrangements of this sort are looked down upon as an undesirable expedient of the poor. *Saṭeloṭe* exchanges are regarded as risky since difficulties in one marriage may lead to difficulties in the other.

Marriage networks: geographical distribution

Marriage networks may be analysed with respect to both genealogical and geographical distribution. The genealogical distribution of marriages is a function of the degree to which marriages are repeated and the categories of immediate and genealogical 'affines' are made to overlap. The geographical distribution of marriages is a function of the distances at which marriages are contracted and the frequency of intra-village marriages. It is only with the latter that I am concerned here.

If the *vətəndar* Marathas in Girvi, proper and attached members of both Kadam lineages, are compared with the non-*vətəndar* Marathas of Bodkevadi, Dhumalvadi and Jadhavvada, it is apparent that the marriage network of the *vətəndar* Kadams is geographically much more dispersed. Girvi *vətəndar* Marathas marry at an average distance of 30.2 miles. Non-*vətəndars* marry at an average distance of only 7.0 miles. While it is clear, however, that the non-*vətəndars* do not go as far afield to find marriage partners as the high status Kadams, the expression of this difference in average distances is somewhat inadequate. Eighteen Kadam marriages were made at a distance of over one hundred miles and six were made at distances of over six hundred miles. No non-*vatandar* Maratha from Girvi, on the other hand, has married at a distance greater than forty miles.

In Figures 16 and 17 the marriage distances of *vatandar* and non-*vatandar*

Fig. 16   Marriage distances of *vatandar* Marathas in Girvi

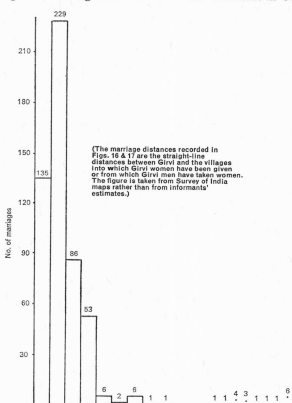

(The marriage distances recorded in Figs. 16 & 17 are the straight-line distances between Girvi and the villages into which Girvi women have been given or from which Girvi men have taken women. The figure is taken from Survey of India maps rather than from informants' estimates.)

Marathas in Girvi are analysed in greater detail. The differences between the two classes of the Maratha population are clear. The greatest number of *vatandar* marriages were contracted at distances of ten to twenty miles. Well over half of non-*vatandar* marriages, on the other hand, are made at distances of zero to ten miles.

The frequency of intra-village marriages is another measure of the geographical distribution of marriages. In Maharashtra there is no rule of village exogamy, but the extent to which intra-village marriage occurs varies widely between the *vǝtǝndar* and non-*vǝtǝndar* sections of the Maratha population. Only 5.2 per cent of the marriages of the *vǝtǝndar* Maratha Kadams are intra-village connections. However, 26.7 per cent of the marriages of non-*vǝtǝndar* Marathas link families living in Girvi.

Fig. 17   Marriage distances of non-*vǝtǝndar* Marathas in Girvi

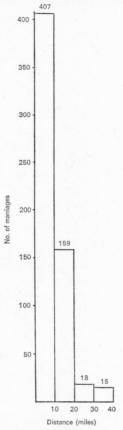

Figure 18 is a diagram of all existing and remembered intra-village marriages among Girvi Marathas.

In general the geographical distribution of affinal kinship is inversely related to the geographical distribution of agnatic kinship. High status *vǝtǝndar* Marathas have large localized patrilineages and widely dispersed networks of affines. *Vǝtǝndars* live with their agnates. The vast majority of their affines live in other villages where they are members of similar large patrilineages. *Vǝtǝndars* have few affines in their own villages. Low

95

status non-*vətəndar* Marathas have small localized patrilineages and locally concentrated networks of affines. They have roughly as many affines as agnates living with them in their villages. There are few intra-village

Fig. 18   Intra-village marriages among Girvi Marathas

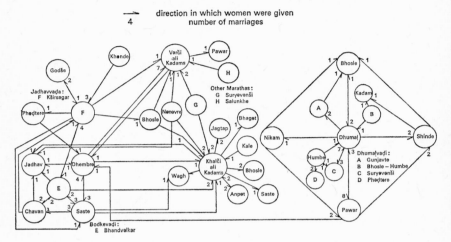

marriages linking *vətəndar* and non-*vətəndar* sections of the Maratha population. Most importantly, the boundary between the two sections of the Maratha caste is crossed by few ties of affinity and their marriage networks are relatively distinct.

Hypergamy

In the literature on Maharashtrian kinship it is often suggested that among Marathas rank and affinity are combined in a system of hypergamy. Professor Karve argues that,

The Maratha clans (*kuḷi*) are arranged in a hypergamous system. All those who are supposed to be true Marathas belong to ninety-six clans. The actual lists given by Maratha writers however generally contain more than ninety-six names. Among these ninety-six there are concentric circles of nobility and status. The highest are called 'Panchkuli' – 'of the five clans'. These are the clans of Jadhav, More, Shirke, Pawar, etc. The next division is 'seven clans' which includes Bhosle and so on.

The rule for marriage is that the five...can marry among themselves or can marry girls from the other clans but do not give their daughters to any one outside the five clans. The 'seven clan' division can marry among themselves, or can give their daughters to the 'five-clan' or receive girls from all the rest except 'the five clan' division. Thus the hypergamous clan arrangement is like that of the Rajputs and Khatris of Northern India. (1965:177)

This hypergamous system of ranked *kuḷi* seems to exist, however, only in the works of Maratha writers. Some informants have heard that there are ninety-six clans, but they say that all clans have the same rank (*dərja*, *patəli*, the same words are applied to caste rank). Some say that the *pənč kuḷi* are more prestigious because they were associated with Shivaji, who was himself a Bhosle, part of Professor Karve's 'seven clan' division. Nevertheless all are agreed that people marry only those whose prestige is equal to their own and that all of the Maratha clans may intermarry. Prestige attaches to lineages rather than to clans and there is no trace of any system of hypergamy which might link Marathas of *vətəndar* and non-*vətəndar* status.

SUMMARY

With regard to the relations between kinship and political stratification several points need to be emphasized. There is a distinction within the dominant Maratha caste between *vətəndars* and non-*vətəndars*. The two categories share the same kinship categories but have different practices. The *vətəndars* have large localized patrilineages and keep extensive written genealogies. They seek to marry other *vətəndars* equal in status to themselves. As a result *vətəndars* contract few intra-village marriages and frequently marry at considerable distances. Non-*vətəndars*, on the other hand, having no prestigious estates in land and office, show a greater tendency to migrate from village to village and consequently have smaller lineages. They keep no written genealogies. Non-*vətəndars* marry other non-*vətəndars*, very often in their own villages and rarely at any great distance. Although *vətəndar* and non-*vətəndar* Marathas are united by common caste identity and to a certain extent by common clan affiliation, they are otherwise quite distinct. Some former non-*vətəndars* have achieved attached status in *vətəndar* lineages and a few *vətəndars* are linked to non-*vətəndars* by ties of marriage, but these bonds cutting across the pattern of political stratification are the exception rather than the rule.

PART 3
POLITICAL ALLIANCES

7
Vertical alliances

In this and the two subsequent chapters I will analyse the political action which I observed in Girvi, Phaltan Taluka, and Satara District between February 1966, when I went to live in Girvi, and September 1967. This was a hectic period in local politics. In Girvi a new Panchayat was elected early in 1966 and a new Credit Society Managing Committee was elected later in the same year. A General Election was held throughout India in January 1967 and in Maharashtra there were zilla parishad and panchayat samiti elections in May 1967. More than half of the villages in Phaltan Taluka elected new panchayats in April 1967 and in Phaltan a new Municipal Council was elected in May 1967. I will not attempt to narrate the political history of this period. Rather I will show how the pattern of political aliances which emerged in these elections and in connected events is related to the social structure of the region and to the arenas and occasions of political action.

Decisions concerning political alliances are made in terms of such antecedent structural frameworks as the governmental and administrative systems, the caste system, the economic system, and the kinship system. An analysis of these systems in Western Maharashtra reveals a fifth and fundamental structural framework which runs through all the others. This structural framework is the division of the population into two categories: the mass of the population with little or no political influence and a small political class consisting mainly of potentially influential, high status, well-connected, and wealthy *vatandar* Marathas.

Since there is a small political class in Western Maharashtra, the members of which have privileged access to political power, political alliances in the region are of two kinds, vertical and horizontal, distinguished by their relations to the two political strata of the population. Vertical alliances link persons who are members of the political class and/ or the political elite with persons who belong neither to the political class nor to the political elite. Horizontal alliances link members of the political elite to one another and to members of the political class. Each type of political alliance has a distinctive distribution with regard to the arenas and occasions of political action. Vertical and horizontal alliances are based,

Political alliances

too, on distinctive social relations and strategic considerations. That is, the two types of alliance have different relations to the governmental and administrative arenas of political action and to the caste, economic, and kinship systems. Finally, political action reflects the fact that, because of the inequalities in the distribution of power, horizontal alliances are more useful to politicians than are vertical alliances.

THE ANALYSIS OF LOCAL-LEVEL POLITICS: FACTIONS AND ALLIANCES

Much of the literature on local-level politics in India is concerned with what are called factions. In this study, however, I avoid the term 'faction' and instead write of 'alliances' and patterns of alliances. Before beginning the substantive part of Part 3, therefore, I must review the relevant literature in order to explain this methodological choice.

'Faction' long has been a term of opprobrium in ordinary political rhetoric (see Lasswell 1931). In the literature on Indian politics, however, 'faction' often is used to refer to political groups which perform positive social functions. The term first seems to have been used in this positive sense by Oscar Lewis (1954, 1955, and 1958) and his colleague, Harvant Singh Dhillon (1955).[1] According to Lewis factions are groups which emerge in conflicts over scarce resources.

More specifically, we have found that new factions developed as a result of (1) quarrels over the inheritance of land; (2) quarrels over the adoption of sons...; (3) quarrels over house sites and irrigation rights; (4) quarrels over sexual offences; (5) murders; and finally (6) quarrels between castes. The villagers sum this all up by a popular saying that both factions and quarrels revolve around wealth, women and land. (1954:503)

Factions, however,

are not political groupings, or temporary alliances of individuals to fight court cases, although some of them take on political functions and become involved in power politics. Rather, they are primarily kinship groupings which carry on important social, economic and ceremonial functions in addition to their factional struggles against one another. (Lewis 1954:503; see also Dhillon 1955:29–30)

Since the pioneering studies of Lewis and Dhillon the study of factions in India has developed in two directions. On the one hand are those who emphasize conflict between factions and the negative consequences of factionalism, the ways in which the pursuit of factional ends militates against the public good. On the other hand are those who emphasize the principles of faction recruitment and the positive functions of faction organization.[2]

102

Factionalism and conflict

The most elaborate theory of factional conflict is that developed in a number of publications by Beals and Siegel.[3] Beals and Siegel argue that factionalism is a dysfunctional result of external stresses acting upon strains within village communities. In their view an Indian village is a group in the sense of

an intercommunicating aggregation of sub-units (individuals or sub-groups) having the conscious intention of perpetuating their existence and achieving certain goals. A group consists of people assembled together for the purpose of achieving co-operation towards a common set of goals. (Beals and Siegel 1960a:107)

Such a group is subject to stresses or changes in its relation with its external environment which may affect its ability to achieve common goals. The group's ability to respond positively to external stresses is a function of the kind and quantity of strains which exist within it. Beals and Siegel define strain

as a potential conflict within the organization; as a general inability to predict the outcome of certain types of situations; and as situations in which a person sees his expectations defeated. (1966:70)

Among the types of strain occurring in Namhalli, a Mysore village, are the potentially conflicting allegiances which a wife owes to her husband and father and which a low caste servant owes to his high caste master and to the head of his own caste. Strain also results from ambiguities in the ranking of castes and in the rules of succession to family headship (Beals and Siegel 1960b:401). In general, the 'universal existence of punitive sanctions is evidence for the existence of strain' as is the occurrence of overt conflict (Beals and Siegel 1960a:112).

In the view of Beals and Siegel factionalism is overt, unresolved conflict within a group which interferes with the group's achievement of its goals (1960a:108; 1960b:399). Factionalism is most likely to occur when

a dominant external society selectively influences the group in a manner which is covert and which tends to accentuate existing cleavages. (1960a:112)

Its form 'is dependent upon the particular nature of the social structure and its built-in strains and cleavages' (1960a:115). Groups characterized by a low degree of strain will be able to resist great external pressures, while those characterized by a high degree of strain will develop factions under the influence of relatively mild stresses (1960b:407, 414). They explicitly reject the theory that conflict results from competition for scarce resources.

From some viewpoints, it appears probable that conflict is least likely to occur over the allocation of scarce goods, for the allocation of scarce goods without conflict is considered a principal function of society. (1966:18)

The Beals and Siegel theory of factional conflict suffers from a number of weaknesses. Their notion that factions are an irrational and dysfunctional response to external stresses is derived from their concept of a village as a group co-operating to achieve shared goals. However, few anthropologists today would accept this notion of the village as a harmonious whole even if imperfections in the form of internal strains are taken into account. The work of Srinivas (1955, 1959) has taught us to see the unity of the village as little more than the unity of the dominant caste and Pocock emphasizes that 'we ought not to speak of the solidarity of caste nor, more emphatically, of the solidarity of the village' (1957:297). In his discussion of factions in Gopalpur, another Mysore village, Beals himself discards the view of the village as a group co-operating to achieve shared goals and reverts to the notion of competition over scarce resources. In this discussion Beals sees each villager trying to make a living, to own many cattle, to make good marriages for his children, and so on. In the pursuit of these ends a villager is bound to come into conflict with his neighbors and kinsmen and to protect himself he must try to find supporters, to form 'alliances and coalitions designed to shield his growing family from the whims of Nature and the uncontrolled impulses of his fellow men' (1962:2).

The notion that potentially conflicting allegiances are a source of strain opening a society to factional conflict is equally open to doubt. Colson (1962) and Gluckman (1963) have shown that conflicting allegiances or cross-cutting ties often act to lessen and limit conflict. Again, Beals himself has given an example of this effect of cross-cutting ties in his account of Gopalpur (1962:66, 73).

'Faction' was introduced into the literature on Indian social structure to describe certain aspects of village politics. In some respects the actions of factions are undeniably disruptive and divisive. But in making these aspects of factionalism their central concern Beals and Siegel are forced to make a distinction between factional conflict and ordinary political activity and virtually to abandon the latter (1966:20–5). Beals and Siegel ultimately restrict their theory to cases of unregulated conflict, but as Bailey (e.g. 1968) and others have demonstrated most of what usually is called factional conflict is regulated, in fact, by a few quite simple principles.[4]

Factions and political organization

The first major step in the study of factions as an aspect of political organization was taken by the symposium on factions in Indian and overseas Indian societies organized by Raymond Firth (see Firth 1957; Pocock 1957; Mayer 1957; Morris 1957 and Benedict 1957). According to Firth factions are

groups or sections of society in relations of opposition to one another, interested in promoting their own objects rather than those of the society as a whole and often turbulent in their operations. (1957:292)

Firth does not regard factions simply as an unrealistic reaction to external stresses, but instead asks what factions do, how they are formed, and how they work. His summary statement directs our attention to two related aspects of factions which have proved to be of particular importance in subsequent investigations. He emphasizes the internal structure of factions and the ties on which recruitment is based. Factions, he states, are political groups, but they are not part of the formal structure of government. They are impermanent groups which are mobilized on specific occasions around the roles of leader and follower. The relationship between leader and follower may be based on kinship, religious or politico-economic ties, on the patron–client relationship, or on any combination of these ties. Firth also stresses that from the individual's point of view factions may be a good way to achieve personal goals and a flexible means of mobilizing support.

Faction organization, however, has proved to be a difficult problem and for some time case study followed case study without producing any new insights. Nicholas, for example, defines factions as follows:

1. Factions are conflict groups. ... 2. Factions are political groups. ... 3. Factions are not corporate groups. ... 4. Faction members are recruited by a leader. ... 5. Faction members are recruited on diverse principles. (1965:27–9)

This definition adds nothing to that of Firth, but Nicholas does raise an issue which points the way to a more fruitful conception of faction organization. He insists that the principles upon which faction members are recruited are different from those upon which coalitions between factions are based and that factions preserve their identity even when they are part of larger coalitions. Nicholas argues that 'the fundamental reason for this is that two faction leaders can never have identical interests' (1965:46). This raises two questions which must be answered at the same time that the internal organization of factions is clarified. What are the principles upon which alliances between separate factions are based? Can two followers in the same faction ever have identical interests?

In his contribution to the Firth symposium Pocock emphasizes a feature of factions on which most observers are agreed. Factions are secondary, composite groups which cut across such primary groups as village, caste, and lineage.

I said just now that a faction may seem to coincide with a more permanent group, but if it did so coincide we should not need to speak of factions but only of conflict between permanent groups, and in the latter case we should probably be led on to speak of a necessary opposition between such groups. Factions, on the contrary, are composed of several such groups or of elements of such groups. (Pocock 1957:296)

As Pocock notes (1957:295) secondary groups such as factions are difficult to describe and analyse, but we now have available to us a concept which is peculiarly suited to problems of just this sort. This concept, that of network, was introduced into anthropological theory by Barnes (1954). In a later review article the same author notes that the concept was

developed in social anthropology to analyze and describe those social processes involving links across, rather than within, group and category limits. The interpersonal links that arise out of common group membership are as much part of the total social network as are those that link persons in different groups, and an analysis of action in terms of a network should reveal, among other things, the boundaries and internal structure of groups. While there are other ways of discovering groups, the network concept is indispensable in discussion [*sic*] those situations where, for example, the individual is involved in 'interpersonal relations which cut right across the boundaries of village, subcaste and lineage' (Srinivas and Béteille, 1964, p. 166). (1968:109)[5]

Mayer has written a series of valuable papers in which he has used Barnes' concept of network to analyse both the principles of recruitment within Indian factions and the principles of alliance among factions (1962, 1966, 1967b; see also 1958b, 1963a and 1963b). Mayer's analysis is based upon a precise distinction between a social field or field of interaction and a set. A social field is equivalent to Barnes' (1968:111) partial network; it consists of the actors in a particular society and all the dyadic relations of a particular sort or sorts which link them. A set, on the other hand, is a finite, bounded, egocentric portion of a network (Mayer 1966:102); it is the equivalent of Barnes' star and zone (1968:112-15). In particular, an action-set consists of an ego and the star or zone which he activates for a particular purpose on a particular occasion (Mayer 1966:108-10).

The action-set exists in a specific context which provides the terms of ego's purpose in forming linkages. When successive action-sets are centred on similar contexts of activity, personnel and linkages may also be similar. By 'superimposing' a series of action-sets, therefore, one may discern a number of people who are more often than not members of the action-sets, and others who are involved from time to time. (Mayer 1966:115)

Those persons who figure in a series of superimposed action-sets in a single social field comprise what Mayer calls a quasi-group. Quasi-groups may occur in any social field and are commonly called factions when they occur in political arenas (1966:116).

Vertical alliances

Mayer notes that the

action-set contains paths of linkages, and is thus a combination of relationships linking people directly to ego, and of those linking people to intermediaries who are themselves in direct contact with ego. (1966:109)

His analysis bears both on the form of paths and on the content of linkages. Thus Mayer hypothesizes that the kind of election campaign which a candidate can run will depend upon the length of the paths forming his action-set, i.e. the number of links between ego and terminal respondents; the number of lateral links directly linking ego's contacts, and the frequency of multi-pronged linkages between ego and his respondents (1966:110–12). The content of the linkages in an action-set is always transactional; '...linkages exist because they carry transactions furthering in some way the interests of the parties concerned' (1966:112). Such transactions have two aspects. The transactor's interest in receiving support for himself or indirectly for ego is the inward aspect; the respondent's interest in receiving some benefit in return for support is the outward aspect. One also may distinguish between patronage and brokerage transactions. In the former 'the transactor has the power to give some benefit which the respondent desires' while in the latter the transactor is a middle-man promising 'to obtain favors for the respondent from a third person' (1966:113–14; see also Mayer 1967b).[6]

The argument which follows best can be understood in this context as a contribution to the analysis of the transactional linkages or alliances which comprise political action-sets. Here I would add to Mayer's distinctions between inward and outward aspects of transactions and between patronage and brokerage a further distinction between intrinsic and extrinsic aspects of linkages. The intrinsic aspect of the linkage is the transaction itself. The extrinsic aspect is a kind of pretence for interaction, e.g. 'he is of my caste', which is not essential to the transaction. Data on politics in rural Western Maharashtra indicate that linkages or alliances in political action-sets are of two kinds, vertical and horizontal, differing in both their intrinsic and extrinsic aspects.

DISTRIBUTION OF VERTICAL POLITICAL ALLIANCES

Vertical alliances involving persons outside the political class are most likely to occur when a member of the political elite or someone who aspires to membership in the elite needs to marshal support to defend or to acquire a position of influence. In India it is usually necessary to marshal support only during elections, for elections are the most important occasions when positions of influence can be acquired or must be defended. However, because the politics of rural Western Maharashtra are dominated by a privileged political class, electoral support is not required as frequently as it might be in a more egalitarian political system. When electoral support is required the means by which it is obtained are influenced also by the existence of the political class.

The political career of K. R. Bhoite

The political career of Krishnachandra Raghunathrao Bhoite illustrates the degree to which a successful politician depends on vertical alliances with persons outside the political class. It also illustrates the ways in which such alliances are formed.

Bhoite first became involved in local politics in 1962. He stood successfully as Congress candidate for the Phaltan–Khandala seat in the Maharashtra Legislative Assembly in 1967, but until he campaigned for that office he did not have to recruit support outside the political class by entering into vertical alliances. He still has not found it necessary to form such alliances to any great extent.

Bhoite is a well educated, young, *vətəndar* Maratha. His *bhaubund* held the Patilship of Aradgaon, a village on the western boundary of Phaltan Taluka near Khandala Peth. He attended high school in Lonand and then moved to Phaltan to study at Mudhoji College where he took his B.A. After graduation Bhoite continued to study part-time while employed as a clerk in the Shriram Co-operative Sugar Factory. He took his M.A. from Mudhoji College and is now writing a thesis on democratic decentralization for an external Ph.D. at Poona University.

In 1962, when zilla parishads and panchayat samitis were established in Maharashtra, Bhoite left the Shriram Co-operative Sugar Factory and stood for election to the Aradgaon Panchayat. He was elected to the Panchayat *binvirodh* (without opposition). Until he stood for the Maharashtra Legislative Assembly this village panchayat election was the only occasion on which Bhoite might have required support from the general electorate. In this case, however, the need was obviated by the lack of opposition.

In subsequent *binvirodh* elections Bhoite was elected Sarpanch by his fellow Aradgaon Panchayat members, to membership in the Phaltan Panchayat Samiti by the panchayat members of his electoral division, and Chairman of the Panchayat Samiti. Bhoite was formally elected to the latter office by the Panchayat Samiti members, but the decision was actually made by the Satara District Congress Committee. The Satara DCC deliberations were attended by the Rajasaheb of Phaltan who backed Bhoite and whose voice probably carried the greatest weight; by R. B. Bhagat, a *vətəndar* Maratha from Pimparad who is President of the union in the Shriram Co-operative Sugar Factory and of the Phaltan Taluka Congress Committee; by S. R. Bhosle, a member of the Board of Directors of the Shriram Co-operative Sugar Factory and of the family which held the Patilship of Phaltan, and by M. R. Bhoite, a Maratha who holds important offices in Phaltan Taluka and Satara District co-operative societies. None of the members of the Phaltan Panchayat Samiti were invited to participate in the Congress decision, but the Council accepted the Congress choice without open opposition. As Chairman of the Phaltan Panchayat Samiti Bhoite was also a member of the Satara Zilla Parishad.

Bhoite was elected Panchayat Samiti Chairman in 1962 as the ally of the Rajasaheb of Phaltan and with the Rajasaheb's support. He continued to be the Raja's ally for some years and appeared to support the Raja right up to the time when he was given the Congress ticket for the 1967 General Election in Phaltan-Khandala. The Raja gave him an honorary teaching post in Mudhoji College. When M. G. Date, a leading Phaltan Brahmin and ally of S. R. Bhosle, challenged the Rajasaheb for control of the Phaltan Education Society the latter had Bhoite elected Secretary of the Society's Governing Council. The Raja also chose Bhoite for the relatively minor post of Phaltan Taluka Congress Committee Secretary. B. R. More – for some years an ally of the Raja but a man with ambitions of his own, a *vɔtəndar* Maratha, *mehuṇa* (WB) of Y. B. Chavan, President of the Shriram Education Society, member of the Board of Directors of the Shriram Co-operative Sugar Factory and briefly President of the Phaltan Municipality – named Bhoite to the Governing Council of the Shriram Education Society.

Bhoite's success in Phaltan Taluka may be attributed to his alliance with the Raja of Phaltan, Malojirao Naik Nimbalkar. Naik Nimbalkar represented Phaltan in the Legislative Assembly from Independence until 1957, when he was a member of the Bombay Cabinet, and again from 1962 until 1967. He also has been President and Treasurer of the Maharashtra Pradesh Congress Committee. He is Permanent President of the Phaltan Education Society. One or another of his sons has been Chairman of the Shriram Co-operative Sugar Factory since it was established in 1957. Through his allies he has maintained control of the Phaltan Urban Co-operative Bank and the Phaltan Taluka Purchase and Sale Union. The Raja is the most powerful man in Phaltan. In recent years he has been in a position to mediate or control most of the links between Phaltan men and the wider political arena. He is the central point in the network of Phaltan political alliances.

However, when Krishnachandra Bhoite was elected Chairman of the new Phaltan Panchayat Samiti he achieved a position from which he could act with a degree of independence in the district and state political arenas. He dealt with district leaders in the Satara Zilla Parishad, where, as Panchayat Samiti Chairman, he was Phaltan's most important representative. He also was invited to attend meetings of the Satara District Congress Committee.

Satara District politics are dominated by Yeshvantrao Chavan. Chavan was elected to the Legislative Assembly from North Karad in 1952, 1957 and 1962. In 1956 Chavan became Chief Minister of Bombay with the support of Morarji Desai, who felt that he was the Maharashtrian most acceptable to Gujarat (Brecher 1966:48), and he continued as Chief Minister of Maharashtra after the division of Bombay into linguistic states in 1960. In 1962 he succeeded V. K. Krishna Menon as Defence Minister in the Union Cabinet, entering Parliament in an uncontested 1963 by-election in Nasik. His friend Kisan Veer, a Shimpi from Wai, was MP in North Satara from 1962 to 1967 and the allies of Chavan and Veer controlled the Satara DCC and Zilla Parishad. Chavan's main opponent in Satara is D. S. (Balasaheb) Desai, a *vatəndar* Maratha from Patan who in 1966 was Maharashtra Home Minister and who is thought to aspire to the Chief Ministership. Desai's *mavəs bhau* (MZS), R. D. Patil, was Chairman of the Satara District Central Co-operative Bank (see Sirsikar 1970:177–84).

In national politics Chavan is a supporter of Prime Minister Indira Gandhi and an opponent of Morarji Desai. Balasaheb Desai is thought to be a supporter of Morarji Desai. The Rajasaheb of Phaltan, who, it was said, arrested Chavan when he fled to Phaltan during the 1942 Quit India movement, is also a supporter of Morarji.

When Bhoite entered the Satara District political arena as Phaltan Panchayat Samiti Chairman his first step was to ally himself with K. B. (Babanrao) Adsul. Adsul is a Mali from Taradgaon, a large village a few miles west of Phaltan where Malis comprise about half the population. He now lives in Phaltan where he owns a small press. He is a Secretary of the Satara DCC and at that time was also Secretary of the Shriram Education Society. Bhoite and Adsul planned many public functions in Phaltan: openings of new schools, public health facilities, wells, and so on. They always made a point of inviting Chavan's main allies in Satara, Kisan Veer, B. D. Bhilare (DCC President), and Yeshvantrao Parlekar (Zilla Parishad President), to their functions. In this their behavior was in marked contrast to that of Naik Nimbalkar who, as a former Ruler, Minister and MPCC President, felt that his proper role was at a 'higher level'. The result of the efforts of Adsul and Bhoite was to draw to themselves the attention and gratitude of three men who, along with Balasaheb Desai, Chavan and Baburao Ghorpode (Zilla Parishad Vice-President), sat on the

Satara District Congress Election Committee in 1967. It was this committee which recommended a slate of candidates for Satara to the Maharashtra Pradesh Congress Committee.

People in Phaltan began to discuss the Congress nominations for the
15 February 1967 General Elections in the summer of 1966. Bhoite was
widely mentioned as a possible candidate although he denied it in public
and continued to work with the Raja. In June 1966 he explained that he
did not want to 'get across the Raja'. He thought that the Raja would
probably get the Congress ticket and he would ask for it himself only if he
saw that the Raja was unlikely to get it. In the event, the Rajasaheb asked
that the Congress ticket be given to his son, Vijaysingh, the Chairman of
the Shriram Co-operative Sugar Factory, and Bhoite emerged as the most
prominent opposition candidate.

Bhoite was officially awarded the Congress nomination on 8 November
1966. Afterwards it was rumored that Chavan had intended to give him the
nomination all along. Certainly this would be in accord with one partici-
pant's remark that 'in our party democracy decisions are made at the top'.
In any case he cemented his hold on the nomination when, in October
1966, he helped arrange a series of alliances that allowed Kisan Veer, who
was giving up his seat in Parliament so that Chavan could stand for election
in Satara, to retain a position of power in the District. Veer won election as
Chairman of the Satara District Central Co-operative Bank against the
incumbent, R. D. Patil. Although neither man intervened publicly,
Balasaheb Desai was known to support Patil, his *mavas bhau*, and Chavan
was known to support Veer. Bhoite and Adsul, neither of whom were
members of the Bank, helped Veer win the support of four of the sixteen
Directors who elected the Chairman: M. R. Bhoite; N. M. Saste, a
vatandar Maratha from Nirgudi; Dattaji Bedke, Chavan's *javi* (BDH) and
a member of a rich Maratha family in Phaltan, and Dadasaheb Godshe, a
Maratha from Khatav. Bedke was elected Vice-Chairman of the Bank,
replacing M. R. Bhoite. The latter hoped to win support in his bid to be
elected Chairman of the Maharashtra Apex Marketing Society. Bhoite and
Saste also wanted support in the Phaltan Ginning and Pressing Society,
of which the former was Chairman and the latter a member of the Managing Committee.

In his campaign for election to the Maharashtra Legislative Assembly
from Phaltan-Khandala K. R. Bhoite was opposed by the Raja's son,
Vijaysingh. Vijaysingh stood as an Independent, but allied himself with the
local Jan Sangh, with a coalition of opposition parties called the Sampoorna
Maharashtra Samiti, and with G. B. Mane. Mane, an important Buddhist
Mahar leader in Phaltan, stood for election in the Phaltan-Man reserved

constituency with the Raja's support. For the first time Bhoite was faced with the necessity of recruiting popular support. He had won high office in the zilla parishad system and nomination to the Legislative Assembly on the strength of his alliances with other members of the political elite. Now, with a powerful and popular family opposing him, he could not avoid the need for popular support, as he had in the 1962 Aradgaon Panchayat election, by arranging with other elite leaders to be chosen *binvirodh*.

Only in his own village, Aradgaon, was Bhoite's support based on direct vertical alliances with voters from outside the political class. In other parts of his constituency Bhoite attempted to form horizontal alliances with other elite leaders who, by virtue of their own vertical alliances, could deliver the votes of their followers to him. He prepared for his campaign by making a list of such influential men in each village in the western half of Phaltan Taluka. Most of them were *vatandar* Marathas.

In many cases his campaign was based on a series of horizontal political alliances. His link with Saswad, a village where he polled very well, was a double one.[7] Bhoite was allied with Jayvantrao Anpat, a *vatandar* Maratha who was Saswad's Sarpanch and one of the Secretaries of the Phaltan Taluka Congress Committee. Anpat, in turn, was allied with other *vatandar* Marathas in Saswad who served as Polling Agents for Bhoite on election day and saw to it that their supporters voted correctly. Bhoite's link with Shindevadi voters was a triple one. One of Bhoite's closest allies was Namdev Jadhav, a rich Maratha trader who was Chairman of the Phaltan–Lonand Agricultural Produce Market Committee and a member of the Board of Directors of the Shriram Co-operative Sugar Factory. Bhoite married Jadhav's wife's sister and Jadhav helped Bhoite build a house in Phaltan. Jadhav's mother was a Shinde from Shindevadi and he was allied there with a *vatandar* Maratha named T. R. Shinde, a member of the Governing Council of the Shriram Education Society. Through the help of his own allies in Shindevadi, Shinde was able to deliver a large majority of the local vote to Bhoite.

Bhoite acquired his elite allies in a number of ways. In Khandala he received virtually unanimous support from the Congress organization. Khandala men were disappointed that one of their number had not been given the Congress ticket, but they were not involved in any of the organizations controlled by the Raja of Phaltan and their interests were best served by continued loyalty to Chavan and his powerful Satara Congress organization. The President of the Khandala Peth Congress Committee, the Chairman of the Khandala Purchase and Sale Union and the Chairman of the Khandala Panchayat Samiti all spent many days visiting villages with the candidate.

Vertical alliances

Bhoite's situation in the Phaltan half of his constituency, where he received a majority in only a few scattered polling stations, was much more difficult. There his allies fell into three categories. To begin with he had several close allies who joined him when he was Panchayat Samiti Chairman and who helped him win the Congress nomination. These included Namdev Jadhav, Babanrao Adsul, N. M. Saste, M. R. Bhoite and Haribhau Nimbalkar. Although Nimbalkar is now in the Congress, he was Phaltan's Communist MLA from 1957 until 1962. He is President of the Phaltannagar Palika Kamgar Union and of the Phaltan Taluka Sakhar Kamgar Union in Sakharvadi. He also owns a press and publishes Shiva-sandesh, a small bi-monthly newspaper.

After he won the nomination Bhoite received the support of S. R. Bhosle, a Congressman and opponent of the Raja from before Independence; Bhosle's ally M. G. Date; and of their friends, including the Bedkes. These men did not want the Congress nomination to go to the Raja's son, but if it had been possible they would have preferred Bhosle's own son, a lawyer practising in the Bombay High Court, to Bhoite. They rallied around Bhoite after he was nominated but they continued to oppose several of his friends, especially Namdev Jadhav, M. R. Bhoite and Haribhau Nimbalkar.

Finally, Bhoite received support from a number of leaders who held office in institutions such as marketing co-operatives and the zilla parishad system which extend beyond the boundaries of Phaltan Taluka. Politicians in these institutions depend as much or more upon their alliances in Satara as they do upon their alliances in Phaltan. Among Bhoite's most important allies in this category were Jayvantrao Anpat, Saswad Sarpanch; Bhuvasaheb Dhumal, Panchayat Samiti member from Adarki Bk. and Chairman of the Phaltan Taluka Purchase and Sale Union; M. B. Bhosle, Sakharvadi Sarpanch and Panchayat Samiti member; R. N. Phadtare, Zilla Parishad Councillor; M. R. Khalate, Khunte Sarpanch and Panchayat Samiti member, and B. B. Nalavade, Aljapur Sarpanch and Panchayat Samiti member. All of these allies were *vatandar* Marathas.

The campaign for the Legislative Assembly conducted by Bhoite and his allies rested heavily on his two main assets: the popularity of Y. B. Chavan, Satara's modern Shivaji; and Congress strength in Khandala. Chavan, with Balasaheb Desai and Bhoite, addressed several mass rallies in both Khandala and Phaltan. Other Congress rallies featured Vinaikrao Patil, Maharashtra Pradesh Congress Committee President, and V. P. Naik, Chief Minister.

Bhoite concentrated his own efforts in Khandala. Babanrao Adsul and Bhoite campaigned there almost daily and visited nearly every village.

Political alliances

Most days Bhoite and Adsal were escorted by important Khandala leaders, expecially the President of the Khandala Peth Congress Committee and the Chairman of the Khandala Panchayat Samiti. The candidate and his friends usually had tea at the house of a leading villager and talked with a few of the important men. For example, at Palshi, one of the largest villages in Khandala, Bhoite was taken to the house of one of the local *vatandar* Marathas. Among the people he met were the present Sarpanch and his predecessor, both members of the same *vatandar* lineage as the host. The Khandala men, with their knowledge of the local situation, took the lead in such meetings. They introduced the candidates to the villagers, explained that he was well educated, an experienced Congress worker, and Chavan's choice. In nearly every village Bhoite and his allies were assured of strong support. Their main aim was to arrange for polling agents to insure that the voting went as planned on election day.

Bhoite's efforts in Phaltan were very limited. He knew that there was strong opposition to him in Phaltan and that the election depended on the result in Khandala. He held several meetings in Sakharvadi, where he had important allies in local government and in the unions, but neither he nor his allies attempted to visit many of the other villages.

K. R. Bhoite's political career illustrates several characteristics of vertical alliances in Western Maharashtra. In the first place, vertical alliances are often a minor ingredient in a politician's success. Many offices are filled by indirect elections in which only elite leaders have the right to vote. Where offices are filled by direct election the need for popular support often is obviated by agreements among elite leaders to avoid contests. Secondly, when a politician does require popular support, most commonly in a contested direct election, he does not recruit it by entering into direct vertical alliances, whether based on issues or patronage, with voters throughout a large political arena such as an assembly constituency. Direct vertical alliances occur most frequently within single villages. When a politician needs popular support he recruits it by forming horizontal political alliances, single or multiple, with other elite leaders who can deliver the votes of their own villages.

Naik Nimbalkar's Assembly campaign: role of the Sugar Factory

The 1967 Legislative Assembly campaign of Vijaysingh Naik Nimbalkar, the Rajasaheb's son and Chairman of the Shriram Co-operative Sugar Factory, expands but otherwise confirms the above analysis of the distribution of vertical political alliances. Naik Nimbalkar's campaign was very like that of K. R. Bhoite. Bhoite concentrated his efforts in Khandala while Naik Nimbalkar worked mostly in Phaltan, but the campaigns of both men were based on similar networks of alliances. Naik Nimbalkar's campaign was distinguished from Bhoite's by the way in which the former made use of his control of the Shriram Co-operative Sugar Factory.

The Raja of Phaltan was instrumental in establishing the Shriram Co-operative Sugar Factory in 1954 when he was still a member of the Bombay Cabinet. He has maintained control of it ever since. After his defeat in the 1957 General Election the Factory became the main base of the Raja's power. Indeed, some of his opponents in Phaltan complain that he treats the Factory and its resources as his 'privy purse'.

In their management of the Shriram Co-operative Sugar Factory the Rajasaheb and his son have to balance the conflicting interests of two groups: cane producing shareholders and employees. Producer shareholders want a good price for their cane and dividends on their shares. Employees want bonuses. Cane prices, share dividends and employee bonuses all come out of the Factory's gross income from the sale of sugar and by-products at the close of the crushing season.

Most producer shareholders are *vatandar* Marathas. Of the eighty-seven producer shareholders in Girvi, for example, sixty-four are members of the two Kadam lineages of *vatandar* Marathas. Producer shareholders have votes in Factory affairs and may enter into horizontal political alliances with members of the political elite.

I do not have detailed information on Factory laborers. However, I was told that few of them are *vatandar* Marathas. Most live in Phaltan. Those who do not belong to the political class are linked to the Raja by vertical political alliances.

The Raja and his son, with their ally R. B. Bhagat, President of the Phaltan Taluka Shriram Sahakari Kamgar Union, hold the support of the laborers by paying them bonuses which the opposition directors, courting the support of the producer shareholders, claim are far too high.

The Naik Nimbalkars made good use of their control of the Sugar Factory in their Assembly campaign. Many of the Raja's hardest working elite allies were producer shareholders who were then or are now his supporters on the Board of Directors, although this was not his only link with many of them. He was helped also by the laborers. They often were heard marching in a body from the Factory to their homes in Phaltan chanting Vijaysingh's election slogans. During one period many were given leave from work to help campaign in the villages of Phaltan Taluka. They gathered at the Raja's Palace where Bhagat, the union leader and the Raja's right-hand man, gave them handbills and campaign instructions. They were then driven in trucks, normally hired by the factory to transport cane, to villages where they distributed the handbills from door to door.

Political alliances

During the 1967 General Election the Shriram Co-operative Sugar Factory was to Naik Nimbalkar in Phaltan what offices in panchayats or credit societies were to other politicians in their own villages. The Factory was the locus of Naik Nimbalkar's direct vertical alliances with non-elite supporters and the base from which he was able to form horizontal alliances with other elite leaders. I have argued that direct vertical alliances are confined to villages. They also occur in larger settlements such as Phaltan town. Within such settlements vertical alliances are based on the patronage which can be distributed by an elite leader who controls a panchayat, credit society, co-operative factory, or a large landed estate.

The use of issues to generate support

Electoral support from persons outside the political class is generally recruited directly by means of vertical alliances within one's own settlement and indirectly by means of horizontal alliances with other elite leaders who can deliver the votes of their own settlements. In theory it would be possible to recruit support directly from many settlements, circumventing local elite leaders, by exploiting issues with widespread appeal. However, this tactic is rarely used.

In Maharashtrian politics the most successful use of an issue to gain electoral support was the 1956–9 Samyukta Maharashtra Samiti agitation for a Marathi-speaking state. In the 1952 General Election the Congress lost only three of ten Legislative Assembly seats in Satara District and only one of four Parliamentary seats, two of which also included Kolhapur. In 1957, however, the Congress, which then favored retention of the bilingual Bombay State, suffered massive defeats in Western Maharashtra at the hands of the Samyukta Maharashtra Samiti. In Satara the party lost seven of ten Assembly seats and both Parliamentary seats. It must be admitted, however, that the issue of a Marathi-speaking state appealed to elite leaders as well as to persons outside the political class. It was used to form horizontal as well as vertical alliances.[8]

In Phaltan during 1966–7 only one issue was used to recruit support directly, by-passing local leaders. This issue concerned the relations between the owners of land in Sakharvadi, on the one hand, and the Maharashtra State Farm Corporation which rents the land and the laborers who cultivate it, on the other.

The Nira Right Bank Canal was brought into the northern part of Phaltan Taluka in 1926. The privately owned Phaltan Sugar Works were established in Hol-Sakharvadi in 1932. With the encouragement of the Raja of Phaltan, the factory owners reached an agreement with the Bombay Government and with farmers in the area to guarantee themselves an adequate supply of sugar-cane. The government agreed to supply water. The government also helped persuade small farmers to lease their land to the factory for thirty years at a very low rent. The leased land was then non-irrigated and the farmers did not have the capital to develop it. They understood that the factory would develop their land, construct feeder canals and so on, and return it to them at the end of the lease period. However, when the leases expired the land was taken over by the State Farm Corporation which grows cane for the sugar factory with hired laborers. Most of the owners are said to have found employment in Bombay. Few are employed as laborers by the State Farm Corporation.

The owners of the land want it returned to them. The Phaltan Sugar Works owners advocated the formation of a farming co-operative for the whole of the land so that they will be assured of an adequate supply of cane. The union of agricultural laborers, led by Haribhau Nimbalkar and M. Bhise, a Brahmin, wants the State Farm Corporation to retain the land because the laborers would lose their jobs if the owners cultivated it themselves.

In 1967 the factory owners and the union leaders as well as Hol-Sakharvadi's Sarpanch, M. B. Bhosle, and its Zilla Parishad Councillor, R. N. Phadtare, supported the Congress and K. R. Bhoite. When they left the Congress, the Raja and his son, Vijaysingh, tried to recruit electoral support in Sakharvadi directly by demanding that the State Farm Corporation return its land to the owners. Their use of this issue was successful in spite of the united opposition of Sakharvadi leaders. In the General Election Vijaysingh carried three out of the four polling stations in Hol-Sakharvadi with 1279 votes to 1101 for Bhoite out of a total of 2586.

Control of local elite leaders

Politicians rarely attempt to use issues to form direct vertical alliances with non-elite supporters outside their own settlements because few issues are attractive enough to compete with the benefits and sanctions controlled by local elite leaders. Even if a politician finds an issue which has widespread popular appeal it is likely that other elite leaders can, if they wish, deny him the electoral support of their settlements.

The results of the 1967 General Election in Girvi demonstrate the power of elite Maratha *vatəndars* over the votes of their villages. There were 1946 registered voters in Girvi in 1967 (see Chapter 3, Fig. 3). Of these, 293, or about 15 per cent, were bogus, either because they were not actually resident in Girvi or because they were registered twice. As the 1967 election approached all of the *vatəndar* Maratha Kadams (443 votes), the non-*vatəndar* Marathas of Bodkevadi (275 votes), the Ramoshis (223 votes) and the Mahars (105) were known to favor G. B. Mane, Vijaysingh Naik Nimbalkar's ally in the Phaltan–Man constituency. The Kadams were united and enthusiastic in their support of Mane and Naik Nimbalkar. Other villagers were reluctant to express support for the Congress and Congressmen were not even permitted to campaign in Girvi. However, it was generally agreed that the non-*vətəndar* Marathas of Dhumalvadi (230 votes), the Malis (153 votes), the Dhangars (27 votes), the Nhavis (17 votes), the Kumbhars (23 votes), and the Muslims (26 votes), with a total of 476 votes, all favored the Congress candidate, Dr Prabavathi Sonavane.

The voting in Girvi was overseen by half a dozen polling agents working for Mane, all influential Kadams. There were no Congress polling agents in Girvi. As each voter approached the polling station, he was stopped by one of Mane's agents who told him how to vote and for whom. Another agent stood inside the polling station and checked the name of each voter off a list of registered voters as he entered. Mane's agents also found people to go into the voting booths to help voters who were blind or infirm. Most such voters were assisted by a *vərči ali* Kadam student who belongs to a joint family whose members include the Chairman of the Lift-Irrigation Society, a member of the Panchayat, and a member of the Managing Committee of the Multi-Purpose Credit Society.

When the votes were counted it was found that Dr Sonavane received only 101 of the 956 valid votes. Mane received 758 and 97 were given to two independent candidates. Many people did vote for the Congress, although they would not admit it in public. However, many other Congress supporters were frightened into staying home or into voting for Mane. It is also quite possible that some of Mane's votes in Girvi were cast illegally by persons impersonating registered voters who did not come to the polling station or who were not actually resident in Girvi (see Bailey 1965:18).

Results of the 1967 General Election in Phaltan–Khandala

I have argued that vertical political aliances occur primarily between residents of the same settlement. When politicians have to marshal support outside their own settlement they do so indirectly by forming horizontal alliances with elite leaders in other settlements. This analysis of the distribution of vertical political alliances is confirmed by the results of the 1967 General Election in the Phaltan–Khandala Assembly constituency (see Appendix).

A total of 21,591 valid votes were cast in the Khandala Mahal portion of the constituency. K. R. Bhoite received 16,183 or 75.0 per cent and

Vijaysingh Naik Nimbalkar received 2941 or 13.6 per cent. Bhoite received a majority of the valid votes in thirty-two of the thirty-four polling stations in Khandala. His success in Khandala may be attributed to the support which he received from all of the major Congress leaders in the Taluka: the President of the Khandala Peth Congress Committee, the Chairman of the Khandala Purchase and Sale Union, the Chairman of the Khandala Panchayat Samiti, and so on.

Bhoite failed to carry only one Khandala polling station. In Khed Bk. he received only 16.1 per cent of the vote to Naik Nimbalkar's 72.8 per cent. Bhoite carried the Bholi polling station with less than a majority. In Bholi Bhoite received 45.5 per cent of the valid votes, Naik Nimbalkar 8.0 per cent and Balasaheb Chavan, a minor Independent candidate, 39.4 per cent. Bhoite's lack of success in these two villages may be attributed to his failure to form horizontal alliances with important local leaders. In Khed Bk. Vishnu Dhoiphode, a well known Communist leader in the Sampoorna Maharashtra Samiti, was allied with Naik Nimbalkar. Bhoite recognized that Dhoipode had his village firmly under control and did not even attempt to campaign there. In Bholi Bhoite's vote was cut by the ability of Balasaheb Chavan, a resident of Bholi, to control many of the votes in his own village.

The situation in the Phaltan portion of the Phaltan-Khandala constituency was very nearly the reverse of that in Khandala. Of 30,932 valid votes cast in Phaltan, Naik Nimbalkar received 19,979 or 64.6 per cent and Bhoite received 8557 or 27.7 per cent. Naik Nimbalkar carried thirty-three polling stations with between 42.0 and 91.4 per cent of the valid votes. Bhoite carried eleven polling stations with between 47.9 and 81.2 per cent of the valid votes. One polling station was carried by a minor candidate.

Naik Nimbalkar's success in Phaltan was due to his control of important institutions, especially the Shriram Co-operative Sugar Factory. His control of the Sugar Factory, the Urban Co-operative Bank, and the Phaltan Education Society gave him the means to form direct vertical alliances with many residents of Phaltan town, his own settlement, where he received 86.5 per cent of the 10,695 valid votes cast in fourteen polling stations. It also gave him the means to form horizontal alliances with important leaders in other villages.

Bhoite carried eleven polling stations in Phaltan and did relatively well in several others. His successes in Phaltan are primarily a reflection of his horizontal alliances, most of which are based on his control of the Phaltan Panchayat Samiti and on his association with the Congress and Y. B. Chavan. For example, Bhoite received 50.7 per cent of the valid votes in Kalaj where he was allied with H. J. Kadam, *vatandar* Maratha Chairman of the Kalaj Multi-Purpose Credit Society and class (*d*) co-opted member of the Phaltan Panchayat Samiti.

He carried one of the four Hol-Sakharvadi polling stations with 50.1 per cent of the valid votes and did relatively well in two of the others in which he received 40.3 and 42.0 per cent of the valid votes. In Hol-Sakharvadi Bhoite was allied with R. N. Phadtare, the Zilla Parishad Councillor from the Hol-Sakharvadi electoral division, and with M. B. Bhosle, the Hol-Sakharvadi Sarpanch and Panchayat Samiti member. He also had the support of union leaders Haribhau Nimbalkar and M. Bhise and of the management of the Phaltan Sugar Works.

Bhoite was allied as well with Jayvantrao Anpat, the Sasvad Sarpanch, and with N. P. Dhumal, Tambve Sarpanch. He carried Sasvad with 81.2 per cent of the valid votes and Tambve with 70.7 per cent. Bhoite's alliance with T. R. Shinde, through Namdev Jadhav, gave him 66.7 per cent of the valid votes in Khunte No. 2 (Shindevadi). Other horizontal alliances allowed him to carry the Raodi Bk.-Raodi Kh.-Kusur, Khamgaon, and Kapadgaon-Koregaon polling stations.

Bhoite did relatively well in Kapashi-Aljapur, where he received 40.9 per cent of the valid votes, and in the second Taradgaon polling station, where he received 42.3 per cent of the valid votes. His success in Kapashi-Aljapur was due to his alliance with B. B. Nalavade, *vətəndar* Maratha, Sarpanch and member of the Phaltan Panchayat Samiti. In Taradgaon he was supported by one of his oldest allies, K. B. Adsul.

Bhoite's position in the Panchayat Samiti enabled him to form vertical alliances with the voters in his own village, Aradgaon, which he carried with 79.5 per cent of the valid votes. He also carried both polling stations in neighboring Hingangaon. Hingangaon is part of Bhoite's Panchayat Samiti constituency, but Bhoite himself attributed his success there to the fact that Hingangaon is dominated by Bhoites, members of his own clan (*kuḷ*). It should be noted, however, that he was opposed by J. M. Bhoite, the Zilla Parishad Councillor from the Taradgaon electoral division and a Hingangaon *vətəndar* Maratha, and that he did better in the first Hingangaon polling station, which contains the villages of Sherichivadi and Salpe, than he did in the second, which contains most of the Hingangaon Bhoites. It is likely, therefore, that Bhoite's ability to deliver patronage to his own constituency is a more important element in his success there than the kinship bonds which he shared with putative agnates.

Except in Sakharvadi, where Naik Nimbalkar won the support of the landowners who had lost their property to the State Farm Corporation, neither candidate did at all well in polling stations where they lacked influential allies. On the other hand, neither candidate did badly in polling stations in which they were able to secure horizontal alliances with all or some of the local elite leaders.

THE CONTENT OF VERTICAL POLITICAL ALLIANCES

The power of elite leaders over their non-elite followers derives from the social relations which link elite leaders and the political class generally with the rest of the population. The most important are those which involve the *vətəndar* Marathas, the predominant element in the political class of Western Maharashtra. Some of these social relations serve as a basis for appeals to group solidarity. Most vertical political alliances, however, are based on economic relations in which the political class controls valuable resources. The *vətəndar* Marathas are in a privileged position with regard to the former social relations, but economic relations pertain to all the elements of the political class: *vətəndar* Marathas, Malis, and Dhangars in the villages where they are dominant, plus Brahmins and Jain Gujars in the market towns.

Common caste affiliation is a link between the political class and the mass of the population in only two instances. In those settlements in which Brahmins, Gujars, Dhangars, and Malis belong to the political class there are no other groups to whom they can appeal on the basis of caste solidarity. *Vətəndar* Marathas, however, can exploit caste ties in appeals to non-*vətəndar* Marathas, the largest single group in Western Maharashtra. *Vətəndar* Marathas are the arbiters of two kinds of caste status. In the early decades of the twentieth century they permitted the people then known as Kunbis to claim full Maratha status. More recently, many non-*vətəndars*, former Kunbis, have been permitted to claim full *vətəndar* Maratha status by attaching themselves to *vətəndar* Maratha *bhaubunds* (see Chapter 6, p. 81 ff). In both these instances *vətəndar* Marathas have formed vertical political alliances based on the exchange of high caste status for political support. In the former they exchanged status in their struggle against the power of the Maharashtrian Brahmins (see Latthe 1924). In the latter they are exchanging status for support in new political institutions based on universal suffrage.

Members of the political elite who are recruited from outside the political class can appeal to their caste mates for political support also, but the efficacy of such appeals is limited. Such a politician's caste fellows are likely to constitute a very small part of the population of his village, although they may form a significant portion of some election wards. Furthermore, such a politician's appeals to caste solidarity must compete with the economic power of the *vətəndar* Marathas and other elements of the political class.

Political alliances

With regard to caste as a basis for vertical political alliances, then, *vətəndar* Marathas are in an advantageous position. They are able to exchange caste status for political support on a scale which no other group can match.

Ties of kinship rarely form a basis for vertical political alliances. Because of the rule of caste endogamy members of the political class do not have ties of kinship with members of castes which do not form part of the political class in their settlement. The only possible exception to this generalization is the Maratha caste. The Maratha caste is divided into two sections, *vətəndars* within the political class and non-*vətəndars* outside the political class, which may be linked by ties of kinship. However, such ties are rare (see Chapter 6, p. 94 ff). Only 5.2 per cent of the marriages contracted by *vətəndar* Marathas in Girvi are intra-village marriage links. Few of the intra-village marriage connections in which *vətəndar* Marathas are involved link them to large non-*vətəndar* Maratha lineages. Most link the *vətəndar* Marathas with isolated families which, for one reason or another, have moved from their original villages to live in Girvi with their affines. Of the thirty-six intra-village marriages involving *vətəndar* Marathas in Girvi twenty-two link them to such isolated families. They have had fourteen marriage links with the large non-*vətəndar* Maratha lineages in Bodkevadi and Jadhavvada and none at all linking them with the Marathas of Dhumalvadi (see Chapter 6, Fig. 18).

Economic relations are the main structural basis of vertical political alliances. In addition to high caste status *vətəndar* Marathas and other groups in the political class, such as Brahmins and Gujars, control a disproportionate share of the wealth of their settlements. Their wealth enables them to exert economic power as employers of agricultural labor. It also enables them to invest in co-operative societies on a larger scale than other groups and, hence, to control credit and a great deal of the non-agricultural employment (see Chapter 5).

THE GIRVI PANCHAYAT ELECTION, 1966

The Girvi Panchayat has thirteen members elected from five geographically defined wards (see Map 3 and Fig. 3). Three members each are elected from Vitthal, Lakshmi, and Shriram wards and two members each from Janubai and Hanuman wards. Two seats are reserved for women, one in Vitthal and one in Shriram ward, and one seat in Lakshmi ward is reserved for a member of the Scheduled Castes. Each voter may caste as many votes as there are seats in his ward. He may cast all his votes for a single candidate or he may divide them between several candidates.

Although the *vətəndar* Maratha Kadams comprise only 24.8 per cent of the population of Girvi, they have won a commanding position in every Panchayat election except the first, in 1952. Six of the thirteen Panchayat members elected in 1966 were *vətəndar* Marathas. So commanding was their position that members of the two Kadam patrilineages were able to compete for control of the Panchayat without fear that other groups would bring about their defeat by exploiting the divisions among them.

To win control of the Panchayat the Kadams had first to secure election in those wards in which they were represented. However, because the *vətəndar* Maratha Kadams are completely absent from Lakshmi ward, constitute less than a tenth of the voters in Janubai, less than a third in Shriram, and less than half in Vitthal and Hanuman wards, they could not hope to control the Panchayat simply by winning election in their own wards. They also had to obtain the support of other Panchayat members. Although I was able to observe only the second, indirect, stage of the 1966 Panchayat elections, it was clear that control of caste status and of economic resources were important factors in the ability of the *vətəndar* Marathas to secure election for themselves and to win the support of other members.

The result of the first, direct, stage of the 1966 Girvi Panchayat elections are shown in Figure 19. The first point to be noted about these results is that in all but one of the four wards in which Kadams won election a significant portion of their potential voters were attached members of their lineages. Eighty of one hundred and forty-one *vətəndar* Maratha voters in Hanuman ward belonged to attached groups. Twenty-seven of thirty-two *vətəndar* Maratha voters in Janubai ward and thirty-one of one hundred and fifty-four in Vitthal ward also belonged to attached groups. Although I do not know exactly how the residents of the village voted nor even, since the actual vote was far lower than the potential vote, which residents actually exercised their franchise, it seems likely that the support of the attached members of their lineages was an element in the electoral success of the Kadams.

Many of the attached groups have had some claim on *vətəndar* status for many years, but the claims of 47.6 per cent of the attached *vətəndar* Marathas are of very recent origin. The Kotvals (Genealogy 1*f*) and Pundes (Genealogy 1*g*) of the *vərči ali* lineage and the Kokates (Genealogy 2*i*) of the *khalči ali* lineage were all non-*vətəndar* Marathas only three or four years ago. The proper *vətəndar* Maratha Kadams seem to be exchanging caste status for political support. The impetus for this form of exchange has probably come from the introduction of political institutions based on universal suffrage. Prior to Independence the *vətəndar* Marathas had an hereditary right to their power in the village. They then had every reason

Fig. 19   Results of the 1966 Girvi Panchayat Election

Ward	Seat	Name of candidate	Caste	Votes	Result
Vitthal	R	Mrs V. M. Kadam (Genealogy 1a, M2)	Maratha (vətəndar)		EU
Vitthal	G	S. D. Bodre	Ramoshi	240	E
Vitthal	G	R. B. Kadam (Genealogy 1a, K27)	Maratha (vətəndar)	219	E
Vitthal	G	B. G. Kadam (Genealogy 1a, J17)	Maratha (vətəndar)	136	D
Janubai	G	M. A. Kadam (Genealogy 1a, L29)	Maratha (vətəndar)	177	E
Janubai	G	J. B. Bhandvalkar	Maratha (non-vətəndar)	132	E
Janubai	G	M. A. Dhembre	Maratha (non-vətəndar)	46	D
Lakshmi	R	B. R. Nikalje	Mahar		EU
Lakshmi	G	B. S. Dhumal	Maratha (non-vətəndar)	194	E
Lakshmi	G	M. T. Dhumal	Maratha (non-vətəndar)	121	E
Lakshmi	G	D. A. Phadtare	Maratha (non-vətəndar)	101	D
Shriram	R	Mrs S. G. Kadam (Genealogy 2c, J4)	Maratha (vətəndar)		EU
Shriram	G	D. D. Kadam (Genealogy 2d, I8)	Maratha (vətəndar)	206	E
Shriram	G	S. G. Jadhav	Mali	191	E
Shriram	G	B. S. Kadam (Genealogy 2f, I12)	Maratha (vətəndar)	116	D
Hanuman	G	H. D. Kadam (Genealogy 2a, I4)	Maratha (vətəndar)	109	E
Hanuman	G	R. M. Kumbhar	Kumbhar	101	E
Hanuman	G	B. G. Kadam (Genealogy 1a, L20)	Maratha (vətəndar)	97	D
Hanuman	G	B. K. Kadam (Genealogy 2a, I11)	Maratha (vətəndar)	54	D
Hanuman	G	S. A. Kadam (Genealogy 2a, H1)	Maratha (vətəndar)	32	D

G = General, R = Reserved, EU = Elected Unopposed, E = Elected, D = Defeated.

to exclude other Marathas from *vətəndar* status. Now the *vətəndars* must win their power in elections. They can easily trade some of their status, which no longer gives them an hereditary right to office, for valuable electoral support.[9]

One *vətəndar* Maratha, Mugatrao Kadam (Genealogy 1a, L29), won election from Janubai ward where his lineage mates, proper and attached, comprised less than a tenth of the registered voters. The result is all the more surprising since Mugatrao polled ahead of all the other candidates even though the losing candidate, Mansingh Dhembre, was a member of the largest single group of voters in the ward, the Dhembre *bhaubund* of Bodkevadi. For some reason Dhembre was unable to obtain the support of his agnates.

Mugatrao's success may be ascribed to several factors. He could count on support from the thirty-two members of his own lineage in Janubai ward. He also could exert economic power over the Ramoshis and some of the non-*vatəndar* Marathas. Mugatrao's joint family, including his five brothers and his father, is one of the wealthiest in the village. They own 56.65 acres of irrigated land and 107.03 acres of dry land in Girvi. They also own fifty acres of canal irrigated land near Phaltan and rent fifty acres more. In Girvi they employ twelve men and twelve women, mostly Mahars and Ramoshis, as *geḍis* on a yearly basis. During the cotton harvest they often hire as many as 100 pickers for several weeks. Mugatrao's eldest brother, Keshavrao (Genealogy 1*a*, *L*25), is a former Sarpanch. Keshavrao holds the Shriram Co-operative Sugar Factory contract for cane harvesting in Girvi which means that he schedules the harvest and hires the men who cut, load and haul the cane. After I left India Keshavrao was elected Vice-Chairman of the Shriram Sugar Factory. Mugatrao's youngest brother, Devrao (Genealogy 1*a*, *L*30), is a member of the Managing Committee of the Girvi Credit Society. The family holds the office of *vərči ali mukəddəm*. It was Mugatrao's economic power, some of it deriving from his family's land, some from their control of village institutions, and some from their alliance with the Raja of Phaltan, that enabled him to win the election in Bodkevadi.

Having secured their own election, the Kadams had to win the support of other Panchayat members. Here their economic power came to the fore. Their most dependable supporters on the Panchayat were the Ramoshi, Mahar, and Mali members. The Ramoshis and Mahars are dependent upon the Kadams for agricultural employment. The Ramoshis and Malis are dependent upon the Kadams for credit. All but one of the members of the Managing Committee of the Girvi Credit Society are *vatəndar* Marathas. They have taken the lion's share of the Society's loans themselves, but it is significant that the Ramoshis and Malis have been given comparatively large shares also. Of the Rs. 629,465 lent by the Society between 4 January 1965 and 29 June 1967, Rs. 34,450 went to Malis and Rs. 29,350 went to Ramoshis. Although both received much less than the *vatəndar* Marathas, they still received more than the non-*vatəndar* Marathas, on both an absolute and a *per capita* basis. There are more than three times as many non-*vətəndar* Marathas in Girvi as there are either Ramoshis or Malis (see Fig. 2), but the non-*vətəndars* have received only Rs. 27,150 in loans from the Credit Society. With regard to these three castes, then, the Kadams are attempting to exchange economic patronage for political support. As long as they can form vertical political alliances based on employer–employee and creditor–debtor relations with the Malis, Ramoshis, and Mahars, there is little chance that the political power of the *vətəndar* Marathas will be successfully challenged.

SUMMARY

The 1967 General Election in Phaltan demonstrated that vertical political alliances occur within single settlements. The Raja of Phaltan has vertical alliances in Phaltan town with persons who are employed as laborers in the Sugar Factory or who are otherwise dependent upon him. The Raja does not use his control of the Sugar Factory to form direct vertical alliances with people in Jinti or Girvi. Rather, he forms horizontal alliances with leaders such as Keshavrao Kadam (Genealogy 1a, L25) in Girvi who, by virtue of vertical political alliances within their own settlements, can deliver support to the Raja when he needs it. Elite leaders do not form direct vertical alliances with persons in settlements other than their own because the power of the elite in each village is generally sufficient to prevent such interference.

The 1966 Girvi Panchayat election suggests that within individual settlements vertical political alliances are based primarily on ties of economic dependence linking *vətəndar* Marathas with other groups in the population. Their landed wealth enables the *vətəndar* Marathas to exert economic power as employers. Their investments in institutions such as village credit societies enables them to exert economic power as creditors. As arbiters of two kinds of valued caste status *vətəndar* Marathas are also in a position to exchange status for political support. Status, however, is a less fluid asset than economic power. The supply is limited by the number of status distinctions and by the number of potential recipients. A particular item of status such as membership in a *vətəndar* lineage must be conferred on a particular recipient all at once and once conferred it cannot be withdrawn easily.

8
Horizontal alliances

Horizontal political alliances link elite leaders with other elite leaders and with members of the political class who have not entered the elite. They occur in all political arenas and on all occasions of political action. The number of horizontal alliances is greater in more inclusive areas, but nowhere do they disappear entirely. Many positions of influence over the distribution of political patronage are obtained in periodical elections by means of direct or indirect appeal to the mass of the voters. However, the actual distribution of patronage is decided continuously by a small group of elite leaders. Therefore, even though vertical alliances are often unnecessary, a successful politician must maintain his horizontal alliances constantly intact.

With horizontal as with vertical political alliances the crucial factor continues to be patronage transactions of one sort or another, but in other respects the two kinds of alliance are quite different. Vertical alliances are either inter-caste links or else links between *vatandar* and non-*vatandar* Marathas. They generally involve economic or status transactions for which kinship rarely is a pretext. Horizontal alliances, on the other hand, tend to be intra-caste, linking one *vatandar* Maratha with another, although inter-caste links involving Brahmins, Gujars, and so on also occur. They involve patronage or support transactions for which kinship is not infrequently a pretext. However, the kind of kinship connections which are available to politicians vary with the inclusiveness of the political arena. In no case is there a one-to-one correspondence between political alliances and ties of kinship.

HORIZONTAL POLITICAL ALLIANCES IN GIRVI

The *vatandar* Maratha Kadams are clearly dominant in Girvi. They are the traditional Patils of the village. They own the greatest share of the land and comprise, if the attached groups are included, nearly twenty-five per cent of the population. They always are accorded ritual precedence in such village festivals as Bendur and the Bhairavnath fair. The horizontal alliances among the dominant Kadams are the most important element in village politics. Other groups are confined to the role of follower.

The primary structural framework underlying horizontal political alliances in Girvi at the present time is the opposition of the two *vətəndar* Maratha *bhaubunds* of the Kadam *kuḷ*. Residents say that there are two parties in the village, *vərči ali* and *khalči ali*. Since the two Kadam lineages are unrelated except as members of the same clan and, in a few instances, as affines of affines there is no particular basis for co-operation between them. Since one holds the Police Patilship and the other held the Revenue Patilship there traditionally have been many grounds for competition.

Management of the village fair

The management of the annual fair in honor of Bhairavnath, the village guardian god, illustrates the dominance of the *vətəndar* Kadams as well as the tendency of each Kadam lineage to unite in opposition to the other. The festival is celebrated in two stages in the second fortnight of Chaitra month (April/May). On the first day Bhairavnath is placed in a *palki* and carried in procession to the shrine of Jagubai on the west side of the village. There, in front of the assembled men of the village, the marriage of Bhairavnath and Jagubai is performed by the Brahmin priest assisted by the *mukəddəm* of the *vərči ali* lineage. When the marriage ceremony is finished Bhairavnath is returned to his temple.

The rest of the fair takes place on a convenient market day about a week later. In the morning Bhairavnath and Jagubai again are placed in a *palki* and carried in procession around the village so that the women may have *dəršən* near their homes. A *tamaša* troupe is hired to perform short dramas, songs and dances and the village wrestlers hold a tournament.

The fair is managed by a committee of leading men. The committee is supposed to be selected by the assembled villagers at the Bhairavnath-Jagubai wedding, but, in fact, the leading men always select themselves, usually several weeks before the first part of the festival. The same men serve on the fair committee year after year. They are always Kadams and they are always equally divided between the *vərči ali* and *khalči ali* lineages. In 1966 the fair committee consisted of Ramrao Bapusheb (Genealogy 1*a*, *K*27), Bhagvantrao Gulabrao (Genealogy 1*a*, *M*6), Babanrao Ganpatrao (Genealogy 1*a*, *J*17) and Rajaram Baburao (Genealogy 1*b*, *E*5) from the *vərči ali* lineage and Ganpatrao Eknath (Genealogy 2*c*, *J*4), Baburao Sitaram (Genealogy 2*f*, *I*12), Shankarrao Appasaheb (Genealogy 2*a*, *H*1), and Sarjerao Sahebrao (Genealogy 2*d*, *J*10) from the *khalči ali* lineage. During recent years Ramrao Bapusaheb has served as the committee's treasurer.

Over the past few years the cost of the fair has ranged from Rs. 991 to

Rs. 1298, the largest expenses being the hire of the *tamaša* troupe and the prizes for the wrestlers. Several weeks in advance of the fair members of the fair committee go from house to house collecting contributions from each family. When the fair is over the committee usually has a balance of several hundred rupees.

The surplus funds are divided between the *vərči ali* and *khalči ali* members of the fair committee. The latter divide the money among themselves, but the *vərči ali* members have joined together to lend their share at an interest rate of six and a quarter per cent per month. In May 1967 they had Rs. 2282 in outstanding loans ranging from Rs. 12 to Rs. 300. The forty-three borrowers included thirteen proper *vərči ali* Kadams, six attached *vərči ali* Kadams, eighteen Ramoshis, four non-*vətəndar* Marathas, and two Brahmins. Except for the Brahmins, all of the borrowers were residents of the *vərči ali* Kadams' own Vitthal ward.

Disputes over the allocation of the unspent balance of fair funds have threatened to disrupt the fair on several ocasions. The *khalči ali* Kadams claim that they do not receive a fair share of the surplus. The *vərči ali* Kadams reject this charge. They argue that the division of the surplus among the committee members should be proportional to the amount collected in contributions. If the *khalči ali* members want a greater share of the surplus they must see to it that people from their end of the village contribute more.

In 1965 the dispute over the surplus funds produced an open split. The Bhairavnath-Jugubai wedding was celebrated as usual and the procession a week later was performed jointly, but the two Kadam lineages held separate wrestling tournaments and each lineage hired its own *tamaša* troupe.

By 1966 the dispute had been smoothed over and a single fair was held again. The *vərči ali* Kadams retained control of the fair finances, but they agreed to give Rs. 150 to a member of the committee from the *khalči ali* lineage. It was said that the money was intended to be used to pay for the installation of lights in the Maruti Temple but no work had been done.

In 1967 this compromise was threatened by a dissenting *vərči ali* Kadam, Bhagvantrao Gulabrao (Genealogy 1*a*, *M*6), a member of a wealthy family split by internal conflict and isolated in village politics. Bhagvantrao embarrassed his fair committee colleagues in front of the villagers assembled for the Bhairavnath-Jagubai wedding by protesting against the grant of Rs. 150 to the *khalči ali* member. Other leading Kadams tried to hush Bhagvantrao, but he would not sit down. The argument ended only when the entire assembly mercifully was distracted by the discovery of a snake in its midst. Some suggested that the village agree to a formula for the collection of money for the fair, but nothing was settled. It was feared that the fair would be cancelled, but the compromise between the *vərči ali* and *khalči ali* Kadams was preserved and the fair was held without further disagreements.

The conflicts revolving around the management of the annual Bhairav-nath fair display the major elements of Girvi politics. Free from statutory limitations the *vətəndar* Maratha Kadams are able to do as they please on the fair committee. The course of events is determined not by the vertical alliances linking the Kadams with other groups, but by the horizontal alliances which the Kadams have with each other. The dominant feature of these horizontal alliances is a tendency for each Kadam lineage to unite in opposition to the other. Not infrequently, however, competition between families leads to splits in *bhaubund* unity.

Horizontal alliances in panchayat politics

The same factors emerge from an analysis of Panchayat politics in Girvi. However, although the Kadams have almost complete freedom in the traditional fair committee, they are under several restraints on the statutory Panchayat. There is no formal procedure for selecting the fair committee, so the elite Kadams are free to select only themselves. The thirteen Panchayat members, on the other hand, are chosen by universal suffrage from five geographically defined wards (see Fig. 3 and Map 3). One seat on the Panchayat is reserved for a member of the Scheduled Castes. No ward is comprised solely of *vətəndar* Maratha Kadams and each voter may caste as many votes as there are Panchayat members to be elected from his ward. It would be difficult, therefore, for the Kadams to win more than the six seats they obtained in the 1966 Panchayat election. The elite Kadams hold 46.2 per cent of the Panchayat seats with only 24.8 per cent of the village population, but on the Panchayat their dominance is somewhat masked by the presence of non-*vətəndar* Marathas and members of other castes. Masked though it is the dominance of the Kadams remains quite complete.

I have discussed the vertical political alliances which entered into the Girvi Panchayat election of 1966 in Chapter 7. Vertical alliances were important in the election of some Panchayat members. They also played a role in the formation of a majority party on the Panchayat and in the in-direct election of the Sarpanch since seven of the members belong neither to the political elite nor to the political class.

Horizontal political alliances among the *vətəndar* Kadams came to the fore after the direct election of the Panchayat when the members turned to the task of choosing their Sarpanch. However, horizontal alliances also entered into the election of Panchayat members as the candidates attempted to form slates which anticipated the formation of Panchayat coalitions after the election. The division of the Kadams into two localized patri-lineages influenced the formation of alliances at both stages. However, lineage membership had a slightly different impact at each stage.

The election of the Panchayat. As the election approached the two leading candidates for Sarpanch were Mugatrao Appasaheb Kadam (Genealogy 1*a*, *L*29), a member of the *vərči ali* lineage, and Dattatrya Dhondiram Kadam (Genealogy 2*d*, *I*8), a member of the *khalči ali* lineage. I have noted already that Magatrao's family is one of the wealthiest and most influential in the village (see Chapter 7, p. 125). Dattatrya Kadam was the incumbent Sarpanch. He and his six brothers own 12.88 acres of wet land in Girvi and 40.29 acres of dry.

The two leading candidates faced opposition from within their own lineages. Several *vərči ali* Kadams, jealous of the prominence of Muga-trao's family, wanted to back Ramrao Bapusaheb (Genealogy 1*a*, *K*27) for Sarpanch. Ramrao's brother, Amrutrao (Genealogy 1*a*, *K*25), was then Chairman of the Girvi Credit Society. The move in favor of Ramrao was initiated by Suryajirao (Chiman) Kadam (Genealogy 1*a*, *M*4), whose brother's wife, Vijaymala Kadam, was the unopposed lady candidate in Vitthal ward. In the *khalči ali bhaubund* there was some thought that one term as Sarpanch was enough and that Dattatrya Dhondiram ought to step down in favor of Hanmantrao Dolatrao (Genealogy 2*a*, *I*4). In the end, however, Mugatrao's family persuaded Ramrao not to run for Sarpanch, perhaps by promising to support him for Upa-Sarpanch and his brother for re-election as Credit Society Chairman.[1] Hanmantrao never emerged as an open candidate for Sarpanch.

In the final balloting Mugatrao was the only *vərci ali* candidate in Janubai ward. Two other *vərči ali* men, Ramrao Bapusaheb (Genealogy 1*a*, *K*27) and Babanrao Ganpatrao (Genealogy 1*a*, *J*17), were candidates in Vitthal ward and a fourth, Bhujangrao Govindrao (Genealogy 1*a*, *L*20), stood for election in Hanuman ward. Vijaymala Malharrao, wife of Malharrao Kadam (Genealogy 1*a*, *M*2), was the unopposed *vərči ali* candidate for the women's seat in Vitthal ward. Of these all but Babanrao Ganpatrao were publicly committed to supporting Mugatrao for Sarpanch and had his support in the election. Babanrao Ganpatrao supported Datta-trya Dhondiram Kadam for Sarpanch, thus opposing members of his own *bhaubund*.

Five *khalči ali* Kadam men, Hanmantrao Dolatrao, Balvantrao Kedari (Genealogy 2*a*, *I*11), Shankarrao Appasaheb (Genealogy 2*a*, *H*1), Datta-trya Dhondiram, and Baburao Sitaram (Genealogy 2*f*, *I*12), contested the

Panchayat election from Hanuman and Shriram wards. Sulochana Ganpatrao, wife of Ganpatrao Eknath Kadam (Genealogy 2c, *J*4), was the
unopposed *khalči ali* candidate for the women's seat in Shriram ward.
Two *khalči ali* Kadams, Sulochana Ganpatrao and Hanmantrao Dolatrao,
supported Dattatrya Dhondiram for Sarpanch. Balvantrao Kedari and
Shankarrao Appasaheb supported Mugatrao and Baburao Sitaram leaned
in that direction.

In the first stage of the 1966 Girvi Panchayat election groups of elite
Kadams allied on the basis of common patrilineage membership were
returned from the wards in which their respective lineages were represented. Mugatrao Appasaheb and his *vərči ali* allies won election in Vitthal
and Janubai wards. Dattatrya Dhondiram and his *khalči ali* allies won election in Hanuman and Shriram wards. *Bhaubund* based alliances dominated
the election. Several candidates, Babanrao Ganpatrao in Vitthal ward,
Balvantrao Kedari and Shankarrao Appasaheb in Hanuman ward, and
Baburao Sitaram in Shriram ward, tended to support the Sarpanch
candidate from the opposite *bhaubund*, but their choices, like those of the
successful candidates, were determined by *bhaubund* affiliation. They had
to stand for election in geographically defined wards dominated by their
own lineages and they were excluded from their lineage slates. In such
circumstances they could hope to receive influential support only from the
opposing *bhaubund*.

The Sarpanch election. In the first stage of the Panchayat election candidates looked forward to competition between lineages, but for the moment
they were forced to compete within lineages. In the second stage of the
election, when the Panchayat members chose their Sarpanch, the emphasis
changed. Competition within *bhaubunds* remained, but competition
between *bhaubunds* came to the fore.

In the January 1966 panchayat election the *vərči ali* party emerged with a
seven to six majority. The *vərči ali* party consisted of lineage members
Mugatrao Appasaheb, Vijaymala Malharrao, and Ramrao Bapusaheb
plus their non-political class supporters, Shripati Dagadu Bodre, Jayvant
Buva Bhandvalkar, Bapu Shivram Dhumal, and Bapu Ramchandra
Nikalje. The *khalči ali* party consisted of lineage members Dattatrya
Dhondiram, Hanmantrao Dolatrao, and Sulochana Ganpatrao and their
non-political class supporters, Ramchandra Maruti Kumbhar, Shivram
Ganpatrao Jadhav, and Mahadev Tukaram Dhumal. Observers in the
village felt that these alliances would hold up and that Mugatrao Appasaheb Kadam would be elected Sarpanch.

The election of the new Sarpanch was delayed several weeks when

Bhujangrao Govindrao Kadam unsuccessfully tried to have the courts reverse the victory of R. M. Kumbhar. When the thirteen Panchayat members finally met in March the *vərči ali* party nominated Mugatrao for Sarpanch and Ramrao Bapusaheb for Upa-Sarpanch. At the last moment, however, it was discovered that Vijaymala had allied herself with the *khalči ali* party. The *khalči ali* group nominated Vijaymala for Sarpanch and Dattatrya for Upa-Sarpanch. This unexpected development caused so much confusion that the Revenue Department official who was presiding postponed the election for two weeks. By the end of that period a compromise had been arranged. Mugatrao and Dattatrya withdrew and Vijaymala and Ramrao were elected unopposed.

At first sight Vijaymala's alliance with the *khalči ali* party appears to be perfectly reasonable power politics. The *vərči ali* party had a majority of only seven to six. In such situations coalitions are unstable and the costs of keeping allies are very high. If just one person shifts then the majority party changes. Therefore, persons in a position to give the majority to either party can demand a high price for their support. In this case Dattatrya Dhondiram Kadam's party was able to win a majority on the Panchayat at the cost of the Sarpanchship.

In many respects the analysis of these alliances in terms of power politics is adequate. Certainly if Mugatrao's majority had been more than one Dattatrya Dhondiram's maneuver would not have been successful. However, there is more to it than that. An analysis of the factors behind Vijaymala's alliance with the *khalči ali* party reveals the kinds of tensions which tend to divide alliances based on lineage membership.

The Vijaymala-*khalči ali* alliance was arranged by Dattatrya Dhondiram Kadam and Vijaymala's husband's brother, Suryajirao (Chiman) Kadam. Chimanrao, a young law student, is a political entrepreneur of the first rank whose efforts culminated in his election as Chairman of the Phaltan Panchayat Samiti in September 1970. Chimanrao and Dattatrya first asked Ramrao Bapusaheb, Mugatrao's ally and the *vərči ali* candidate for Upa-Sarpanch, to join them. Ramrao had been interested in the Sarpanchship earlier in the election and they hoped he would now be willing to challenge Mugatrao. Ramrao refused the offer, however, partly from a sense of *bhaubund* loyalty and partly to avoid damaging his brother's position as Chairman of the Credit Society. It was only then that Chimanrao and Dattatrya decided to elect Vijaymala Sarpanch with *khalči ali* support.

The willingness of Vijaymala's husband and of her husband's brothers to ally themselves with the opposing *vətəndar* lineage has its origin in a dispute over succession to the office and prerogatives of the *vərči ali* lineage *mukəddəm* (see Chapter 6, p. 86–7). The last male member of the senior line of the *vərči ali* Kadam lineage was Nanasaheb Bhagvantrao (Genealogy 1a, *J*3). Nanasaheb owned a very large, ruined, but once elegant *vaḍa* (palace) on the west side of Girvi (southwest of House No. *K*8, Map 3) and eighty acres of land. He was married to a woman of the Gwalior royal family and he lived in Gwalior where he had an office in the royal household. Since Nanasaheb did not live in Girvi his duties as *mukəddəm* were performed by Malojirao Khanderao Kadam (Genealogy 1a, *M*1), the last Girvi Revenue Patil and Vijaymala's husband's father's brother's son. Nanasaheb's land was cultivated by a number of tenants. Yadhavrao Balvantrao Kadam (Genealogy 1a, *K*19), Mugatrao's father's brother, was living in Gwalior too. Nanasaheb had two daughters, but no sons. He proposed to adopt Yadhavrao as his heir, but before the adoption ceremony could be performed Nanasaheb died. A complicated dispute then arose as to who was Nanasaheb's rightful heir. The dispute was fought over the ownership of Nanasaheb's *vaḍa* and land, but the prerogatives of the lineage *mukəddəm* went with the estate.

One of the claimants was Yadhavrao. He based his claim on his intended adoption, but he was already in possession of the disputed estate. The Girvi Talathi was persuaded to record Yadhavrao as occupant of Nanasaheb's estate in 1941 or 1942. At the same time Appasaheb Balvantrao, Mugatrao's father, became his brother's tenant and began to act as *mukəddəm*.

A second claimant was Malojirao Khanderao. Malojirao argued that Yadhavrao's adoption was invalid. He claimed that he should inherit Nanasaheb's estate and succeed to the *mukəddəm*ship because he was the most senior remaining member of the lineage and Nanasaheb's closest agnatic relative.

A third claimant was Nanasaheb's daughter's daughter, the wife of a wealthy *jagirdar* in Khandesh, who argued that she should inherit because she is Nanasaheb's nearest relative.

The dispute was taken to court and eventually appealed all the way to the Supreme Court in Delhi. Before the Supreme Court heard the case, however, a compromise was reached. Nanasaheb's granddaughter got three-quarters of the estate and Yadhavrao got one-quarter.

When the court case was settled, about four years ago, the dispute returned to Girvi. Neither owner lived in Girvi and they wanted to sell the land. Two groups tried to purchase Nanasaheb's estate, but both found it difficult to raise the money, Rs. 64,000. On the one hand were Appasaheb and his six sons, including Mugatrao, aided by some of their affinal relatives. On the other hand was a group consisting of Malojirao and

Vijaymala's husband's family, the genealogically senior men of the lineage. The latter were unable to raise the money and Appasaheb's family gained full occupancy rights to Nanasaheb's *vaḍa* and his land.

Appasaheb's family already had possession of the estate as Yadhavrao's tenants and had used the power it gave them to exercise the prerogatives of *mukəddəm*. They continue to act as *mukəddəm* today. They sometimes say they have a right to the office because they succeeded Yadhavrao who was the adopted heir of Nanasaheb and who subsequently died without sons. More often, however, they say they purchased the office along with Nanasaheb's land and *vaḍa*.

Chimanrao's family feels that the office of *mukəddəm* ought to be theirs since they are the genealogically senior *vərči ali* family still resident in Girvi.[2] They resent what they consider to be the usurpation of the ritual leadership of the village by Mugatrao's family and they were glad to take advantage of the chance to prevent Mugatrao from becoming Sarpanch.[3]

At the time of the Sarpanch election there was no connection other than membership in the same *kuḷ* between the family of Chimanrao and Vijaymala and that of Dattatrya Dhondiram. It later emerged that a marriage which resulted in the two families having a common affinal connection was arranged at the same time as the political alliance. In December 1966 Dattatrya's sister was married to Chimanrao's sister's son. Chimanrao played a leading role in the marriage ceremony. He is credited with arranging the marriage of his sister's son just as he did the alliance. The announced dowry was Rs. 8000, far and away the largest dowry I encountered in Girvi.[4] Several Girvi observers declared that the financial position of Chimanrao's sister's son was not sound enough to warrant such a large dowry and that if the figure of Rs. 8000 were true, only Rs. 2000 were paid in public, it was wildly extravagant. Some felt that Dattatrya had used the marriage of his sister to pay for a political alliance which allowed him to maintain his influence in the Panchayat.[5] Chimanrao and Dattatrya remained rather distant consanguineal relatives so there can be no question of their political alliance being based on an affinal relationship.

Horizontal alliances in Credit Society politics

As a political arena the Girvi Multi-Purpose Credit Society is comparable to the fair committee and to the second stage of Panchayat politics. In all three arenas horizontal alliances are predominant. The Managing Committee of the Credit Society is elected by the Society shareholders each of whom has one vote. The largest group of shareholders are the *vətəndar* Maratha Kadams (38.8 per cent). All candidates for the Managing Committee stand at large so there are no constituencies dominated by non-

vatandars. As in the case of the fair committee and the second stage of Panchayat politics, so in the Credit Society the Kadams are free to do as they please with a minimum of regard for the actions of other members. In the Credit Society, too, the division of the Kadams into two patri-lineages defines the alternative forms of horizontal political alliances. Most of the time each lineage unites against the other, but intra-lineage competition regularly leads to the formation of alliances which cut across lineage boundaries.

In August 1966 twelve men submitted nomination papers for the nine-member Managing Committee of the Girvi Multi-Purpose Credit Society. Six of the candidates were members of the *varči ali* Kadam lineage: Shamrao Govindrao (Genealogy 1*a*, *L*19), Shamrao's brother Dattaji Govindrao (Genealogy 1*a*, *L*21), Devrao Appasaheb (Genealogy 1*a*, *L*30), Amrutrao Bapusaheb (Genealogy 1*a*, *K*25), Rajaram Baburao (Genealogy 1*b*, *E*5), and Kashaba Anandrao (Genealogy 1*d*, *E*1). Five candidates belonged to the *khalči ali* Kadam lineage: Ganpatrao Eknath (Genealogy 2*c*, *J*4), Lakshman Maruti (Genealogy 2*a*, *H*13), Ramchandra Madhavrao (Genealogy 2*b*, *J*1), Sarjerao Sahebrao (Genealogy 2*d*, *J*10), and Khanderao Bajirao (Genealogy 2*f*, *I*13). The twelfth candidate, Sarjerao Shankar Nikalje, was a Mahar. One of the *varči ali* candidates, Shamrao Govindrao, and two of the *khalči ali* candidates, Ganpatrao Eknath and Ramchandra Madhavrao, were persuaded to withdraw and the remaining nine were elected unopposed (*binvirodh*) in September.

On 10 October the Managing Committee met to elect its new Chairman. At that time all of the *khalči ali* members supported Khanderao Bajirao for Chairman. Amrutrao Bapusaheb, the incumbent Chairman, was supported for re-election by two fellow members of the *varči ali* lineage, Devrao Appasaheb and Kashaba Anandrao. Another *varči ali* member, Rajaram Baburao, was also a candidate. Since he was unable to secure a majority for himself Khanderao Bajirao withdrew and the three *khalči ali* members transferred their support to Rajaram Baburao. Rajaram then had four votes, but he was unable to secure a fifth. Dattaji Govindrao was willing to vote for Rajaram, but his father, Govindrao Madhavrao (Genealogy 1*a*, *K*13), forbade it. Nor could he secure the vote of Sarjerao Nikalje. Unable to bargain for his vote independently, Nikalje was subject to the will of whoever had control of his person at the moment. On the 10th he was controlled by Amrutrao.

With neither side able to secure a majority the election was postponed until 14 October to allow further negotiations. Amrutrao cut away the *khalči ali* support for Rajaram by offering to vote for Sarjerao Sahebrao if he could not win himself. Sarjerao was confident of the support of the other two *khalči ali* members. He hoped to get a fifth vote from Sarjerao Nikalje. Nikalje was employed as a *gǝḍi* on a yearly contract by Sarjerao Sahebrao's lineage mate, Baburao Sitaram Kadam (Genealogy *2f*, *I*12), and he thought Baburao would be able to influence Nikalje. However, Devrao Appasaheb and Kashaba Anandrao continued to seek a majority for a *vǝrči ali* candidate and Sarjerao Sahebrao knew that he would lose Amrutrao Bapusaheb's support as soon as they were successful.

By the 14th Devrao and Kashaba had secured a *vǝrči ali* victory. They won the support of all the *vǝrči ali* members except Rajaram by offering the Society Chairmanship to Dattaji Govindrao. They obtained the winning vote of Sarjerao Nikalje by taking him to Amrutrao's house on the 13th while Baburao Sitaram was away from Girvi and keeping him there until the Managing Committee meeting began. Dattaji's nomination was moved by Devrao and seconded by Kashaba. Rajaram was nominated by Sarjerao Sahebrao, but no one would second the nomination so Dattaji was elected unopposed.

Bhaubund membership was the main influence on alliance formation in the Credit Society. Throughout the election maneuvers the three *khalči ali* members acted as a unit. They preferred to secure the election of one of their own number, but failing that they were willing to vote for Rajaram in order at least to have a Chairman who would depend on them. Except for Rajaram, who hoped to win the election himself, the *vǝrči ali* members of the Managing Committee also acted as a unit. Amrutrao offered to vote for Sarjero Sahebrao against Rajaram, a member of his own lineage, but his offer actually served to protect *vǝrči ali* interests. By exploiting *khalči ali* lineage loyalty to deprive Rajaram of his *khalči ali* support Amrutrao helped to secure the election of a *vǝrči ali* candidate who depended upon *vǝrči ali* support. Sarjerao Nikalje's was the deciding vote, but he was a party only to vertical, not horizontal, alliances. Although the *vǝtǝndar* Kadams had given him office, they had not given him political influence. Economically dependent on the Kadams and deprived of the protection of the absent Baburao Sitaram he had no choice but to do as the Kadams nearest him commanded. As Baburao Sitaram commented when he saw Devrao Appasaheb, Ramrao Bapusaheb, Kashaba Anandrao, and Dattaji Govindrao delivering Nikalje to the Society office, they had him 'in a box'.

Summary: horizontal alliances in village arenas

In Girvi the pattern of horizontal political alliances is closely related to patrilineal descent. Competition between separate, localized patrilineages underlies most horizontal alliances. In the remaining cases competition within one or the other patrilineage leads to alliances which cut across lineage boundaries. Even though competition occurs within as well as between lineages, intra-lineage competition remains a minor theme and the patterning of alliances in terms of descent is not broken down. That is, within the Girvi political class of *vətəndar* Maratha Kadams alliances are not formed at random. One does not form alliances with persons who are simply Kadams like oneself. It makes a difference whether the Kadam concerned is a member of one's own lineage or of the opposing lineage. Although competition within one's own lineage may occasionally lead one to form an alliance with members of the opposing lineage, most alliances are with lineage mates.

Caste is not a factor in horizontal political alliances in Girvi because only Marathas belong to the Girvi political class. In villages such as Taradgaon, where there are as many Malis as Marathas, horizontal alliances may be caste based (see also Orenstein's *Gaon* 1965). Caste is also a factor in horizontal alliances in urban areas such as Phaltan, but in most villages in the area a single caste is clearly dominant.

The panchayat system has brought some non-Marathas into Girvi politics, but they participate as dependents rather than as equals. A place on the Panchayat has not given the non-Marathas any real influence. There is a Mahar representative because it is required by law. Although Ramoshi representation is perhaps unavoidable since they are concentrated in a single ward, it is probably more important that they are useful to the *vərči ali* Kadams who control them. In some respects the Ramoshi member is more useful than another *vərči* ali Kadam because he is less independent.

It is impossible for affinal kinship (*soyre*) to influence horizontal political alliances within Girvi because all the members of the political class belong to the same exogamous, agnatic clan (*kul*). Affinal kinship may be much more important in villages where the Revenue and Police Patilships are held by lineages which belong to different clans or in joint panchayats which include two or more formerly separate *vətən* villages. There is no evidence that political alliances in Girvi are based on ties of non-agnatic consanguineal kinship.

HORIZONTAL POLITICAL ALLIANCES IN PHALTAN TALUKA

The relationships between horizontal political alliances and such structural frameworks as caste and kinship alter as one moves from political arenas which include only one village to arenas which include more than one village. In single village political arenas the political elite and political class generally consist of members of only one caste. Therefore, caste cannot be a factor in horizontal alliances even though it may enter into some vertical alliances. However, because castes are distributed unevenly in the villages of Western Maharashtra and because some minority castes are concentrated in towns (see Chapter 4), the political elite and political class of more inclusive arenas consists of members of several castes. In more inclusive political arenas, therefore, caste may be a factor in the formation of horizontal alliances.

In single village political arenas the political elite and political class generally consist of members of one or at most two localized patrilineages which in most cases are prevented from intermarrying by the rule of exogamy. Within a leader's own village, therefore, all of the politically significant persons are likely to be his agnates, near or distant. Few, if any, will be his affines and if any are his non-agnatic consanguines his tie with them through women will be subsidiary to his tie with them through men. In more inclusive political arenas the situation is reversed. Few of the political leaders in a taluka or district are related in any way. However, since Maratha patrilineages are localized and since most Marathas marry at a distance if two leaders are related they are more likely to be affines than agnates. If they are non-agnatic consanguines they are unlikely to be related through men as well as through women.

Kinship and horizontal political alliances in Phaltan Taluka

Throughout the period of my field work some of the Rajasaheb's most important allies in Phaltan were persons related to him by ties of fairly close kinship. For example, in 1966 the Raja and his son were supported in the Shriram Co-operative Sugar Factory by B. S. Naik Nimbalkar (*vətəndar* Maratha of Wathar), V. R. Naik Nimbalkar (*vətəndar* Maratha of Nimbalak), Namdev Jadhav (Maratha of Phaltan), Vishvasrao Ranavare (*vətəndar* Maratha of Jinti), S. K. Beldar (Beldar of Andrud), Sahebrao Mane (*vətəndar* Maratha of Asu), and D. R. Doshi (Gujar of Phaltan). Two of his Sugar Factory allies, B. S. Naik Nimbalkar and V. R. Naik Nimbalkar, were distant members of his own large patrilineage. The former was Vice-Chairman of the Sugar Factory from 1965 to 1966 and supported the Raja on the Managing Committee of the Shriram Education Society. The latter was elected to the Board of Directors of the Sugar Factory by the co-operative society shareholders. In addition to his activities in the Shriram Sugar Factory, he supports the Raja on the Phaltan Taluka Purchase and Sale Union, the Phaltan Taluka Supervising Union and the Governing Council of the Shriram Education Society.

Another of the Raja's Sugar Factory allies, Vishvasrao Ranavare, was a classificatory affine (see Fig. 20). A member of the Raja's real mother's brother's *kul* (the Raja was adopted on the *gaḍi*), although from a different localized lineage, Vishvasrao also is connected with the Raja through

Keshavrao Appasaheb Kadam (Genealogy 1*a*, *L*25) of Girvi. Vishvasrao was Vice-Chairman of the Sugar Factory from 1966 to 1967. He was nominated for the Zilla Parishad by the Raja's coalition of opposition parties and won the Hol-Sakharvadi seat in May 1967. Vishvasrao was the Raja's choice for Panchayat Samiti Chairman, but he was forced to withdraw when Chimanrao Kadam (Genealogy 1*a*, *M*14) threatened to switch to the Congress unless the job were given to him.

Keshavrao Appasaheb Kadam (Genealogy 1*a*, *L*25) was elected to the Board of Directors of the Shriram Co-operative Sugar Factory in the elections originally scheduled for 1966 but postponed until 1967. He succeeded Vishvasrao as Vice-Chairman of the Board of Directors. Keshavrao is Vishvasrao's *mehuṇa* (MBD & WB). He is also the Raja's classificatory consanguine through Raosaheb Ranavare of Nimbhore who was *mama* (MB, FZH) to both.

Kinship also enters into some of the alliances which centered on Y. B. Chavan, S. R. Bhosle and K. R. Bhoite in the 1967 Congress General Election campaign. I have mentioned already that Dattaji Bedke, the new Vice-Chairman of the Satara District Central Co-operative Bank, is

Fig. 20 Kinship connections linking the Raja of Phaltan to some of his allies

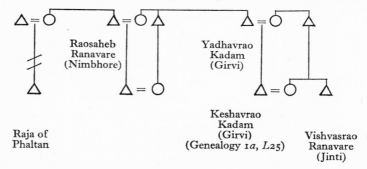

Chavan's *javi* (BDH), that B. R. More is Chavan's *mehuṇa* (WB) and that Namdev Jadhav is Bhoite's *saḍu* (WZH). The first two are affinal relationships while the third is consanguineal (*bhauki*). One of S. R. Bhosle's closest allies on the Board of Directors of the Shriram Co-operative Sugar Factory and in the campaign was D. G. Pawar, a wealthy *vəṭəndar* Maratha from Asu who is Bhosle's *vyahi*, an affinal connection; Bhosle's son is married to Pawar's brother's daughter.

Some horizontal political alliances in arenas which include more than one village can be understood in terms of the kinship connections between the persons involved. In the more inclusive arenas a significant number of alliances are based on non-agnatic consanguineal kinship and affinal kinship, while in the less inclusive, single village arenas only agnatic kinship has a bearing on political choice. The actors involved in Phaltan are aware of the relation between kinship and politics and often feel that it has explanatory value. For instance, when K. R. Bhoite had won the Congress nomination to the Legislative Assembly he said that the only people who were really angry at the rejection of the Raja's son were his relatives, the Marathas in Wathar, Girvi, Nimbhore and Jinti.

Some caution needs to be used here, however, because it is often difficult to tell which comes first, politics or kinship. The marriage of Dattatrya Kadam's (Genealogy 2*d*, *I*8) sister and Chimanrao Kadam's (Genealogy 1*a*, *M*4) sister's son was seen by some observers as a payment for Vijay-mala's political services on the Girvi Panchayat rather than as the basis for an alliance. Similarly, K. R. Bhoite and Namdev Jadhav probably did not become allies because they married sisters. It is more likely that they saw they had political interests in common and that Bhoite married Jadhav's wife's sister to seal the bargain.

It is true that if one considers only marriages involving politically active persons there is often a close correspondence with political alliances at the time of marriage (cf. Barth 1959a:107). Most marriages have nothing to do with politics, but people do not, at least, marry their enemies. However, one's affines may become enemies. For example, Sahebrao Mane, a *vatandar* Maratha from Asu, married D. G. Pawar's brother's daughter. When his first wife died he married her sister, maintaining his connection with Pawar. But when the Raja offered him a chance to become a Director of the Shriram Co-operative Sugar Factory Mane joined the faction opposed to Pawar's. B. R. More hoped that he would be given the Congress nomination in 1967 since he is Chavan's *mehuṇa*. When the ticket went to Bhoite, instead, More nearly joined the Raja. He finally decided to stay in the Congress, but he took his revenge on Bhoite's friends, alleging that Babanrao Adsul was corrupt and depriving him of his Secretaryship in the Shriram Education Society. Keshavrao Appasaheb Kadam (Genealogy 1*a*, *L*25) worked for the Raja in 1966–7, but in 1957 he was one of the first to oppose him. Once formed, kinship relationships are relatively permanent. Political interests, however, are constantly changing. No politician could afford to be bound by ties of kinship in his choice of allies. When I asked S. R. Bhosle why Sahebrao Mane had opposed his close affine, D. G. Pawar, he replied that in politics kinship 'is irrelevant'.

Some horizontal political alliances are based on kinship relationships, but this fact does little to advance one's understanding of the total pattern of horizontal political alliances. Only a small number of the alliances in more inclusive political arenas can be based on kinship. No leader has a sufficient number of suitably placed relatives, whether consanguineal or affinal, to enable him to base a successful coalition on kinship alone. In political activity outside the village arena kinship is often useful but never sufficient.

Caste and horizontal political alliances in Phaltan Taluka

The politics of institutions which are based on exclusively rural constituencies or on constituencies which include both urban and rural areas are dominated by Marathas, most of whom have *vatandar* status. Sixty-seven of ninety-five offices in such institutions in Phaltan are held by Marathas, six by Malis, five by Dhangars, three by Jains, three by Brahmins and, at most, two by each of several other minority castes (see Chapter 3, Fig. 5). As a result of Maratha dominance caste is rarely relevant to the horizontal alliances of elite leaders in such institutions. No coalition of minority castes could hope to challenge the dominant position of the Marathas, even if some dissident Marathas were to join them. Maratha domination is so secure that non-Maratha leaders can best achieve influence by allying with Marathas. Marathas, in turn, are free to form alliances with minority caste leaders without fear of damaging their caste's dominant position. Granted that most elite leaders are Marathas, what matters in the formation of horizontal alliances is not a man's caste, but the office he holds.

In institutions which are based on predominantly urban constituencies, however, Marathas are in a much weaker position. Only eighteen of forty-nine offices in such institutions are held by Marathas. Brahmins have twelve offices and Jains have nine. In urban based institutions caste affiliation is relevant to the formation of horizontal alliances. Like kinship, caste is there to be exploited when it is useful to do so, but it may be ignored when that is useful.

In 1965 it was said that the Brahmins were allied with the Jains and the Mahars against the Marathas in Phaltan Municipality. It is true that from 1963 until mid-1967 the Municipal Council was divided into two parties roughly along these lines. The Council President was G. B. Mane, a respected Buddhist Mahar lawyer. Mane was supported by the other Mahar member and by three Brahmins, two Jains, one Dhangar and one Maratha. The opposition party consisted of three Marathas, one Shimpi, one Vani Lingayat, one Ramoshi and one Koshti. However, these coalitions were only one phase in a series of shifting alliances in which caste was not the major determining principle.

When the Council was elected in 1962 there were three parties. Brahmins and Marathas belonged to each and Jains belonged to two. At that time the Raja's group consisted of two Marathas, one Brahmin, one Jain, one Vani

Lingayat, one Ramoshi, one Shimpi and one Koshti. The Rashtriya Gadi group consisted of the two Mahars and one Maratha. A third group of independent members consisted of two Brahmins, one Jain, one Maratha and one Dhangar. Mane's winning coalition was formed when the Rashtriya Gadi group joined the independent group and persuaded the Koshti member to absent himself. It was not until 1963 that the third Brahmin and the second Jain joined Mane. It was still later that one of the Marathas left Mane to join the opposition group. Mane's coalition broke up in the middle of 1966 and the pattern of alliances shifted again in April 1967.

There is no doubt that caste is important in municipal affairs. The political class of Phaltan town is composed of several castes in addition to the Marathas. Horizontal alliances on the Municipal Council are often made without regard to caste affiliation, but in other cases caste is probably the determining factor. The dominance of the Marathas, although it is less pronounced than in the countryside, remains central as far as caste is concerned.

There is evidence that when urban politicians do base their decisions on caste the non-Marathas tend to unite in opposition to the Marathas. The Marathas are alert to this danger and have taken steps to counter it. When the municipal election wards were revised for the 1967 municipal election the multi-number wards which, with the rule that allows each voter to cast as many votes as there are members to be elected from his ward, favored minority communities were abolished. The ward boundaries also were redrawn to disperse the voting strength of minority groups in separate constituencies. One Brahmin member of the Municipal Council decided not to stand again because the people who had voted for him in 1962 were scattered in three different wards in 1967. I was unable to check the caste composition of Phaltan municipal election wards, but the results of the 1967 municipal election did strengthen the Marathas' position. They had four of sixteen seats in the old Council, elected from multi-member wards, and six of nineteen in the new Council. The Brahmins had three seats in the old Council but none in the new and the Jains had two seats in the old Council but only one in the new.

But while competiton between Marathas and non-Marathas does occasionally determine the course of municipal affairs, competition within the Maratha caste is more often the dominant factor. Even in the period 1963–7 the apparent Maratha versus non-Maratha conflict was not the whole of municipal politics. Behind each of the parties in the Municipal Council was one of the two major leaders of Phaltan. The opposition party in the Council was allied with the Rajasaheb. The party in power was allied with S. R. Bhosle, a descendent of the Phaltan Revenue Patils and one of the highest ranking *vatandar* Marathas of the Taluka. The caste composition of the parties in the Council varied, but the competition between the two powerful Marathas, Naik Nimbalkar and Bhosle, remained constant.[6]

DISTRIBUTION OF HORIZONTAL POLITICAL ALLIANCES: OCCASIONS

While analysing the relations between horizontal political alliances and such structural frameworks as caste and kinship in political arenas of varying inclusiveness I have dealt mainly with alliances formed during elections. One reason for this is that many elections were held during the period of my fieldwork. Another is that horizontal alliances are a major element in any politician's electoral success since electoral support in the more inclusive political arenas is recruited indirectly by means of horizontal alliances with elite leaders who control the votes of their own settlements. Finally, the pattern of alliances often is easier to observe during elections when politicians are both more active and more in the public eye.

Analysis of the pattern of horizontal alliances formed during elections is instructive, but too great an emphasis on electoral politics is misleading. Elite leaders mobilize their vertical alliances infrequently and primarily during elections. Horizontal alliances, however, are sought on all occasions for they are of use in deciding day-to-day political questions as well as in marshalling electoral support.

The example of Phaltan town is instructive in this regard. Between 1962 and 1967 there were no municipal elections in Phaltan. In the intervening years, however, the process of alliance formation went on without pause, producing three distinct coalitions and four administrations. The collapse of the second major coalition in the Phaltan Municipal Council illustrates very clearly the kind of non-electoral ends which horizontal political alliances are expected to serve.

As I explained above, when the Phaltan Municipal Council was elected in 1962 the sixteen members were divided into three groups. The Rajasaheb had eight allies on the Council: Dr V. V. Mahagaonkar (Brahmin), Mrs S. S. Shah (Jain), V. P. Unavane (Koshti), M. S. Pawar (Maratha), B. R. More (Maratha), R. R. Bhandvalkar (Ramoshi), N. S. Hendre (Shimpi), and K. V. Phanse (Vani Lingayat). The Rashtriya Gadi group consisted of G. B. Mane (Mahar), T. B. Ahivale (Mahar), and N. B. Nimbalkar (Maratha). There were also five independent members allied with S. R. Bhosle and M. G. Date: B. V. Nimbkar (Brahmin), Mrs A. Chamche (Brahmin), M. B. Choramle (Dhangar), Dr P. J. Rajvaidya (Jain), and N. S. Mandre (Maratha). The Rashtriya Gadi group allied itself with the five independents. They persuaded Unavane to be absent on the day of the vote and elected Rajvaidya President and Mane Chairman of the Standing Committee.

Rajvaidya was President for about a year and a half. He was removed from office, but not from the Council, by the Maharashtra Government acting in response to a petition from the Raja's allies. The Council was unable to agree on a successor and Mane was finally chosen over More by drawing names from a hat. The Council remained divided eight to eight and Mane's party was unable to pass its budget. The deadlock finally was broken when Dr Mahagaonkar switched sides, giving Mane a nine-to-seven majority. Mrs Shah later switched to Mane and later still Mandre left Mane to join the Raja's group. The resulting coalitions held up until June 1966. The only change occurred in 1965 when R. R. Bhandvalkar resigned, increasing Mane's majority to three.

The new Maharashtra Municipalities Act took effect on 27 June 1966. The old Phaltan Municipal Council was dissolved. Its members continued in office but new Council officers were elected who were to hold office until the next municipal elections, not later than 31 December 1967. Under the new legislation Council officers could be removed by a simple majority instead of the three-quarters majority required by the old law.

In the June 1966 election of a new Council President the two opposing parties merged. B. R. More, formerly the Raja's ally, was elected President and Mrs Shah, an ally of Bhosle and Date, was elected Vice-President, both *binvirodh* (without opposition). The two parties divided the Council Committees between them. The Standing Committee consisted of B. R. More (Chairman), M. S. Pawar and N. S. Mandre from the group formerly allied with the Raja plus Mrs Shah and G. B. Mane from the group allied with Bhosle and Date. The Sanitation, Medical and Public Health Committee consisted of Mrs Shah (Chairman), B. V. Nimbkar, Dr Mahagaonkar from the Date-Bhosle group with Mandre and Phanse from the former Raja group. The Water-Supply and Drainage Committee consisted of Mrs Chamche, Choramle and Ahivale from the Date-Bhosle group with M. S. Pawar (Chairman) and Unavane from the Raja group.

Mane's supporters felt that under the new law an unstable majority of nine to six was not worth preserving. The Raja would require the support of only eight members in order to turn the President out of office, whereas before he would have required the support of twelve members. When it became necessary to keep a solid core of seven supporters instead of only three the costs of maintaining Mane's coalition outweighed the benefits.

Nimbkar, Date and Bhosle were pleased as well to deprive the Raja of More's support. Some of the Raja's opponents hoped that More would use his influence with his relatives (one of More's sisters is married to Y. B. Chavan and another is married to D. S. Jagtap, a Deputy Minister in the Maharashtra Cabinet) to get the municipal boundary redrawn to include the Shriram Co-operative Sugar Factory, thus greatly improving its tax base.[7] Mane regretted the loss of the Presidency but knew that under the new law he would not have been able to keep it long in any case.[8]

B. R. More served as Phaltan Municipal President for less than a year. He resigned in March 1967, less than three months before the next municipal elections, when the Raja formed a majority prepared to support a resolution of no confidence. The resolution alleged that More acted without consulting other Council members. More's supporters, however, claimed that three issues led to his defeat. More wanted to concentrate on only one public work, the water-supply system, and to stop all of the others. All of the Council members 'swallow' money from public works, it was said, so this hurt them all. As revenues came in More tried to pay off all the municipal debts. More dealt with municipal creditors directly. He offered to pay them immediately if they would agree to make a contribution to the Shriram Education Society, of which More is President. It was said that this hurt municipal employees who normally demanded bribes before making payments to creditors. Finally, More irritated the Raja by trying to bring the Shriram Co-operative Sugar Factory inside the municipality and by supporting the Congress in the General Election.

Only six Council members, More, M. S. Pawar, B. V. Nimbkar, Dr Mahagaonkar, Mrs S. S. Shah and Mrs Chamche, opposed the no confidence motion. These included all of the Council officers, a majority of the Standing Committee and of the Sanitation Committee, and two of the five members of the Water-Supply Committee. Thus, those out of power were willing to support the motion while those in power opposed it.

On the Phaltan Municipal Council, as in other political arenas, the formation and maintenance of horizontal political alliances and the calculation of the costs and benefits involved is a constant concern of elite political leaders. Positions on the Council from which influence over the distribution of patronage may be exercised are won or lost at periodical elections. It is then, if ever, that vertical political alliances are necessary. The actual distribution of patronage, though, is not decided by universal suffrage. Patronage distribution is continuously decided by the Council members. It is not determined by their vertical alliances but, rather, by the horizontal alliances which they form among themselves. In order to win positions of potential influence elite leaders may need to form vertical alliances during elections. Between elections, and during elections as well, actual influence is won by means of horizontal alliances with other elite leaders.

9
Alliances and political stratification

As I suggested in Chapter 1 and as much of the material presented in the previous chapter demonstrates, one of the most striking features of horizontal political alliances in Western Maharashtra is their instability. This might appear to make the task of analysis extremely difficult, but, in fact, if the instability of horizontal alliances is placed against the other features of the political system it provides a key for the isolation of the crucial factors in political action.

Coalitions in the Shriram Co-operative Sugar Factory

An examination of coalitions formed on the Board of Directors of the Shriram Co-operative Sugar Factory since its founding in 1957 provides further confirmation for the view that horizontal alliances are unstable. The first Board of Directors of the Sugar Factory was appointed by the Bombay Government. Vijaysingh M. Naik Nimbalkar was Chairman and M. G. Date was Vice-Chairman. Other non-official members were M. B. Bedke (Maratha, Phaltan), K. K. Borawake (Mali, Phaltan), D. G. Pawar (*vətəndar* Maratha, Asu), R. M. Gawade (*vətəndar* Dhangar, Gokhali), M. N. Doshi (Gujar, Gunavare and Phaltan), T. R. Shinde (*vətəndar* Maratha, Khunte-Shindevadi), S. R. Bhosle (*vətəndar* Maratha, Phaltan), Kondiram J. Ranavare (*vətəndar* Maratha, Jinti) and Sahebrao Bhosle (*vətəndar* Maratha, Hol).

The first Sugar Factory election was held in 1960. The entire Board was up for election and the slate supported by the Rajasaheb was returned without a defeat. V. M. Naik Nimbalkar, M. G. Date, D. G. Pawar, Sahebrao Bhosle, and K. K. Borawake were re-elected by the producer members. Sakharam G. Parkale (*vətəndar* Maratha, Asu), Bapusaheb Nimbalkar (*vətəndar* Maratha, Nimbalak), Vishvasrao Bapusaheb Rana-vare (*vətəndar* Maratha, Jinti) and D. V. Gaund (*vətəndar* Dhangar, Gunavare) were elected by the producer members for the first time. Also elected to the Board for the first time were R. T. Shah (Gujar, Phaltan), representative of the traders, and K. B. (Babanrao) Adsul (Mali, Taradgaon), co-operative society representative. The opposition slate in

Political alliances

1960 was led by several incumbent Directors who were not supported by the Raja for re-election: S. R. Bhosle, M. B. Bedke, R. M. Gawade and T. R. Shinde. It also included B. R. More, Bhausaheb Naik Nimbalkar, V. R. Naik Nimbalkar, Yeshvantrao Ranavare (*vətəndar* Maratha, Jinti), Mahadev Baliram Bhosle (*vətəndar* Maratha, Hol), Namdev Jadhav (Maratha, Phaltan) and M. R. Bhoite (Maratha, Phaltan).

If the alliances formed in the 1960 Sugar Factory election are taken as a starting point then by 1965 the coalitions were almost completely reversed. The reversal did not take place all at once, however, but rather was the result of small shifts in each of the yearly elections. Figure 21 is a list of most candidates for election to the Board by producer members in the years 1961 through 1965.

Fig. 21   Shriram Sugar Factory election alliances

Management slate

1961
  Shamrao Beldar
    (Beldar, Andrud)
  Yeshvantrao Ranavare
    (*vətəndar* Maratha, Jinti)
  ? ? Khatke
    (Dhangar, Gokhali)

1962
  V. M. Naik Nimbalkar
  B. R. More
  Sakharam G. Parkale

1963
  Bapusaheb M. Naik Nimbalkar
    (*vətəndar* Maratha, Phaltan; ElB
    of V. M. Naik Nimbalkar)
  Bhausaheb Naik Nimbalkar
  Sahebrao Mane
    (*vətəndar* Maratha, Asu)

1964
  Vishvasrao Ranavare
  D. Beldar
    (Beldar, Sangvi)
  plus two others – all defeated

1965
  Vijaysingh Naik Nimbalkar –
    elected
  Vishvasrao Ranavare – elected
  Shamrao Beldar – elected
  V. R. Naik Nimbalkar – elected by
    co-operative society shareholders

Opposition slate

1961
  no organized opposition – all
  management candidates were elected

1962
  no organized opposition – all
  management candidates were elected

1963
  S. R. Bhosle – defeated
  M. G. Date – defeated
  D. G. Pawar and Babasaheb
  Nimbalkar retired

1964
  S. R. Bhosle – elected
  K. K. Borawake – elected
  D. G. Pawar – elected
  Babasaheb Nimbalkar – elected

1965
  M. G. Date – defeated
  Nanasaheb Pawar – defeated
    (*vətəndar* Maratha, Asu; B of
    D. G. Pawar)
  Rambhau M. Gawade – defeated
  Dattaji Bedke – candidate for elec-
    tion by co-operative society share-
    holders (son of M. B. Bedke)

Alliances and political stratification

The 1960 Sugar Factory election was closely fought, but when the slate allied with the Raja was returned without defeat the opposition dissolved. Many men who had opposed the Raja in 1960 now saw that the Raja had a strong grip on the Factory and joined him when they had the chance. Yeshvantrao Ranavare joined the Raja's slate in 1961. He was followed by B. R. More in 1962, Bhausaheb Naik Nimbalkar in 1963, and V. R. Naik Nimbalkar in 1965.

Men who supported the Raja in 1960 left him when his attempts to maintain personal control over the Factory conflicted with their own ambitions or when he refused to support them for re-election. M. G. Date, who contributed a large part of the initial capital of the Society and who wished to continue as Vice-Chairman, was replaced in that office by D. G Pawar in April 1960. In 1963 Date stood for election to the Board with S. R. Bhosle even though Bhosle's 1960 campaign had been directed especially against Date, the only Brahmin on the Board. In 1964 Bhosle was joined by K. K. Borawake, D. G. Pawar, and Babasaheb Nimbalkar, all of whom had been dropped from the Raja's slate in earlier elections.

By 1965 the Rajasaheb was supported in the Shriram Co-operative Sugar Factory by six Directors, including his son, three of whom, Bhausaheb Naik Nimbalkar, V. R. Naik Nimbalkar and Namdev Jadhav,[1] had opposed him in 1960. He was opposed by four Directors three of whom, Borawake, Pawar and Babasaheb Nimbalkar, had been his allies in 1960. The only stable factor in the Sugar Factory is the long standing opposition between the Raja's family and S. R. Bhosle.

Consequences of unstable horizontal alliances

The consequences of the frequent shifts in horizontal political alliances among the political elite extend in two directions. The relationship between horizontal alliances and the caste and kinship frameworks of political choice is attenuated. The dependence of horizontal alliances on vertical alliances and vice versa is reduced also. The choice of one does not depend upon the choice of the other.

Since elite politicians frequently change their horizontal political alliances their choices are not limited by ties of caste or kinship. Caste and kinship both become mere extrinsic pretexts for transactions, the content of which is derived from other frameworks. At one point the Mahars, Brahmins, and Jains on the Phaltan Municipal Council formed the core of a controlling majority which excluded most of the Maratha members. If out of the whole series of shifting alliances on the Municipal Council one looked only at this coalition one might be led to believe that caste conflict, Marathas versus non-Marathas, is the determining factor in municipal politics. But if the whole series of alliances from 1962 until 1967 is examined it is clear that Council members frequently choose their allies without regard to caste affiliation.

Similarly, in 1966 three of the Rajasaheb's alliances in the Shriram Co-operative Sugar Factory were based on kinship. The Raja's son was supported on the Board by Bhausaheb Naik Nimbalkar and V. R. Naik Nimbalkar, his distant agnates, and by Vishvasrao Ranavare, his classificatory consanguine. But if one examines the whole series of Sugar Factory alliances it is clear that kinship is not the sole determining factor. Both Naik Nimbalkars opposed the Raja in 1960. Although Vishvasrao Ranavare has always supported the Raja, other Jinti Ranavares have opposed him. S. R. Bhosle and D. G. Pawar are allies as well as affines, but they have not always been allies and Pawar's other close affine on the Board, Sahebrao Mane, is now his opponent.

In Girvi horizontal political alliances must either be within or between two patrilineages of the same clan (*kul*). Because the political class is more homogeneous in Girvi than it is in more inclusive political arenas the range of political choice is narrower. A greater proportion of political alliances are based on ties of kinship. However, even within this restricted arena there are occasions when leaders choose to ignore ties of common agnatic descent. At any given moment, a large proportion of horizontal political alliances seem to be based on ties of kinship. But if shifts in alliances over time are examined the influence of kinship ties is seen to be less important.

Vertical political alliances are relatively stable. Therefore, the instability of horizontal alliances means that an elite leader's choice of vertical allies does not determine his choice of horizontal allies. Nor does his choice of horizontal allies determine his choice of vertical allies.

In general, an elite leader's following consists of politically weak economic dependents. In most cases it is not composed of a caste or class whose interests might be parallel to those of some followings and opposed to those of others. Since all elite leaders have roughly the same sort of vertical alliances they do not form horizontal alliances on the basis of the special interests of their followings. Rather they seek to form horizontal alliances which will further their own ambitions, which will allow them to provide sufficient patronage to their followers to avoid their capture by competing elite leaders, and which will protect the interests of the political class.

THE GREAT *versus* THE POPULACE

The division of the population into a privileged political class and a powerless populace is the most important structural framework underlying political choice in Western Maharashtra. Groups based on caste and descent as well as networks of persons based on non-agnatic consanguineal and affinal kinship exist, but they are much less significant. One does not find competing groups based on caste and kinship. One does find many signs of conflict between the political class and the populace.

Limited use of popular appeal

Few men attempt to enter politics on the basis of their own popular appeal. As a rule they begin as the ally of some such powerful person as the Rajasaheb of Phaltan or Yeshvantrao Chavan who has them elected. As Mosca (1939:154) observes,

When we say that the voters 'choose' their representative, we are using a language that is very inexact. The truth is that the representative *has himself elected* by the voters, and, if that phrase should seem too inflexible and too harsh to fit some cases, we might qualify it by saying that *his friends have him elected*.

I have already noted that politicians attempt to win popular support indirectly by forming alliances with other elite leaders who can deliver the votes of their own followers. Not infrequently the elite is able to arrange to have candidates stand for election unopposed (*binvirodh*). Fifty-one panchayat elections were held in Phaltan Taluka in the spring of 1966. Of these only twenty-four were contested. In the other twenty-seven all candidates stood unopposed. I obtained the results of thirteen of the contested panchayat elections involving forty-three wards. There was no contest in four of the forty-three wards. In addition, ten of twenty-one seats reserved for women were won without a contest.

Indirect election

The system of indirect election, widely used in the political institutions of Western Maharashtra, protects the political elite from popular control in two ways. It makes it very difficult for a politician to challenge the elite on the basis of popular support alone. It also makes it possible for elite leaders to achieve high office without appealing to the electorate at all.

Even if a politician were very popular the political system would make it very difficult for him to appeal to the electorate over the heads of other elite members. The power in any institution is concentrated in the hands of the chairman. The chairman, not the members of the managing committee, controls the co-operative society. The panchayat samiti is run by its chairman, not by council members. The chairman of an organization is invariably elected indirectly, by the committee or council members, rather than directly by all voters. A politician who looks to voters instead of members of the elite may get himself elected but will find that he has no share of power.

Political alliances

Indirect election is especially important in the co-operative system. Co-operative societies are hierarchically linked by the system which allows a society to elect representatives to other societies in which it has invested. The first officers of co-operatives are appointed by the government. As a result of these features of the co-operative system a politician can advance all the way to state office without ever having to win a popular election.

The career of M. R. Bhoite is a good illustration of the opportunities inherent in indirect election. Bhoite began his political career as an ally of the Raja of Phaltan. A lawyer, he was employed by the Raja in a number of ways. Most importantly the Raja involved him in the co-operative system and had him elected Chairman of Phaltan's Lakshmi Co-operative Bank. This put Bhoite in a position from which he could reach out into the District and free himself from the Raja. Bhoite helped merge the Lakshmi Co-operative Bank with the new Satara District Central Co-operative Bank and was rewarded by being elected Vice-Chairman of the big new bank.

Bhoite then was able to use his position in the District to advance his interests in Phaltan. He organized the Cotton Ginning and Pressing Co-operative in Phaltan and was appointed Chairman of its first Board of Directors. This gave him a base in Phaltan which he was able to turn into still another important post in the District. The Board of the Phaltan Ginning and Pressing Society chose Bhoite to be its representative in the District Purchase and Sale Union. The General Body of the Union elected him to its Board of Directors and the Board of Directors elected him Chairman. As Chairman of the Satara District Purchase and Sale Union Bhoite is also a member of the General Body of the Maharashtra Apex Marketing Society and he was recently elected to the Apex Society's Board of Directors. In Satara Bhoite is an associate member of the Zilla Parishad representing the Purchase and Sale Union.

Here, then, is a man who has never faced a popular election but who is on the verge of achieving state office as Chairman of the Maharashtra Apex Marketing Society. The career of K. R. Bhoite (not a relative of M. R. Bhoite) in the zilla parishad system was similar. When he stood for election to the Aradgaon Panchayat Bhoite might have faced an electorate based on universal suffrage, but he avoided that possibility when he was elected without a contest. Until he left the zilla parishad system to stand for the Legislative Assembly he was never involved in a direct election again. He was elected Sarpanch by the members of the Aradgaon Panchayat. He was elected to the Phaltan Panchayat Samiti by the members of the nine village panchayats in his electoral college. The members of the Panchayat Samiti elected him Chairman of that body and hence to membership in the Satara Zilla Parishad.

Alliances and political stratification

I already have argued in Chapter 7 that politicians recruit popular support through horizontal alliances with other elite leaders. The control which elite leaders have over persons in their own settlements who do not belong to the political class makes it difficult to recruit support directly. The system of indirect election makes it pointless even to attempt to win widespread popular support directly. It is only by allying with other elite leaders that one can win a share of power in Western Maharashtra.

Consensus decision procedures

Many decisions in Indian councils are made by consensus. That is, the decision is not brought to a vote and has at least the appearance of being unanimous. Although the word 'consensus' is used in India's English-language press it has no exact equivalent in the vernacular used by politicians in Western Maharashtra. In Marathi uncontested elections are said to have been decided *binvirodh* ('without opposition'). Council decisions that are made without a vote are decided *sarvanuməta mənjur* ('unanimously'). This does not mean that the decision has the consent of everyone concerned. But if there is opposition it is not openly expressed. In general politicians do not attempt to reach compromise decisions acceptable to all concerned. A majority is not averse to imposing its views on a minority. Contested decisions often appear to be uncontested, however, because those who oppose them remain quiet unless they can mount an effective opposition.

Council business: 'sərvanumata mənjur' (*'unanimous'*) *decisions.* I once talked with two leading Phaltan politicians who were discussing a recent meeting of the Satara District Central Co-operative Bank which one of them had attended. One man said that the meeting had been in what he ironically termed a 'democratic mood'. He went on to explain that the normal procedure at such meetings is for the chairman to read the list of questions decided unanimously and then to announce that the meeting is closed and that tea will be served. On this occasion, however, everyone wanted to ask questions about everything.

My informant's remark correctly characterizes the procedures used in meetings of the Phaltan Panchayat Samiti and the Satara Zilla Parishad. All but one member of the first Satara Zilla Parishad belonged to the Congress. Before each Council meeting the Congress members gathered in the bungalow of the Zilla Parishad President. There it was decided who would move and second each of the motions on the Zilla Parishad agenda. When that was settled the members walked together to the Zilla Parishad hall. The official meetings were remarkably brief. The President announced

153

each motion. An assistant of the Chief Executive Officer explained it. A Council member briefly moved approval in one or two sentences. Another Council member seconded the motion. The President announced that the motion was passed unanimously.

Clearly no decisions were made at the Zilla Parishad meetings. The Council merely ratified decisions made elsewhere. Nor were decisions made at the Congress caucus. The caucus only arranged the script and chose the cast for the performance of the public meeting.

Zilla Parishad decisions were really made by the President, Vice-President, the chairmen of the subject committees, and the Chief Executive Officer. Within the limits set by the state government these men decided how much money to spend on family planning, primary school construction, hybrid seeds, road construction and so on. Beyond this a formula of proportionality (see Lijphart 1968:110–11 and 127–9) was used to minimize potential conflict on the Zilla Parishad. The money allocated to primary schools, for example, was divided equally among the Zilla Parishad constituencies. Each Councillor was then invited to recommend ways in which the money could be spent in his own constituency.

Similar procedures were followed in the Phaltan Panchayat Samiti. Most decisions were made by the Chairman and the Block Development Officer. As in the Zilla Parishad, however, they only decided how much to spend on various kinds of projects. Panchayat Samiti members were given a veto over the allocation of money within their own constituencies. For example, in October 1966 Vasantrao Janavale, the Dhangar Zilla Parishad Councillor from Girvi, vetoed a grant of Rs. 500 to Dhaval, a village in his constituency, even though the proposal was supported by the Dhaval Sarpanch, also a Panchayat Samiti member. Normally such public disputes were avoided by the use of a private caucus in the Chairman's office before the formal meeting. On this occasion, however, Janavale had missed the caucus.

Decision-making procedures in the Girvi Panchayat are somewhat different. All decisions are formally unanimous. Questions before the Panchayat are never brought to a vote. But behind the formal unanimity lies the power of the elite *vatandar* Marathas. Decisions are actually made outside the Panchayat by the Kadams. However, in order to participate in the benefits available through the system of local government their decisions must be formally ratified by the Panchayat.

Panchayat members in Girvi who opposed decisions supported by the political elite do not do so openly; they simply stay away from Panchayat meetings. Officially decisions can be blocked if enough people stay away because the Panchayat cannot act without a quorum. However, there are two ways in which the elite Kadams can avoid this problem and bend the Panchayat to their ends. Panchayat rules permit decisions which would have been made at a meeting which was postponed because it lacked a quorum to be made without a quorum when the meeting is reconvened. Evidence of a quorum consists of the signatures in the minute book of the members who were present. This provision provides the elite leaders with another means to obtain decisions from a reluctant Panchayat. On some occasions they enter decisions in the Panchayat records even when a quorum is not present and then collect sufficient additional signatures later.

Election of officers: 'Binvirodh' ('*unopposed*') *decisions.* I was frequently told that the indirect election of the chairman of an institution was *binvirodh*, 'unopposed'. In every case that I was able to investigate this claim was simply not true. Such positions do not go begging. One candidate in an election may withdraw reluctantly at the last moment when he sees that he cannot possibly win, but this does not mean that such an election is uncontested. It merely means that the contest to some extent is cloaked from the public eye.

Consider, for example, the election of the Chairman of the Satara District Central Co-operative Bank in October 1966 (see Chapter 7). Kisan Veer, an ally of Yeshvantrao Chavan, was the only person nominated for the office. He was declared elected unopposed and afterwards many observers averred that the election really was *binvirodh*. Nevertheless, other observers admitted that the incumbent, R. D. Patil, an ally and *mavəs bhau* (MZS) of Balasaheb Desai, fought hard to win re-election. Able to win the support of only three of the sixteen Directors, Patil withdrew from the contest at the last minute enabling the Board of Directors to preserve a facade of unanimity.

Investigation of other *binvirodh* elections yields similar results. Formally, K. R. Bhoite was elected Chairman of the Phaltan Panchayat Samiti *binvirodh*. In fact, however, Bhoite was opposed by Vasantrao Janavale, a Dhangar from Girvi who had been active in the Congress for some years. Janavale had been Executive Officer of the Sarvodaya Scheme in Phaltan. It was widely felt that he had a claim to be Chairman of the new Panchayat Samiti since it took over the functions of his own organization. However, when he was faced with a Congress decision to support Bhoite Janavale chose to withdraw from the contest rather than force the issue to a vote. The Chairman and Vice-Chairman of the Girvi Panchayat were elected *binvirodh*, but only after protracted negotiations reflecting important conflicts in the village led to the withdrawal of the other candidates.

Political alliances

I was able to observe a formally *binvirodh* election in some detail when the Phaltan Municipal Council elected a new President to succeed B. R. More in April 1967. The Raja had no difficulty assembling a majority opposed to More, but it was not easy to get his allies to agree on a supporter. Among those actively seeking the office were N. S. Hendre, a Shimpi, and K. V. Phanse, a Vani Lingayat, but there was opposition to both candidates.

On the day of the election the Raja met in his Palace with Babanrao Kshirsagar, a Phaltan Brahmin, and Nagkumar Gandhi, a Phaltan Gujar. Neither man held office in the Municipal Council, but both had been helping the Raja poll the views of Council members. Gandhi and Kshirsagar reported that they were unable to find a candidate whom everyone could accept. Unanimity could only be obtained by accepting conditions from some members. The Raja and his advisers felt that it would be unwise to accept conditions. They decided to settle for a candidate supported by a majority. It was expected that this meant Phanse.

By that time all the Council members who were willing to work with the Raja, excluding only More and another, had gathered in the Palace. One at a time they were shown into the Raja's room where each was asked to state his preference. After he had seen each member individually the Raja called them all into his room and announced that the candidate with the greatest support was Phanse. It was agreed that no one else would contest the election. Kshirsagar wrote out the nomination papers and all the members left to attend the official Council meeting in the Municipal Hall.

The official meeting took about fifteen minutes. Phanse was nominated and elected by secret ballot. There were no other candidates. Mane and Phanse made brief speeches, the meeting was declared adjourned, and tea was served.

In all these cases there was a contest, but it was decided outside the official arena. The official arena, the council concerned, did nothing more than unanimously ratify the decision which was made elsewhere.

The functions of consensus. The use of decision-making procedures which produce at least the appearance of consensus has several functions. Most broadly it serves to exclude the non-elite public from knowledge of and participation in political decisions. When members of the political class decide among themselves who will sit on the Managing Committee of the Girvi Credit Society or on a village panchayat the rest of the people are deprived of the power of their votes. Consensus procedures also allow the political elite to make their decisions in secrecy behind a facade of unanimity. Meetings of the Zilla Parishad and Panchayat Samiti are open to the public including members of the press. Meetings of council officers and officials and of Congress caucuses, however, are private. The claim that an election such as that of the Satara District Central Co-operative Bank Chairman is *binvirodh* is used by elite leaders to prevent the public from learning that there are divisions within the elite and from knowing who supported whom. If such information were available to the public it might limit the elite's freedom of action.

Within the elite consensus decision-making procedures are used by elite leaders to maintain the unity of large coalitions. In the Satara Zilla Parishad and Phaltan Panchayat Samiti major policy decisions are left to the council officers and administrative officials. Unity is maintained among council members by dividing patronage more or less equally and by allowing each member to control the distribution of patronage in his own constituency. If conflicts do arise they are settled in private. Opposition leaders recognize that consensus is exploited in this way even though it may, in the abstract, be an ideal worthy of attainment. It is not so much consensus that is sought as unity in the face of potential opposition and defeat. Where there are real conflicts, as on the Phaltan Municipal Council from 1962 until 1967, the pretence of consensus dissolves and no compromises are possible.

Consensus procedures permit elite leaders who do not hold council office to influence council decisions at the same time that they exclude the public from exercising any control. They do so by reducing elected councils to the role of publicly ratifying decisions made privately outside the council meetings. All of the wealthy *vətəndar* Maratha Kadams in Girvi participate in the decisions which are publicly ratified by the Girvi Panchayat. Similarly the Rajasaheb took a leading part in the election of Phanse as the new President of the Phaltan Municipal Council even though he is not a Council member. The same thing happened in New Delhi when the 'Syndicate' and Congress President Kamaraj used consensus procedures to elect Shastri as Nehru's successor, thus participating in a choice that officially belonged exclusively to the Congress Parliamentary Party (see Brecher 1966).

Consensus serves the interests of the elite but not those of the electorate. It allows elite leaders to monopolize political power and to do so in private, cloaked by unanimity. It protects them from embarrassing disclosures and preserves their freedom of action. The loser in a political contest can say that he really was not defeated. The winner can say that he is the choice of everyone, the right man for the job.

This is not to say that consensus is an entirely cynical value. No doubt many people believe that consensus procedures do produce the right decisions and select the right men, and they may. But it is doubtful if politicians are completely sincere in their performances. The role of consensus in Indian democracy is similar to the role of the theory of balance or countervailing powers in Western democracies (see Mills 1959:242–68). Consensus, like the idea of a harmony of interests,

serves as an ingenious moral device invoked, in perfect sincerity, by privileged groups in order to justify and maintain their dominant position. (Carr 1949:80)[2]

The two most important conclusions which emerge from this analysis of consensus decision-making procedures in rural Western Maharashtra have been anticipated by Bailey in his paper, 'Decisions by Concensus in Councils and Committees' (1965). In the first place, the use of consensus decision-making procedures reflects the fact that panchayats and other bodies are what Bailey calls 'elite councils'.

Elite councils are those which are, or consider themselves to be (whether they admit it openly or not), a ruling oligarchy. The dominant cleavage in such a group is between the elite council (including, where appropriate, the minority from which it is recruited) and the public: that is to say, the dominant cleavage is horizontal. The opposite kind of council is the arena council. These exist in groups in which the dominant cleavages are vertical. The council is not so much a corporate body with interests against its public, but an arena in which the representatives of segments in the public come into conflict with one another. (1965:10)

As Bailey notes, elite councillors do not represent conflicting interests to which they are answerable. On the contrary, they 'have a strong incentive to present a front of consensus and keep their ranks closed in the face of their public' (1965:10). In the second place, it is clear that

So far from consensus being a sign that everyone in the village is of one mind and one heart, it may be a sign that the dissidents either feared to enter the ring at all or had already been worsted by crooked means beforehand. (Bailey 1965:18–19)

In many cases 'consensus' is a canard much like the 'unity of the village'; in reality it is the unity of the dominant group, the elite (see also Morris-Jones 1960 and Mayer 1958b).

The economics of political patronage

Although the public has little control over the political elite, members of the elite are not altogether indifferent to their followers. A leader's alliance with other members of the elite are related to his alliances with his followers through the distribution of patronage. A leader obtains and maintains a following through his ability to provide or withhold patronage. He obtains control over some sorts of patronage through his alliances with other elite leaders. In return he is able to provide his elite allies with support during elections.

If a leader is to keep his following he must be guided in his choice of alliances primarily by considerations of patronage. He cannot afford to let his choice be limited by considerations of caste or kinship, by ideological considerations, or by personal loyalty to his allies. If he does allow himself to be so limited he may find that he has lost his followers because he could not provide them with sufficient patronage. Together with the freedom from popular control which results from the use of consensus decision procedures this economic link between horizontal and vertical alliances is a factor underlying the instability of elite alliances. The costs of breaking alliances are generally low while the costs of continuing them may be very high. That is, if a leader continues to provide his followers with sufficient patronage they will not withdraw their support when he alters his horizontal alliances, but they may do so if he persists in his horizontal alliances even when they no longer provide him with access to patronage.[3]

Like consensus decision-making procedures, the economics of political patronage contribute to the stability of elite dominance at the same time that they contribute to the instability of horizontal alliances. The political elite in a particular village may be a small minority, but it does not exercise its dominance in isolation from other villages or from more inclusive political arenas. Local dominance occurs in a regional context. Elite members in one area or at one level of political activity are able to help maintain the dominance of elite members in other areas and levels by the opportune distribution of patronage.

POLITICAL STRATEGY

Given the division between the narrow, privileged political class and the politically weak populace, reinforced by the system of indirect election and the use of consensus decision-making procedures and moderated by the economics of patronage, politicians allow themselves to be limited in their choice of allies by considerations of caste and kinship at their own risk. The effect of the discontinuity in the distribution of power in Western Maharashtra, the fundamental structural antecedent of political choice, is to reduce the influence of the caste and kinship frameworks of political choice. It also reduces the influence of vertical political alliances.

Within the political class, then, horizontal alliances are formed primarily in terms of the governmental and administrative frameworks. It is there that patronage may be obtained. As Chimanrao Kadam noted when discussing the course of the 1967 General Election in Phaltan, 'everyone is concerned about his own place ['*jaga*' or 'office'] – doesn't want anyone to touch his place'. In seeking influence in the governmental and administrative frameworks of Western Maharashtra politicians are guided by a few simple rules of strategy.

To gain or maintain power in one political arena politicians regularly seek alliances in other distinct or more inclusive arenas. Politicians who operate in the same political arena are rarely dependable allies because there are potential grounds for competition among them. Politicians in separate or in more and less inclusive arenas are able to co-operate more easily because they do not seek the same political ends. Thus much of the power of Keshavrao Appasaheb Kadam (Genealogy 1a, L25) and his brothers in Girvi comes from their alliance with the Raja of Phaltan. This alliances puts them at an advantage in the village political arena for it allows them to control the access of Girvi residents to patronage from the Shriram Co-operative Sugar Factory. Similarly, now that K. R. Bhoite is competing with the Raja in Phaltan he depends on his alliances with Y. B. Chavan and Kisan Veer in Satara District. The Raja of Phaltan, who attempts to compete with Chavan at the district and state level, depends on alliances at the national level with such leaders as Morarji Desai.

Politicians who are supporting members of ruling coalitions regularly break their alliances and transfer their support to an opposition party. They do so when they can give the opposition a majority in return for a leading position for themselves. This was the tactic used by Vijaymala Kadam to win election as Sarpanch of the Girvi Panchayat and by Chimanrao Kadam, in the form of a threat, to win election as Chairman of the Phaltan Panchayat Samiti.

Conversely, politicians who are in office regularly replace their allies before they can become a threat. Starting with M. G. Date in 1961, the Raja has repeatedly discarded his supporters in the Shriram Co-operative Sugar Factory, especially Vice-Chairmen who might aspire to a turn as Chairman.

Finally, politicians who cannot win office for themselves seek to split opposing coalitions by offering their support to an opposition leader. This tactic brightens their prospects for the future while in the meantime securing them at least a minimum share of influence on the conduct of affairs. Dattatrya Dhondiram Kadam's party used this tactic in the Girvi Panchayat election of 1966. The *khalči ali* Kadams attempted it again in the Credit Society election of the same year. Unable to win election for one of their own number they offered to support Rajaram Baburao, one of the *varči ali* Kadams. G. B. Mane's allies on the Phaltan Municipal Council, unable to maintain control of the Presidency because of new legislation governing municipalities, exploited this tactic when they helped elect B. R. More the new President. They lost the Presidency, but they were able to retain some influence by insuring that the new President was elected with their support rather than that of their opponents.

SUMMARY

At first sight it seems that there is little order in the pattern of horizontal political alliances in Western Mahrashtra. One's allies of today are likely to be one's opponents of tomorrow and vice versa. The population is divided into groups based on caste and descent. Members of different patrilineal descent groups are linked by networks of affinal and non-agnatic consanguineal kinship. But, although one can sometimes observe politicians exploiting such groups and networks, it is not possible to derive the pattern of political alliances solely from the antecedent caste and kinship frameworks. Nor is it possible to derive the pattern of horizontal alliances from the pattern and content of vertical alliances.

Underlying the apparent disorder, however, is the discontinuity in the distribution of power and the privileged position of the political class. The discontinuity in the distribution of power affects the pattern of horizontal alliances in two ways. It weakens the influence of vertical alliances and of caste and kinship ties. At the same time it increases the influence of rules of political strategy which are derived from the modern governmental and administrative framework of political choice. It is these rules of strategy which produce the instability and apparent disorder of horizontal political alliances. It is possible for elite leaders to act without reference to their non-elite supporters and in ways which lead them into conflict with their caste mates and kinsmen. Such behavior is often necessary if a politician is to follow rules of strategy which will enable him to achieve influence and to provide patronage to his followers.

10
Conclusions

SUMMARY

An alliance in the sense in which I have used the term here is a kind of
exchange or transaction involving decisions to extend or withhold support
or patronage. In both its transactional and its decision-making aspects it is a
feature of what Firth and Barth call social organization. Regarded in this
light, I argue, it becomes apparent that there is a simple pattern underlying
the seeming patternlessness of political alliances in rural Western Maharashtra. This pattern consists not in irrational personal antagonisms attri-
butable to the personality characteristics of Indian politicians (cf. Brass
1965:168–82), but rather in the relations between political action and
certain antecedent structural frameworks.

The governmental and administrative institutions of Western Maharashtra comprise one such major antecedent structural framework. These
institutions are the arenas within which political alliances are made. They
determine many of the rules and provide many of the rewards for successful political strategy.

An analysis of the personnel who hold office in these institutions suggests that there is a small political class with privileged access to positions
of influence. The political class is composed primarily of *vətəndar* Marathas
with the addition of Brahmins and Jains in the towns. The existence of this
privileged political class is the second major antecedent structural framework.

All of the groups in the political class have high caste status. The
vətəndar Marathas also have numerical dominance in most villages of the
region and they are found in substantial numbers in the market towns as
well. The Brahmins and Jains are very small castes, but they are a significant part of the population of the towns in which they are concentrated.

The *vətəndar* Marathas share a Dravidian system of kinship with the
rest of the non-Brahmin population, but they are distinguished from the
other non-Brahmins by the size of their patrilineages and the geographical
distribution of their affinal networks. *Vətəndar* Marathas have very large
localized patrilineages. These are divided into juxtaposed domestic
groups, but they are not segmented into sub-lineages. Marriage networks

Conclusions

link *vətəndar* Maratha lineages in widely dispersed villages, but they do not link *vətəndar* Marathas with non-*vətəndar* Marathas in the same village.

The political class of rural Western Maharashtra is a privileged economic class too. Its members own a disproportionate share of the landed wealth of the region and they own a controlling share of most of the region's co-operative societies. As employers of agricultural labor and as creditors the members of the political class are able to exert economic control over much of the rest of the population.

The main feature of the pattern of political alliances in rural Western Maharashtra, the instability of coalitions with its attendant seeming patternlessness, is the result of the discontinuity in the distribution of power and the dominance of a small, privileged political class. Non-*vətəndar* Marathas and members of other castes must depend upon the *vətəndar* Marathas, Brahmins, and Jains for patronage. The followings attached to elite leaders by vertical alliances based on economic relations and on the distribution of patronage are not differentiated by caste or class and do not form distinct interest groups. They have little influence on the formation of horizontal alliances within the political class. A leader must provide his following with patronage, but he does not represent a special interest which can be served only by a limited range of horizontal alliances.

The dominant position of the political class also reduces the influence of its internal caste and kinship structure on the formation of horizontal alliances. Leaders may ally with caste fellows or kinsmen if it suits them, but in most circumstances they do not risk losing power if they ignore such ties.

Since elite leaders are constrained in their choice of horizontal alliances neither by the vertical alliances between the political class and its dependents nor by the internal caste and kinship structure of the political class, what really matters are the rules of political strategy. Some of these rules are a function of the structure of the political arenas peculiar to Western Maharashtra, while others are common to all coalition formation (see Barth 1959b; Riker 1962). The frequent shifts in horizontal alliances are the result of strategic considerations. In many situations influence can be obtained or maintained best by breaking old alliances and forming new ones with persons who were previously one's opponents. Although horizontal alliances sometimes seem to be based on such antecedent structural frameworks as caste or kinship, strategic considerations regularly produce shifts which shatter most of the apparent connections. In some cases caste status or membership in a descent group may be exchanged for political support, but most of the time caste and kinship are mere extrinsic pretexts for transactions involving other, quite unrelated values.

A remark which the Rajasaheb of Phaltan, Malojirao Naik Nimbalkar made to some of his closest allies in the spring of 1967 when they were planning their strategy for the upcoming local government elections succinctly summarizes these general conclusions. The Raja said that there were about a hundred and twenty 'places' (sing. *jaga*) in Phaltan Taluka: twelve seats on the Managing Committee of the Shriram Co-operative Sugar Factory, sixteen on the Panchayat Samiti, eight on the Managing Committee of the Urban Co-operative Bank, twenty-three in the Shriram Education Society, and so on. If they distributed their support for these places cleverly, the Raja and his friends would retain control of the Taluka. If they gave support to the wrong people, they would lose. The Raja's remark indicates that neither ideology, nor personal loyalty, nor rights and obligations arising from caste or kinship are the necessary bases of successful alliances. Rather, alliances are shaped primarily by strategies of personal advancement. If X supports Y's campaign for the Legislative Assembly, Y will back X for Chairman of the Zilla Parishad Education Committee. The importance of such personal considerations in alliance formation is a consequence of the discontinuity in the distribution of political power in Western Maharashtra. There is a political class the members of which are largely free, in their political decisions, from obligations of caste, locality, kinship, and personal loyalty. Most of the time they can, and, indeed, must, form alliances simply in terms of their own personal advancement. In such a situation the major factor in shaping political strategy is the system of administrative and governmental arenas within which prestige and control of patronage may be won.

Several more specific points may be made in addition to these general conclusions. In much of the literature on factions in local-level politics (see Chapter 7, p. 102) caste and kinship are regarded as important determinants of political action. The data which I have presented suggest, on the contrary, that caste and kinship are more often extrinsic pretexts for alliance than they are the intrinsic transactional content of alliances. Much of the previous literature assumes that caste identity and kinship connection are sources of common and/or mutual political interests.[1] In reality, however, there are few direct connections between caste and kinship, on the one hand, and political interests on the other. Furthermore, only in a limited number of situations is it possible to use the values that are attached to caste and kinship as items of exchange in alliance transactions.

POLITICAL ALLIANCES AND KINSHIP

The literature on factions contains two contradictory arguments concerning the relationship between political alliances and kinship. Lewis argues that political alliances are determined very largely by mutual interests derived from ties of descent. Factions, according to Lewis,

are primarily kinship groupings which carry on important social, economic and ceremonial functions in addition to their factional struggles against one another. (1954:503; for a similar view see Dhillon 1955)

While Lewis argues that agnates tend to be allies, Barth (1959a and 1959b) and Leach (1961) argue that where patrilineal inheritance is the rule agnates have common, potentially competitive interests and tend to be enemies. Briefly, the argument runs as follows. The rule of inheritance determines who are to be coparceners of a joint estate. These persons are likely to be competitors and each will seek allies from outside the group of co-owners.

Both arguments contain an element of truth, but stated baldly in this manner both are contradicted by the facts. In Lewis's Rampur, as in Girvi, the history of changes in factional alliances demonstrates that villagers are not limited in their choice of allies by ties of agnatic descent. Conversely, persons who share a joint estate by virtue of a rule of unilineal inheritance or descent are no more enjoined to compete than they are to co-operate. In Girvi, as we have seen, alliances cut across lineage boundaries but there are limits on competition among agnates and a tendency for each *vətəndar* Maratha lineage to unite against the other. Similarly, in Pul Eliya,

Co-resident members of a 'compound' [many of whom are co-heirs of a joint estate] have certain hereditary interests which drive them towards mutual co-operation even in the face of much personal hostility. (Leach 1961:243)

Among the Swat Pathans it is close patrilineal kin who are competitors for a joint estate, but brothers often co-operate. Father's brother's children, real and classificatory, may be called *tarbur* ('enemy') but the term is used only at ego's discretion and he will continue to refer to his cousins as siblings if his relations with them are not hostile (Barth 1959a:109 & 1959b:11). Competition between patrilineal co-heirs also is limited in Rampur where, Lewis reports,

There is not a single case of brothers belonging to separate factions, only one case of first and second cousins, and only four cases (out of fourteen) of third cousins. (1958:119)

Another way to consider the political implications of rules of descent and inheritance is to look at the contrast between faction composition and household partition. Mayer, for example, agrees with Leach that

In questions involving property ... agnates tend to be rivals or at least remain separate instead of co-operating ... we can infer that there are frequent partitions of joint households and that the atmosphere is then such that nobody wishes to keep on holding land jointly, though joint farming is economically advantageous. (1969:241)

But while agnates tend to be divided by their interests in patrimonial property, they tend to be united politically. Concerning factions in Ramkheri Mayer writes that

> In most divisions within the subcaste groups in Ramkheri, one finds the co-opera-tion of agnates to be an important, if not the main feature. . . . Among the Rajputs, for instance, factions are based on the branches of each lineage . . . (1960:239)

In Girvi, too, the tensions implicit in the jural equality of brothers lead them, as their father dies and their own children marry, to partition their joint household. It remains true, nevertheless, that among the politically active *vatandar* Marathas agnates tend to be allies even though they are not bound by ties of descent and even though a number of important alliances cut across lineage boundaries. Finally, in his account of Pul Eliya it is Leach's

> constant theme that while the heirs to a common estate (that is full brothers) tend to be opposed to one another, marriage results in a co-operative relationship between brothers-in-law, that is between individuals who are *not* potential owners of the same property. (1961:241)

Although this hypothesis works in many cases, it fails in others. Thus since about 1921 U. Kadirathe and his three full brothers, four of the rich-est and most influential men in the village, have been close allies and partners in opening new land (Leach 1961:112–15, 144, 217–34).

It would appear that both hypotheses are too broad to account for the details of faction composition in Indian villages. Political alliances do not, *pace* Lewis, faithfully reflect ties of common descent, but neither do the conflicting interests of agnates in their common patrimonial estate, *pace* Leach, regularly drive close agnates into opposite political camps.

A more adequate account of the relations between kinship and political alliances must be based on a more discriminating view of kinship and descent. Indeed, by now much of what can be said on this topic ought to be commonplace. In villages such as Girvi, Ramkheri, and Rampur where there are corporate patrilineages the unity of siblings and of close agnatic cousins is a function of the jural authority of the father, derived from descent, and of co-filiation. Within this range common interest in a patri-monial estate may produce hostile relations between brothers, but while their father is still alive his jural authority is likely to put an end to most open hostility. Even after their father is dead and they have partitioned their joint household any hostility between brothers is likely to be mod-erated by moral ties of amity arising from co-filiation and the same consideration may limit hostility between cousins too. When partition disputes have been settled amity tends to reassert itself, but in any case I would not accept the argument that partition is the result of competition for property. My own data (Carter 1971) indicate that partition only begins to occur frequently when brothers have children of their own for whom they are individually responsible. Within the lineage but beyond the sibling range descent today is no longer the basis for the allocation of secular authority. In the past descent served to allocate rights in offices such as Patilships which lineage mates shared but for which they might compete. Ambitious men were not prevented from seeking allies from outside their lineage and in many situations only such allies could be of help, but in making such alliances a man had to balance his chances of winning benefits for himself against the chances of endangering the common interests of his lineage as a whole. In making alliances to achieve an office which was part of the corporate estate of his lineage a man might seek the aid of affines or non-agnatic consanguines, but he was not obliged to do so. As descent is increasingly separated from the modern political system and as descent group members come to share fewer and fewer interests, descent becomes decreasingly relevant for the formation of political alliances. Nevertheless, as the maneuvers involving the *mukəd-dəm*ship of the *vərči ali* Kadam lineage and the Girvi Panchayat show, it still retains some of its force today.

POLITICAL ALLIANCES AND CASTE

The literature on caste and politics revolves around the alleged confrontation between modernity and tradition. India's modern democratic political system, based on universal suffrage, is held to imply that people will vote as individuals. Ascriptive caste groups, however, are held to be elements of the traditional society to which an all-embracing, primordial loyalty is due.[2] To the extent that people support their caste mates instead of voting on the basis of their individual assessments of the issues and candidates there is a conflict between modernity and tradition. As Fürer-Haimendorf observes, this conflict may be resolved in one of three ways:

the system of government may gradually adjust itself to the traditional social order, or the social order may change to such an extent that it will ultimately fit the prevailing type of government, or, lastly, both the social order and the system of government may change until they reach a tolerable degree of consistency. (1963: 53)

Scholars hold diverse views on the manner in which the conflict between modernity and tradition ultimately will be resolved. Selig Harrison fears that the traditional social order will destroy India's democratic federalism and paints a lurid picture of python-like regional caste lobbies twining their 'coils in and out of state political life' (1960:155). Leach, on the other hand, seems inclined to give the victory to the economic and political forces of modernity. In his view

> The caste society as a whole is, in Durkheim's sense, an organic system with each particular caste and subcaste filling a distinctive functional role. It is a system of labour division from which the element of competition among the workers has been largely excluded. (1960:5)

However, when castes are drawn into the political and economic arena as competing groups the fundamental organic principles of caste society are destroyed. Leach argues that

> Everywhere in India and Ceylon today whole caste groups are tending to emerge as political factions but it is misleading to think of such behavior as a characteristic of caste as such. If a whole caste group plays the role of a political faction by competing with other such factions for some common economic or political goal it thereby acts in defiance of caste tradition ... My own view is that wherever caste groups are seen to be acting as corporations in competition against like groups *of different caste*, then they are acting in defiance of caste principles. (1960:6–7)[3]

The Rudolphs, finally, deny there there is any necessary conflict between modernity and tradition. In their view caste is transformed but strengthened by the impact of modern democratic politics while at the same time it provides one of the institutional mechanisms by which the new political system penetrates into traditional society.

In the Rudolphs' view the new form of caste in which modern and traditional elements are combined is the caste association. The caste association is a paracommunity which combines the features of the traditional natural association and the modern voluntary association. The traditional localized *jati*, confined to a few neighboring villages, was a natural association. Membership was acquired by birth. The group was endogamous and most social roles were defined by caste identity. Caste associations emerged when members of different localized *jatis*, often, but not always, with the same caste name, were released from the constraints of local inter-caste relations by new economic and political activities, brought into contact by modern means of transportation and communication, and found that they could pursue mutual political and economic interests by regional co-operation. Ascribed *jati* membership is no longer equivalent to membership in the caste association. Persons qualified by birth

> must also 'join' through some conscious act involving various degrees of identification – ranging from providing financial support to an association's educational, welfare, or commercial activities, to attending caste association meetings, to voting for candidates supported by caste association leaders. (Rudolph & Rudolph 1967:33)

Conclusions

Caste associations use new forms of communication and transportation and new forms of organization characteristic of voluntary associations to broaden caste consciousness and participation by linking together formerly autonomous localized *jatis* in associations that ultimately tend to be regional in scope. Conversely the caste association facilitates the adjustment of traditional society to the demands of the modern political system.

By initiating, managing, and encouraging the efforts of lower castes to become twice-born, to don the sacred thread symbolizing high ritual rank and culture, it in effect if not in intention drains the caste hierarchy of meaning by homogenizing and democratizing it. When most men can wear the sacred thread or achieve power and status without it, it will have lost its capacity to divide and distance them from each other. And by providing a structure for the pursuit of political power, social status, and economic interest, the paracommunity based on caste sentiment and interest makes secular concerns and representative democracy comprehensible and manageable to ordinary Indians. (Rudolph & Rudolph 1967:36; see also Rudolph & Rudolph 1960 and Rudolph 1965)

The Rudolphs believe that caste associations provide the means for horizontal mobilization of caste communities and that in certain circumstances castes may act as political groups in arenas of varying inclusiveness (1967:36–154). Fürer-Haimendorf and Harrison hold similar views. In support of their arguments these authors cite a number of cases, especially conflict between Reddis and Kammas in Andhra (Harrison 1956, 1960), the caste associations of the Nadars in southern Madras (Hardgrave 1969; Rudolph and Rudolph 1967:36–49), and those of the Vanniyars in northern Madras (Rudolph and Rudolph 1967:49–61).[4] Closer examination of these and other cases, however, leads one to doubt that castes ever act as political groups, regardless of whether or not they have caste associations. It is clear that leaders of caste associations offer the support of their fellow caste members to potential allies. It also is clear that the government may offer concessions to caste association leaders in hopes of winning the promised support of the caste. What is not clear is the degree to which caste association leaders can actually deliver the votes of their caste fellows. Hardgrave's research, for example, shows that the leaders of the two Nadar caste associations, the Dakshina Mara Nadar Sangam of Tiruneveli and the Nadar Mahajana Sangam of Madurai, represented at the most the urban Nadar trading communities but not the mass of rural Shanars in southern Tirunelveli District.

The conflict between the Kammas and the Reddis in Andhra has been accepted as one of the clearest examples of caste based politics in India. It now appears, however, that caste conflict was confined largely to the sphere of rhetoric. On the basis of his detailed research in Guntur District, Weiner denies Harrison's claim that the struggle between the Communist

169

and Congress parties in Andhra was really a conflict between Kammas and Reddis. It is true that the Communist Party in Guntur was dominated by Kammas in the late 1940s and early 1950s but so, in fact, was the Congress (Weiner 1967:141–2). Weiner's work indicates that the most important factor in Guntur District politics is the dominance of the district political class. In this situation, as in Western Maharashtra, vertical mobilization and conflicts between competing land-owning families of the same or different castes determine the pattern of political alliances (see Weiner 1967:133–209).

Similarly, much of recent Gujarat politics has been interpreted in terms of conflict between Patidars and Kshatriyas. Weiner's study of Kaira District, however, indicates that there is a 'built-in quarantine effect' in the segmentary nature of the caste system which limits the horizontal spread of caste conflict. In general, Weiner argues,

Each linguistic region is made up of a series of hierarchically arranged castes who typically do not intermarry or have close social relations with castes in other linguistic regions. In any one region a given social group may seek to displace another in the status hierarchy. Politics is one arena in which this struggle takes place. It is difficult for an aspiring caste to reach out to a neighboring state or in many instances even to a neighboring district to establish a political coalition. There is almost no reason to do so, because each aspiring caste may have a different enemy; the dominant caste itself is often limited to one or two districts, if that, and at the very most spreads throughout a single state. The main point is that the political struggles which occur in one district may have relatively little impact on political relationships in a neighboring district. While the limitations in communications may also be a factor, the most significant element is the segmented character of the social system. (Weiner 1967:115–16)

In a study of politics in Dewas District, Madhya Pradesh, Mayer found that caste membership was not a determining factor in political alliances and patronage distribution. Although Rajputs formed the core of a ruling faction in the rural portions of the district, they could not maintain their position on the basis of Rajput support alone. They formed alliances with and distributed patronage to members of other castes, 'not exclusively on a caste basis, but rather as politicians seeking support on a variety of bases' (Mayer 1967a:130; see also 1963a and 1958b). Mayer concludes that

At least as important as the caste, then, is a different unit of loyalty and recruitment. Such a unit may be based on ideology, party programme, and party membership; but at present it tends to be based on the individual's political interest and factional membership. As Bailey has observed, the recruitment of supporters is here a craftsman's job and not the simple application of a mass-produced blueprint. By this, he means that the followings of the candidate or the district party leaders are composed of people recruited on diverse transactional linkages, and that they vary over time according to people's perception of their own interests . . .

Conclusions

Clearly, caste is a factor in the recruitment and maintenance of such followings; but it is only one among several factors. (1967a:135)

Although I would not deny the existence of sentiments of caste solidarity, it does not seem that such sentiments are very efficacious as a basis of political recruitment. My own data indicate that where there is an entrenched political class, and this pattern of political stratification seems to be quite widespread in India, caste is not very important as a determinant of political alliances. Conflicts which appear to pit caste against caste are in reality conflicts between particular leaders, each supported by allies from several castes. The alliances between persons involved in Phaltan municipal politics discussed in Chapter 8 are a case in point. It often is thought that caste solidarity is more likely to be a determinant of political alliances in situations where two castes have relatively equal numbers and influence, but Weiner's detailed studies of district and village politics in Guntur and Kaira show that even in these situations caste is of minor importance.

I would go further than this, however, and argue that the notion that sentiments of caste solidarity or mutual interests derived from caste identity may serve as the basis of political recruitment is based on several misapprehensions regarding the nature of caste. The notion seems to be based on the view that the caste system can be understood as composed of concrete groups, *jatis*, which subsume all of the interests of the persons or actors who belong to them. This is what Dumont calls the substantial fallacy. Dumont has shown that it is more fruitful to regard the caste system as a structure informed by certain ideas, i.e. principles or isolates. In particular, he demonstrates that one central isolate of the caste system is a principle of hierarchy, the opposition of pure and impure, which defines ritual status. As far as political action is concerned, an important characteristic of ritual status is that it encompasses political and economic dominance but does not subsume it; the two remain differentiated. Thus an appeal to caste solidarity *per se* is an appeal to only one aspect, however important, of an Indian's identity. It is not, except perhaps in a symbolic sense, an appeal to his every interest.[5]

In addition, if Mayer's (1960) perceptive analysis of caste and subcaste in Malwa is taken at its proper value then it becomes clear that the segmentary nature of the caste system is a far more serious bar to the efficacy of political appeals based on caste solidarity than even Weiner supposed. Mayer demonstrates that

On the whole, caste membership is significant for relations with other castes, and subcaste membership for activities within the caste. (1960:5; see also Leach 1960:5 and Dumont 1970:33–6 and 61–4)

171

An individual's identity, interests and role vary with the structural context in which he acts. His identity as a member of a caste is relevant mainly in vertical, hierarchical, inter-caste relations which as a rule occur within the confines of a single village. Outside of his village a man's caste identity fades into the background while his role as subcaste member and kinsman comes to the fore. The important point here is the extent to which

... villages are seen as separate hierarchical systems. The village boundary seems to insulate villages against the need for their commensal rules to be consistent, and so allows variation. Similarly, a man going across the boundary to another village automatically sheds his status as a resident of his own village and can conform to the rules of the host village, which, were he to follow them in his own village, would mean disciplinary action against him. Commensally speaking, then, the village is very much a reality. (Mayer 1960:49)

As a result persons in different villages, even neighboring ones, who share the same caste name may have no mutual interests even in the sphere of ritual caste status *per se*.

Although it would be rash to deny that a villager's caste status means a great deal to him, it is equally rash to believe that political support can be obtained by means of appeals to caste solidarity. An individual's caste status is not necessarily congruent with his economic and political position. Nor is it likely that persons with the same caste name in different villages will share the same ritual interests. Yet it is undeniable that caste associations exist and it remains to be seen on what their appeal rests.

The study of the Gujarat Kshatriya Sabha by Kothari and Maru (1965, 1970) is instructive in this regard. Kothari and Maru write that

The Kshatriya community had in the past enjoyed certain privileges as a caste. With changes taking place in the social and economic organisation, these privileges were infringed at some stage. And this, in turn, led to a rallying together for the preservation of privileges and interests in a deliberate and organised manner. Ascriptive status is here turned into a symbol of mobilisation for building up an interest organisation. (1970:80)

But as Kothari and Maru themselves make clear there was, in fact, no 'Kshatriya community' in the past. On the contrary, the Kshatriya Sabha is a coalition of political allies drawn from a variety of named castes, including 'semi-tribal' Bhils and middle status Bariyas as well as high status Rajputs (Kothari and Maru 1970:72–3). If we are to understand how ascriptive status is exploited to build up coalitions such as this we must drop the notion of caste solidarity and turn to Mayer's notion of an alliance as a transactional link in an action-set. In this case high caste politicians such as Narendrasinh Mahida, a Rajput 'noble', Natvarsinh Solanki, a Rajput Talukdar from Kaira District, and, on some occasions, the Maratha Maharaja of Baroda attempted to achieve power in Gujarat politics by exchanging high caste status for political support against the dominant Patidars. They offered the Sabha's version of Kshatriya status to Bhils and Bariyas in return for support for the Sabha in elections. Note that this is a transaction involving ritual status which some voters desire but do not have and which a group of leaders promise to provide. It is not an appeal to caste solidarity and, in fact, the pattern of political alliances actually cuts across named caste groups. Thus in 1962 Bhailalbhai Patel, a prominent Patidar leader of the Swatantra party, negotiated an electoral alliance with Mahida and Solanki's Kshatriya Sabha. But in Baroda District the Maharaja of Baroda, a former member of the Sabha, was allied with a group of Congress Patidars against a group of Patidar industrialists in Baroda City, the local Kshatriya Sabha and the Patidar-dominated Baroda District Swatantra. In all these alliances caste status is only one item of value being exchanged and there is no evidence that it is the most influential. The Congress countered the Kshatriya Sabha's activities among Bhils, for example, not with offers of caste status but rather with backward class status and all the reserved benefits that go with it (Kothari and Maru 1970:97–8).

It is significant that Mayer concludes his essay on caste and politics by writing that

In general, then, though caste associations and federations may be vitally important in bridging local diversity in the future, they do not appear to have been so yet. Even if and when they do become more important, moreover, it is likely that they will become part of multi-caste parties rather than emerging as separate caste parties, as Morris-Jones suggests. (1967a:137)

One reason that this is so is that while common caste identity may be what I have called the extrinsic aspect of an alliance, it is unlikely to be an element of the intrinsic, transactional aspect of an alliance. It is not the extrinsic pretence for an alliance which carries weight but rather the intrinsic transaction and caste status is likely to figure in action-set linkages only when persons of different caste status are involved. Thus the rich, upwardly mobile, new Chauhans studied by Rowe (1968) tried to win support among their Noniya caste fellows not by appealing to sentiments of caste solidarity but rather by offering them, first, claims to Rajput ritual status and, later, special benefits for low castes promised by the Republican Party. Similarly, a Rajput in Dewas tried to win the support of low caste Bagris by offering them membership in the Dewas branch of the Rajput Parishad (Mayer 1966:109 and 120, n11). My own analysis has shown how the *vatəndar* Marathas of Western Maharashtra have used their high ritual status and membership in a large, internally stratified caste to win the support, first, of the former Kunbis and, more recently, of those few non-

vətəndars who have been admitted to *vətəndar* status. Occasionally it may sound as if Maratha politicians make appeals to caste solidarity, but here, too, I believe, alliances are based on transactions rather than solidarity.

Finally, although the Rudolphs incorrectly emphasize the strength of sentiments of caste solidarity, they are probably correct that the new democratic political system is transforming the traditional social system. It is with regard to this development that Barth's concepts of entrepreneurship and feedback are relevant. Leaders of caste associations are political entrepreneurs attempting to win power by offering to exchange items of value, ritual status and political support, not previously considered equivalent. By so doing they may be altering the encompassing position of ritual status in Indian ideology and, paradoxically, contributing to the secularization of Indian politics and society.[6]

POLITICAL ALLIANCES AND POLITICAL STRATIFICATION

The major features of the pattern of political alliances in rural Western Maharashtra are a function of a single, relatively undifferentiated political class. First, horizontal and vertical alliances may be distinguished by their relations to the two political strata. Horizontal alliances occur within the political class while vertical alliances cut across the boundary between the political class and the masses. The transactional content of the two forms of alliance also is different and they occur in different political arenas. Secondly, when politicians require electoral support they mobilize it indirectly through a network of horizontal alliances with influential leaders in other settlements rather than directly by means of a widespread network of vertical alliances. In the Rudolphs' terminology, the pattern of mobilization is vertical rather than horizontal, centering on notables and their 'vote banks' rather than on interest groups (Rudolph and Rudolph 1967:24–5). Finally, although vertical alliances are relatively stable, horizontal alliances are remarkably unstable. As a consequence of the privileged position of the political class there are few constraints on the choice of horizontal allies other than strategic ones and these are as conducive to instability as they are to stability.

Although the available evidence is scanty, there is reason to believe that the pattern which prevails in rural politics up to the level of the Assembly constituency in Western Maharashtra is found in other regions of India as well. In Guntur District, Andhra Pradesh, for example, there seems to be a regionally dominant political class composed of Kammas, Reddis, and Brahmins. As one would expect the pattern of political mobilization is vertical. Weiner suggests that in Guntur politics in 1962 one won the support of a village by winning the support of its panchayat president and

Conclusions

that, in general, Assembly constituencies went to the party controlling the panchayat samiti.

> In Ponnur constituency, for example, we found that almost every village that the Swatantra assembly candidate carried or that gave the Swatantra candidate a large vote in the 1962 elections had a Swatantra panchayat president. (Weiner 1967:168)

The principal difference between Guntur in 1962 and Maharashtra in 1967 is the great influence of co-operatives, often outweighing panchayats, in the latter. Similarly, in the Telengana region of Andhra there appears to be a political class composed of landed gentry families called *dora* recruited from the Reddi, Velamma, Kamma, and Brahmin castes (Gray 1962, 1963 and 1970).

I also argue that in Western Maharashtra there is a single distinct discontinuity in the distribution of power. That is, the political class is not itself internally stratified and there is within it no distinct subclass with privileged access to positions of power at the district or state levels. It follows, therefore, that there are only two distinct forms of political alliances, horizontal alliances within the political class and vertical alliances between the political class and the masses. However, one might object that if the political elite includes all those who are in a position to influence public decisions, from influential village panchayat members all the way to ministers of the Union Government, then the pattern of alliances must be more complicated, with vertical as well as horizontal links within the political class. Thus it might be argued that although a village panchayat chairman's links with other village leaders are horizontal, his alliance with elite leaders who function at the district level are vertical.

In societies in which this objection holds it is necessary to distinguish different subgroups in the political elite and political class associated with more and less inclusive political arenas. In eighteenth-century English politics, for example, there were at least three distinct subgroups within the political class. The royalty had privileged access to the Crown and an effective and legitimate Parliamentary opposition to the King could not be mounted without the support of a member of the royalty such as H.R.H. the Duke of Cumberland or the Prince of Wales. The peerage had privileged access to the House of Lords and the sons of peers had privileged access to the Commons through both county and borough seats. The landed gentry, the third subgroup, had privileged access to the remaining Commons seats. Peers might form horizontal alliances among themselves and members of the gentry among themselves, but when a member of the royalty or peerage formed an alliance with a member of a lower stratum of the political class the link was vertical. The superior partner was the patron of the inferior (Namier 1957, 1961).

According to Bailey Orissa also has an internally stratified political class. Bailey distinguishes three kinds of political arenas in Orissa: the state government and its associated services, assembly constituencies, and villages. The Orissan political class has two subgroups. The state arena is dominated by a few former princes, big landlords, and members of the professional middle classes drawn primarily from the Karan and Brahmin castes. Bailey writes that

> Orissa has its dominant castes, the Karan and the Brahman. Together they cannot be more than about 8 per cent of the population, but they hold a very high proportion of responsible positions both in politics and in the services. The two castes are rivals, and some of the old manoeuvers of the pre-Independence Congress are to be attributed to this rivalry. But this is not the case today in politics: members of both castes take a leading part in all political parties except the Jharkhand, and lines of cleavage between both parties and within parties are not illuminated by looking at caste membership. The position is that the members of these two castes, together with an increasing number of lower castes nowadays, and with the few members of the Princely families, constitute Orissa's very small middle-class *élite*, and it might be more correct to regard their dominance in politics and the Administration as a class phenomenon, rather than a caste phenomenon. (1963a:106)

Quite different groups are dominant in the village arenas and, although Bailey does not discuss this question in detail, the village level political class must include the Cultivator caste in the coastal region as well as Warriors in hill villages such as Bisipara. According to Bailey there is no subgroup of the political class associated with constituency politics and the competitors in these arenas are either villagers moving out in order to strengthen themselves in their home villages or members of the elite moving down to collect votes to 'qualify themselves to enter the struggle in the elite arena' (1963b:230). Bailey's argument is poorly documented, but it must be admitted that a similar situation prevailed in several regions of British India, with the addition of the British as the highest stratum of the political class (see Broomfield 1966, 1968; Frykenberg 1965; Seal 1968; Johnson 1970; Dobbin 1970; Mukherjee 1970).

Although internally stratified political classes may be found in other regions of India and in Maharashtra during other periods of its history, the political class of Maharashtra today is homogeneous. Socially the composition of the Maharashtra Cabinet is roughly the same as that of the Phaltan Panchayat Samiti or the Satara Zilla Parishad. Indeed, in contemporary India generally, the political class seems to be becoming increasingly undifferentiated. Castes which in Mayer's (1958a) terms are dominant at higher levels of government but lack regional dominance are

Conclusions

being pushed out of their privileged positions. With the introduction of the universal adult franchise and the development of institutions of local government, regionally dominant castes such as the Marathas, Kammas, Reddis, Okkaligas, Lingayats, and so on are extending their power to higher levels of government. Béteille (1967:241) notes that the Madras Cabinet has become a coalition of regionally dominant castes. Increasingly today the same may be said of the highest level of government, the Union Cabinet, as well. In these circumstances all alliances within the political class properly may be regarded as horizontal and all are subject to the same strategic constraints. Not every elite leader is ambitious for higher office, but those that are do not view their links as followers of more powerful leaders as stable, vertical alliances. They continually switch their allegiance from one powerful leader to another in order to further their chances of advancing up the ladder of political office. All elite leaders, at whatever level of political arena, are constrained in their choice of other elite allies by the conditions which protect the elite from popular control and by the economics of patronage. It is true that some elite leaders are much more powerful than others, but it is with respect to the gap between the political class and the masses and not with respect to the hierarchy of office that alliances may be labeled vertical or horizontal.

GENERATIVE MODELS AND ELITE CIRCULATION

Finally, I wish to touch briefly on the third major issue involved in the use of generative models of social organization, that is, the effects of organizational decisions upon antecedent structural frameworks. I already have indicated one area in which such effects can be discerned. Political entrepreneurs who exchange traditional caste status for support in modern democratic politics are producing new forms of cultural integration.

This aspect of generative models also is relevant to the understanding of important aspects of Indian history. I noted in Chapter 1 that the Indian Independence Movement may be understood in part as a process of elite circulation. As Bottomore (1966:48) points out the circulation of elites involves two processes: one in which individuals move between the masses and the elite and another in which social groups struggle for a place in the political class. Although my data are necessarily quite sketchy, I would suggest that both processes of elite circulation result from the application of principles of political strategy, that is, of political organization, which are inherent in political stratification.

Two mechanisms of elite circulation seem to occur in Maharashtra. In the first place, powerful leaders like the Rajasaheb of Phaltan frequently bring powerless newcomers into the elite as dependent and hopefully, therefore, reliable allies. Sometimes these newcomers are members of the dominant *vatandar* class from other areas in which case the elite is moved from place to place but its content remains unchanged. In other cases they are local or non-local members of non-dominant sections of the population in which case the content of the elite is changed. This mechanism produces the first form of individual elite circulation but not the second form of group circulation. Historically the membership of the political class has been influenced by a similar mechanism on a group scale. Sections of the elite interested in increasing the power of some centralized authority, for example, the Brahmin Peshwas and later the British, have attempted to weaken the localized regional strength of the Maratha *vatandars* by allying themselves with various weaker sections of the population. This mechanism tends to produce the second form of elite circulation.

Both of these mechanisms have to do with conflicts within the elite. One should look also at what is happening outside the elite, but it seems less usual for groups or individuals to force themselves into the elite or political class from below than to be drawn into it from above. When groups or individuals who are not part of the political class do begin to acquire power which might threaten established groups there are means of buying them off and cooling their revolutionary ardour. For example, the provision of reserved benefits for Scheduled Castes has greatly reduced the radical activity of the ex-Mahar neo-Buddhists and the 1967 General Election saw several sections of the Republican Party, the political wing of Ambedkar's Mahar movement, in electoral alliance with the Congress. If Mahar leaders revolt against their position in the caste hierarchy by becoming Buddhists they lose the right to hold reserved seats in elective councils and most know full well that they have no chance of winning a general seat.[7] Most of the time the elite is strong enough effectively to counter attempts by disadvantaged groups to obtain a fairer share of political power or to deflect such attempts into token, individual elite circulation. Nevertheless, there seem to be implicit in the organizational principles which derive from the structure of political stratification in India tendencies which lead to a gradual lessening of political inequalities.

Conclusions

Map 3   Main Girvi settlement area (for key and details, see overleaf)

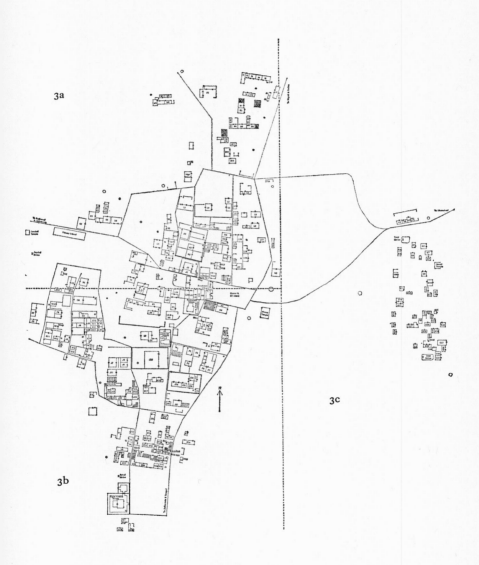

179

Map 3 Main Girvi settlement area

Caste	House no.	Caste	House no.	Caste	House no.
Brahmin	$A_1 - A_5$	Maratha		Nhavi	$P_1 - P_8$
Chambhar	$B_1 - B_{11}$	*Varči ali* Kadams		Parit	Q_1
Dhangar	$C_1 - C_5$	proper	$J_1 - J_{32}$	Patrut	R_1
Gadshi	$D_1 - D_3$	attached	$K_1 - K_{19}$	Ramoshi	$S_1 - S_{43}$
Kumbhar	$E_1 - E_5$	*Khalči ali* Kadams		Shimpi	T_1 & T_2
Lohar	F_1 & F_2	proper	$L_1 - L_{32}$	Sonar	U_1
Mahar	$G_1 - G_{41}$	attached	$M_1 - M_5$	Sutar	$V_1 - V_5$
Mali	$H_1 - H_{20}$	Other Marathas	$N_1 - N_{19}$	Vani Lingayat	W_1
Mang	$I_1 - I_{10}$	Muslim	$O_1 - O_{12}$	Misc.	X_1 & X_2

Ward	House No.
Vitthal	C_4; J_3, J_4, $J_6 - J_{32}$; $K_1 - K_6$, $K_{10} - K_{13}$; N_9, $N_{15} - N_{19}$; O_7, O_8, O_{10}, O_{11}; $S_2 - S_7$, S_{11}, S_{13}, $S_{15} - S_{19}$, $S_{21} - S_{29}$, S_{31}, $S_{34} - S_{39}$; T_1; $V_1 - V_5$. Also Guradara and Outlying Ramoshis.
Janubai	C_3, C_5; F_2; J_5; K_9, $K_{14} - K_{19}$; N_{13}; T_2; U_1; W_1. Guradara and Outlying Ramoshis. Also Janichivadi Malis. Bodkevadi. Jadhavvada.
Lakshmi	F_1; $G_1 - G_{41}$. Dhumalvadi.
Shriram	$H_1 - H_7$, H_{13}, H_{14}; $I_1 - I_{10}$; $L_1 - L_9$, $L_{15} - L_{20}$; N_1, N_2; X_1. Harata Mala and Nava Mala Malis. Attached *khalči ali* Kadams of Bara Biga and Cavarvasti. Proper *khalči ali* Kadams of Pimpalaca Mala.
Hanuman	$A_1 - A_5$; $B_1 - B_{11}$; C_1, C_2; $D_1 - D_3$; $E_1 - E_5$; $H_{10} - H_{12}$, $H_{15} - H_{20}$; J_1, J_2; K_7, K_8; $L_{10} - L_{14}$, L_{23}, L_{24}, $L_{26} - L_{31}$; $N_4 - N_8$, N_{11}, N_{12}; $O_1 - O_6$; P_1, $P_4 - P_8$; Q_1; R_1; $S_{41} - S_{43}$. Shelkevasti Dhangars.

Map 3a

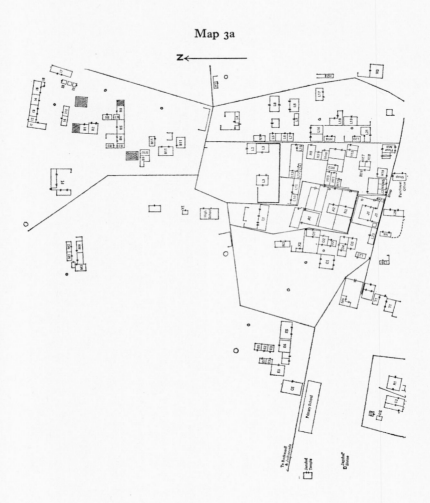

Map 3b

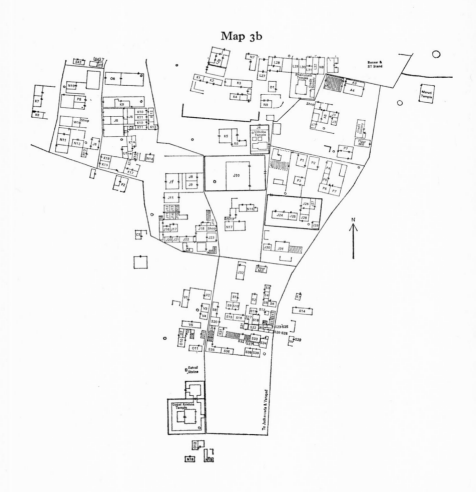

Conclusions

Map 3c

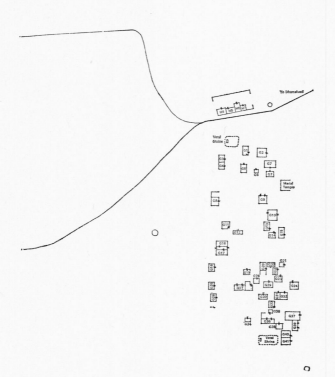

Appendix
Results of the 1967 General Election in Phaltan-Khandala

Polling station	Total valid votes	K. R. Bhoite	V. M. Naik Nimbalkar	Other candidates
		(%)	(%)	(%)
1 *Khandala Mahal*				
Wing (1) Bhatgar Wanhevadi	507	380 (75.0)	51 (10.1)	76 (14.9)
Wing (2) Bhatgar Wanhevadi	480	386 (80.4)	30 (6.3)	70 (14.6)
Shirval (1)	909	758 (83.4)	115 (12.7)	36 (3.9)
Shirval (2)	574	447 (77.9)	105 (18.3)	22 (3.8)
Shirval (3)	601	480 (79.9)	82 (13.5)	39 (6.6)
Bholi	616	280 (45.5)	49 (8.0)	272 (46.5)
Loni Tondal	616	528 (85.7)	22 (3.6)	66 (10.7)
Palshi Mirje	797	574 (72.0)	146 (18.3)	77 (9.7)
Naigaon Sangvi	742	657 (88.5)	25 (3.4)	60 (8.1)
Bhade	838	629 (75.1)	37 (4.4)	172 (20.5)
Wathar Bk.	470	357 (76.0)	73 (15.5)	40 (8.5)
Andori Waghoshi Rui	629	411 (65.3)	75 (11.9)	143 (22.8)
Pimpre Bk.	609	512 (84.1)	56 (9.2)	41 (7.6)
Padegaon	573	317 (85.0)	30 (8.0)	26 (7.0)
Shivajinagar Bhadavade	1029	950 (92.3)	28 (2.7)	51 (5.0)
Kavathe Wadgaon Kesurdi	635	451 (71.0)	50 (7.9)	134 (21.1)
Javale Lohum	529	352 (66.5)	127 (24.0)	50 (9.5)
Karhavadi Atit	564	499 (88.5)	15 (2.7)	50 (8.8)
Bavada	946	760 (80.3)	46 (4.9)	140 (14.8)
Morve	553	440 (79.6)	43 (7.8)	70 (12.6)

Appendix

Polling station	Total valid votes	K.R. Bhoite	V. M. Naik Nimbalkar	Other candidates
		(%)	(%)	(%)
Khandala	743	585 (78.7)	116 (15.6)	42 (5.7)
Pargaon	731	453 (61.9)	223 (30.5)	55 (7.6)
Ajanuj				
Asavali	753	511 (67.9)	134 (18.8)	108 (13.3)
Kanheri	633	410 (64.8)	168 (26.5)	55 (8.7)
Zagalvadi				
Ahire (1)	731	561 (76.7)	78 (10.7)	92 (12.6)
Mhavashi				
Dhavadvadi				
Harali				
Ahire (2)				
Mhavashi	453	341 (75.3)	65 (14.3)	47 (10.1)
Dhavadvadi				
Harali				
Khed Bk.	707	114 (16.1)	515 (72.8)	78 (11.1)
Lonand (1)	673	518 (77.0)	67 (10.0)	88 (13.0)
Lonand (2)	679	569 (83.8)	89 (13.1)	21 (3.1)
Lonand (3)	521	362 (69.5)	128 (24.6)	31 (5.9)
Lonand (4)	571	445 (77.9)	93 (16.3)	33 (5.8)
Nimbodi	605	500 (82.6)	36 (6.0)	69 (11.4)
Padali				
Sukhed	357	268 (75.1)	41 (11.5)	48 (13.4)
Koparde	417	378 (90.6)	19 (4.6)	20 (4.8)
Phaltan Taluka				
Padegaon	443	71 (16.0)	57 (12.9)	315 (71.1)
Raodi Bk.	582	293 (48.6)	128 (22.0)	171 (29.4)
Raodi Kh.				
Kusur				
Khamgaon	846	420 (49.6)	340 (40.2)	86 (10.2)
Murum				
Hol (1)	632	178 (28.2)	311 (49.2)	143 (22.6)
Hol (2)	871	436 (50.1)	399 (45.8)	36 (4.1)
Hol (3)	578	243 (42.0)	282 (48.8)	53 (9.2)
Hol (4)	605	244 (40.3)	287 (47.4)	74 (12.3)
Jinti (1)	846	84 (9.9)	727 (85.9)	35 (4.2)
Jinti (2)	465	170 (36.6)	269 (57.8)	26 (5.6)
Khunte (1)	718	140 (19.5)	547 (76.2)	31 (4.3)
Khunte (2)	451	301 (66.7)	135 (29.9)	15 (3.4)
Shindevadi				
Somanthali	454	43 (9.5)	394 (86.8)	17 (3.7)
Kapadgaon	424	236 (55.7)	149 (35.1)	39 (9.2)
Koregaon				
Aradgaon	699	556 (79.5)	128 (18.3)	15 (2.2)
Taradgaon (1)	920	389 (42.3)	472 (51.3)	59 (6.4)

Appendix

Polling station	Total valid votes	K.R. Bhoite	V. M. Naik Nimbalkar	Other candidates
		(%)	(%)	(%)
Taradgaon (2)	842	272 (32.0)	488 (58.0)	82 (10.0)
Kalaj	764	387 (50.7)	268 (35.1)	109 (14.2)
Tadavale Suravadi	467	61 (13.1)	196 (42.0)	210 (44.9)
Nimbhore	963	129 (13.4)	740 (76.8)	94 (9.8)
Phaltan (14 polling stations)	10,695	1,261 (11.8)	9,252 (82.5)	182 (1.7)
Nandal	623	77 (12.4)	478 (76.7)	68 (10.9)
Saswad	978	794 (81.2)	91 (9.3)	93 (9.5)
Tambve	655	463 (70.7)	159 (24.3)	33 (5.0)
Hingangaon (1) Sherichivadi Salpe	555	394 (71.0)	132 (23.8)	29 (5.2)
Hingangaon (2)	678	325 (47.9)	315 (46.5)	38 (5.6)
Khadki Mirgaon	473	10 (2.1)	422 (89.2)	41 (8.7)
Wathar	817	39 (4.8)	747 (91.4)	31 (3.8)
Bibi (1) Ghadgevadi	465	31 (6.7)	409 (88.0)	25 (6.3)
Bibi (2)	709	92 (13.0)	554 (78.1)	63 (8.9)
Kapashi	606	248 (40.9)	307 (50.7)	51 (8.4)
Adarki Kh.	519	41 (7.9)	373 (71.9)	105 (20.2)
Adarki Bk.	589	139 (23.6)	423 (71.8)	27 (4.6)
3 *Postal Votes*		9	23	
4 *Total*	52,558	24,749 (47.1)	22,943 (43.7)	4,866 (9.2)

Notes

1   On the Bhairavnath fair see Chapter 8, p. 128. Bendur is an agricultural festival in honor of the bullocks which in Satara District occurs in Ashaḍh month (June/July) after the spring planting. In the morning the animals are decorated and in some households a *puja* is performed to them. In the afternoon the gaily decorated bullocks are taken in procession around the Maruti temple. In Girvi proper the procession is made up of lineage and caste groups in the order of their rank in the village, the highest first. The *vərči ali* Kadams, the founders of the village, lead the procession and are followed by the *khalči ali* Kadams, the Malis, the Sutars, the Ramoshis, and the Mahars. In each *vətəndar* Maratha Kadam lineage the leading position is taken by the *mukəddəm*. Separate processions are held in Dhumalvadi and Bodkevadi.

2   The *baluta* system of Maharashtra is equivalent to the *jajmani* system of North India (see Wiser 1936 and Beidelman 1959). The accounts of Loni, a village near Poona, by Coats (1823) and Ghurye (1960) give the best description of the *baluta* system in Maharashtra.

3   Many surnames in Maharashtra are formed by the addition of the suffix '*kər*', here meaning 'resident of', to a place name.

4   Maharashtra is composed of three regions: Western Maharashtra, formerly part of Bombay State; Vidarbha, formerly part of Madhya Pradesh, and Marathwada, formerly part of Hyderabad State. Western Maharashtra includes the Konkon as well as the Deccan Districts, but my argument is restricted to the latter.

5   *Vətəndar* Marathas were the predominant but not the only element in the political class in rural areas. Other important groups were the Brahmins, more influential then than now, and, in some villages, Dhangars (see Ballhatchet 1957; Kumar 1968; Latthe 1924; Seal 1968).

CHAPTER 3

1   '*Gav*' and the other words discussed here are so indefinite that it is difficult to classify settlements in terms of them. Therefore, one can give only an approximate idea of the size of community that informants would call a village. If one assumes that each of the revenue villages listed in the 1961 census corresponds to one and only one village in the sense in which I am now using the word then one can get a rough idea of the range and variation of village size. In 1961 the average revenue village in Phaltan Taluka had 1380 inhabitants. The smallest had 113 inhabitants and the largest had 8824. The latter, however, is unusual since it is the site of the privately owned Phaltan Sugar Works. In terms of their 1961 population the revenue villages of Phaltan Taluka may be grouped as follows:

0–499	18 villages	3000–3499	1 village
500–999	22 villages	3500–3999	3 villages
1000–1499	16 villages	4000–4499	0 villages
1500–1999	10 villages	4500–4999	2 villages
2000–2499	6 villages		
2500–2999	3 villages	8824	1 village

2   Karad: 33,772; Mahableshwar: 6029; Mhaswad: 10,405; Panchgani: 5725; Phaltan: 19,003; Rahimatpur: 9160; Satara: 48,709; Wai: 17,826. A municipality is a settlement with a particular form of government and may be either a town or a village. The two smallest municipalities, Panchgani and Mahableshwar, probably should not be considered towns in the usual sense. They have a municipal form of government because they are important hill stations, not because of their size and complexity. If they are excluded, then the average size of towns in Satara District is 23,145.

3   The only distinction between 'taluka' and 'mahal' is one of size. A mahal is generally smaller than a taluka although in Satara District the only mahal, Khandala, is larger than Mahableshwar Taluka.

4   Population of talukas in Satara District (1961 Census):

Taluka/Mahal	Rural population	No. of revenue villages	Avg. size of villages	Urban area	Total population
Jaoli	80,091	168	476		80,091
Karad	215,787	113	1,910	Karad: 33,772	251,640
				Karad Rural Area: 2081	
Khandala	63,164	46	1,373		63,164
Khatav	155,930	90	1,733		155,930
Koregaon	129,678	75	1,729	Rahimatpur: 9160	138,838
Mahableshwar	12,616	54	234	Panchgani: 5725	24,370
				Mahableshwar: 6029	
Man	80,091	70	1,272	Mhasvad: 10,405	99,410
Patan	180,501	186	970		180,501
Phaltan	113,265	82	1,380	Phaltan: 19,003	140,102
				Phaltan Rural Area 7834	
Satara	142,604	156	921	Satara: 48,709	191,313
Wai	86,920	90	966	Wai: 17,826	104,746
	1,269,561	1,130	1,124	160,544	1,430,105

5   For purposes of administering development grants a standard block is considered to have a population of one hundred thousand, but this figure rarely applies to the old talukas, all of which have been left intact. Therefore, a taluka such as Phaltan, which in 1967 had a population of about one hundred and fifty thousand, receives one and a half times the standard block grant from the Maharashtra State Government.

6   For descriptions of rural administration in India see Khera (1964) and Potter (1964).

7   This provision applied to the local government elections of August 1967. For the 1962 election each electoral division was divided into two electoral colleges consisting of the members of the panchayats in the electoral college area. In 1962 only panchayat chairmen were allowed to be candidates. One panchayat chairman was elected from each electoral college.

8   The basic document on the introduction of the panchayati raj system of local self-government is the *Report of the Team for the Study of Community Projects and National*

Extension Service (New Delhi: Committee on Plan Projects, 1957) often referred to as the *Report of the Balvantray Mehta Committee*. See also Potter (1964), Chapters VII and VIII. For the introduction of panchayati raj in Andhra Pradesh see Weiner (1967), Part II, Chapters 9 and 10 and Appendix 1. The panchayati raj legislation passed by Maharashtra differs in several respects from that of other states. See the *Report of the Committee on Democratic Decentralization* (Bombay: Co-operation and Rural Development Department, Govt. of Maharashtra, 1961) for the history of local government in Maharashtra and an account of the State's thinking on panchayati raj.

9   For a history of the co-operative movement in the Bombay Presidency see Catanach (1970).

10   Four Zilla Parishad Councillors, one President of the Panchayat Samiti, one MLA, and the chairmen or presidents of the Municipal Council, the Phaltan Taluka Purchase and Sale Union, the Phaltan Urban Co-operative Bank, the Shriram Co-operative Sugar Factory, the Phaltan Co-operative Cotton Ginning and Pressing Society, the Phaltan Taluka Supervising Union, the Phaltan Education Society, and the Shriram Education Society.

CHAPTER 5

1   It is not known to what extent the provisions of the law were carried out. Dandekar and Khudanpur state 'that for one reason or the other, a large number of tenancies existing on land during 1947–48 were not recorded to be protected tenants'. (1957:4)

2   After 1952 a landlord could terminate a tenancy only when the land under his personal cultivation did not exceed 16 acres of dry land or 4 acres of wet land or any equivalent combination. Otherwise he could resume only half the land held by a tenant (Dandekar and Khudanpur 1957:6).

3   The largest single non-resident occupant is a *vatandar* Maratha, V. M. Naik Nimbalkar, the Raja of Phaltan's son.

4   But see the description of the use of Girvi Fair Committee funds in Chapter 8.

5   Ramrao's brother was Chairman of the Girvi Credit Society for two years. He was succeeded in 1966 by Govindrao's son. Prior to 1948 when the Girvi Credit Society was founded a Jain merchant who lived in Girvi was the village's biggest moneylender, but he left the village shortly after Independence and his house (Map 3, *J*4) is now owned and occupied by Govindrao Mahhavrao.

CHAPTER 6

1   Other authorities disagree. Enthoven (1922b:21) reports that the Kadam clan has three *devaks*: *haḷad* (tumeric), *kagad* (Screw pine, Pandanus odoratissimus), and *sone* (gold).

2   The prestige attaching to *vatan* land is well illustrated by the following case. S. L. Kadam (Genealogy 1a, *J*26) is a non-resident member of the *varči ali* Kadam lineage. His ancestors owned the palace (*vaḍa*) near the Vitthal temple (see Map 3), but his great grandfather (Genealogy 1a, *G*14) married a daughter of the Maharaja of Baroda and the family went to live in Baroda where they now own considerable property and move in the highest circles. Kadam had nearly 85 acres of *vatan* land in Girvi, 35 of it irrigated, which were cultivated by *khalči ali* lineage tenants. In 1957 the tenants were awarded occupancy

rights under the Bombay Tenancy and Agricultural Lands (Amendment) Act of 1956, but Kadam appealed the award and in an out of court settlement ten years later won the return of 26 acres, 10 of them irrigated. The significant thing is that Kadam immediately made arrangements for one of his Girvi lineage mates to cultivate the land rent free. He went to great expense to keep some of his land not for any economic interests, but solely for reasons of sentiment and prestige. He explained that Girvi is his *vətən* village. Everyone recognizes him as a 'Girvikar Kadam', a *bona fide vətəndar* Maratha, and if he had no land there he would feel that he belonged nowhere.

3   Orenstein reports that in Gaon, a village in southern Poona District, two terms were used for lineage subdivisions, '*ilana*' for 'major division' and '*təksim*' for 'minimal segment' (1965:80–3). None of my own informants used or understood this usage, although they knew that '*təksim*' meant a share of a coparceny and could be used to refer, for example, to a group which held a share in a patilship (see Molesworth and Candy).

4   See also my paper 'Household Partition in Rural Western Maharashtra' (1971).

CHAPTER 7

1   For the opinion that 'faction' was introduced into the Indian literature by Lewis see Dumont (1970:163, 312). The earlier literature on factions in Indian politics is reviewed by Miller (1965).

2   Nicholas writes that: 'There are, broadly speaking, two ways of approaching factions which lead to different though equally useful results: one approach focuses on the analysis of political conflict, the other on the analysis of political organization.' (1965:22)

3   The Beals and Siegel theory is given its fullest expression in their book *Divisiveness and Social Conflict* (1966). See also Beals (1955a, 1955b, 1959 and 1961) and Beals and Siegel (1960a and 1960b).

4   Both Brass and Weiner have noted that factions do perform positive functions for the society as a whole as well as for the individual. Brass accepts that factions may refuse to accept majority decisions, prevent the development of a consenus, and inhibit the organization of interest groups, but he argues that they still perform some useful integrative functions. Factions are active in enrolling primary Congress members and broadening party participation. Factional loyalties protect the unity of the larger Congress party from ideological and communal splits. The position of the Congress is protected also by the fluidity of multi-faction systems (Brass 1965:238–44; see also Brass 1964). Weiner observes that factionalism has helped the Congress party adapt to the new panchayati raj forms of local government (1967:160).

5   Barnes continues that the concept of network 'is appropriate where enduring groups such as parties and factions have not formed, and where individuals are continually required to make choices about whom they should look to for leadership, help, information and guidance.' (1968:109) He errs here in attributing permanence to factions.

6   Holmström feels that Mayer's analysis of linkage content is inadequate. He argues that the links of a political action-set are of two kinds: (*a*) those based on respect and (*b*) those based on disinterested appeals to reason or ideology. 'In matters affecting the public good, appeals to respect tend to be more transactional than appeals to disinterested reason.' (1969:92) But even the most interested transactions have a moral quality and it is this which Holmström labels respect (1969:90–1). No doubt Holmström is right, but except in public speeches I heard few disinterested appeals to reason or ideology. Nor have I

found his concept of respect particularly useful; the purely transactional aspect of alliances seems to have been uppermost in the minds of the persons with whom I have worked.

7   See Appendix 'Results of the 1967 General Election in Phaltan-Khandala'.

8   On the politics of states reorganization in India see Windmiller (1956), Harrison (1960), and Nayar (1966).

9   Why does one Kadam lineage allow the other to acquire attached clients? In addition to its interest in defeating the opposing lineage, each Kadam lineage shares with the other an interest in maintaining their joint dominance. Note that the attached members of each lineage are confined to wards in which proper members of their lineage are concentrated. The *vərči ali* Kadams, for example, do not have attached supporters in wards dominated by *khalči ali* Kadams. Thus attached supporters of one lineage do not constitute a threat to the other lineage.

CHAPTER 8

1   When the new Managing Committee of the Credit Society elected its Chairman in October 1966 Amrutrao Bapusaheb's strongest supporter for re-election was Mugatrao's youngest brother, Devrao.

2   Malojirao Kadam now lives in Phaltan.

3   The antagonism between the families of Mugatrao and Chimanrao was a factor in the 1967 Zilla Parishad election also. In the General Election the Girvi Kadams were united in support of Vijaysingh Naik Nimbalkar and G. B. Mane. After the General Election the Kadams again split. Chimanrao emerged as a leading candidate for nomination by the Raja's party for Zilla Parishad Councillor. He had been of great service to the Raja and had the support of most members of the two Kadam lineages in Girvi. Mugatrao's family opposed Chimanrao and in an attempt to cut away Chimanrao's *khalči ali* support they suggested that the Raja nominate a young lecturer in Mudhoji College who belongs to the *khalči ali* lineage. The Raja rejected that suggestion, however, and eventually decided to give his support to Chimanrao. Although Mugatrao's family was then and still is allied closely with the Raja they still refused to support Chimanrao and offered to pay the campaign expenses of his opponent, the incumbent Vasantrao Janavale who stood for re-election as an Independent.

4   Keshavrao Appasaheb's daughter, Mugatrao's *putəni*, was given a dowry of Rs. 4000 in May 1967.

5   Vijaymala came to most Panchayat meetings but rarely spoke. Dattatrya continued to take a leading role.

6   Bhosle is a member of one of Phaltan's highest ranking *vətəndar* Maratha families. They held the Phaltan Patilship and thus ranked behind the Raja's lineage and that of the Inamdar Naik Nimbalkars of Wathar but ahead of the Patils of less important revenue villages. The long standing conflict between M. M. Naik Nimbalkar, Raja of Phaltan, and S. R. Bhosle has its origins in the pre-Independence politics of Phaltan State. Bhosle was elected to the Phaltan Legislative Council in 1940 and again in 1944. The Council elected him Vice-President (the President was nominated by the Raja) and he was made Law Member of the Raja's Executive Council (the other members of the Executive Council were nominated also). In 1945 Bhosle was dismissed from office by the Raja. According to Bhosle he could be removed from office properly only by a vote of no confidence by the Legislative Council which, in fact, refused to accept his dismissal. The Council was dis-

solved and new elections were held in 1946, but Bhosle and his friends were re-elected. The dispute persisted through the attempt to organize the Deccan States Union and ended only when the outbreak of rioting following the assassination of Gandhi forced the merger of the Deccan States with Bombay (see Menon 1961).

7   The most important source of revenue for the Phaltan Municipal Council is an octroi on goods and animals brought into the town. As long as the Shriram Sugar Factory stands outside the Municipal boundaries its imports are not taxable.

8   Babanrao Adsul and Haribhau Nimbalkar, allies of K. R. Bhoite, also hoped to win More's support against the Raja. In June 1966 during negotiations concerning the new Phaltan administration they led a strike of municipal employees against Mane's administration which ended when More took office.

CHAPTER 9

1   Unfortunately, I do not know when Jadhav was elected to the Board. By 1966 when his friend K. R. Bhoite won the Congress ticket for the General Election Jadhav was in opposition again. But Bhosle and Date were not completely comfortable with all of Bhoite's friends and they did not accept Jadhav as an ally in the Factory.

2   If Dumont (1970) is correct that Hindu ideology stresses hierarchy and holism while modern European ideology stresses individualism then it is appropriate that the political order of the former is justified by an appeal to consensus and that of the latter by an appeal to the balance of power.

3   For more on the economics of patronage see Wilson (1961). Riker's discussion of side-payments (1962:108–23) and Homan's analysis of the role of a group leader in the group's transactions with the external world (1951:170; also Whyte 1955) are relevant too. Mayer discusses some of the implications of community development for political patronage in 'Some Political Implications of Community Development in India' (1963a).

CHAPTER 10

1   Mutual interests are reciprocated and imply a degree of co-operation, while common interests frequently lead to competition (see Dyson-Hudson 1966:87).

2   For examples of the view of caste as a primordial group or as an object of primordial loyalty see Rosenthal (1970) and Béteille (1970:261).

3   Similar views are held by Gough (1960) and Bailey (1963c).

4   The Rudolphs' book also contains an excellent review of the literature on caste and politics up to 1967. For the later literature see Kothari (1970).

5   These remarks are based on Dumont's *Homo Hierarchicus* (1970), especially Chapter 3, 'Hierarchy: The Theory of the Varna'. Dumont is not alone in his view that caste is essentially a ritual institution: see also Hocart (1950), Srinivas (1952) and Harper (1964). One implication of this view is that although Leach (1960) and Bailey (1963c) are in one sense right that caste is a non-competitive system, they at the same time are wrong in thinking that economic and political competition are proscribed. In fact only in the ritual domain is caste non-competitive. It seems to me that Béteille's (1969) critique of Leach and Bailey in which he argues that castes are not non-antagonistic and that political and economic competition may occur errs in part in confusing them with Dumont and arguing that legitimate ritual competition may occur too.

6 See Barth (1966) for a discussion of the role of the entrepreneur in developing new patterns of cultural integration. Stein (1968) presents material which suggests that similar exchanges of ritual status and political support took place in South India in the fifteenth century. Sāḷuva Narasiṃha, a Teluga warrior with headquarters near Tirupati and a major supporter of the Tiruveṃgaḍam Temple at Tirupati, and his agent in the Temple seem to have recruited Sudra political support by providing them with important ritual offices in the Temple. One may speculate that the *bhakti* sect was in some respects the medieval equivalent of the modern caste association. If so then it would imply that the process of integration between caste and politics brought about by the interaction of social organization and social structure is in operation continually. The process has many consequences noted by the Rudolphs, but it is not solely a modern development in India.

7 For examples of the dilemma of low castes faced with the necessity of choosing between status and power see Béteille (1965), Hardgrave (1969), and Parry (1970).

References

Bailey, F. G. (1963a). 'Politics and society in contemporary Orissa', in *Politics and Society in India* (C. H. Philips, ed.) (London: George Allen & Unwin Ltd).
 (1963b). *Politics and Social Change, Orissa in 1959* (Berkeley: University of California Press).
 (1963c). 'Closed social stratification in India', *Archives of European Sociology* 4: 107–24.
 (1965). 'Decisions by consensus in councils and committees: with special reference to village and local government in India', in *Political Systems and the Distribution of Power*, A.S.A. Monographs 2 (London: Tavistock Publications).
 (1968). 'Parapolitical systems', in *Local-Level Politics* (Marc J. Swartz, ed.) (Chicago: Aldine Publishing Co.).
Ballhatchet, Kenneth (1957). *Social Policy and Social Change in Western India* (London: Oxford University Press).
Barnes, J. A. (1954). 'Class and committees in a Norwegian island parish', *Human Relations* 7: 39–58.
 (1968). 'Networks and political process', in *Local-Level Politics* (Marc J. Swartz, ed.) (Chicago: Aldine Publishing Co.).
Barth, Fredrik (1959a). *Political Leadership among the Swat Pathans* (London: LSE Monographs on Social Anthropology, No. 19).
 (1959b). 'Segmentary opposition and the theory of games', *Journal of the Royal Anthropological Institute* 89: 5–22.
 (1966). *Models of Social Organization* (London: Royal Anthropological Institute Occasional Paper No. 23).
Beals, Alan R. (1955a). 'Change in the leadership of a Mysore village', in *India's Villages* (M. N. Srinivas, ed.) (Bombay: Asia Publishing House).
 (1955b). 'Interplay among factors of change in a Mysore village', in *Village India* (McKim Marriott, ed.) (Chicago: University of Chicago Press).
 (1959). 'Leadership in a Mysore village', in *Leadership and Political Institutions in India* (R. L. Park and I. Tinker, eds) (Princeton: Princeton University Press).
 (1961). 'Cleavage and internal conflict: an example from India', *Journal of Conflict Resolution* 5: 27–34.
 (1962). *Gopalpur* (New York: Holt, Rinehart & Winston).
Beals, Alan R. and Bernard J. Siegel (1960a). 'Conflict and factionalist dispute', *Journal of the Royal Anthropological Institute* 90: 107–17.
 (1960b). 'Pervasive factionalism', *American Anthropologist* 62: 394–418.
 (1966). *Divisiveness and Social Conflict* (Stanford: Stanford University Press).
Beidelman, T. O. (1959). *A Comparative Analysis of the Jajmani System* (Locust Valley, N.Y.: J. J. Augustin, Monographs of the Association for Asian Studies, VII).
Benedict, Burton (1957). 'Factionalism in Mauritian Villages', *British Journal of Sociology* 8: 328–42.

References

Béteille, André (1965). 'The future of the backward classes: the competing demands of status and power.' *Perspectives, A Supplement to the Indian Journal of Public Administration* 12:1–39.

—— (1967). 'Elite, status groups, and caste in modern India', in *India and Ceylon: Unity and Diversity* (P. Mason, ed.) (London: Oxford University Press).

—— (1969). 'The politics of "non-antagonistic" strata', *Contributions to Indian Sociology* 3 (NS):17–31.

—— (1970). 'Caste and political group formation in Tamilnad', in *Caste in Indian Politics* (Rajni Kothari, ed.) (New Delhi: Orient Longmans Ltd).

Bottomore, T. B. (1966). *Elites and Society* (Harmondsworth, Middlesex: Penguin Books) (first published 1964).

—— (1967). 'Cohesion and division in Indian elites', in *India and Ceylon: Unity and Diversity* (P. Mason, ed.) (London: Oxford University Press).

Brass, Paul R. (1964). 'Factionalism and the Congress Party in Uttar Pradesh', *Asian Survey* 4:1037–47.

—— (1965). *Factional Politics in an Indian State* (Berkeley: University of California Press).

Brecher, Michael (1966). *Succession in India* (London: Oxford University Press).

Broomfield, J. H. (1966). 'The regional elites: a theory of modern Indian history', *The Indian Economic and Social History Review* 3:279–90.

—— (1968). *Elite Conflict in a Plural Society: Twentieth Century Bengal* (Berkeley: University of California Press).

Carr, E. H. (1949). *The Twenty Years Crisis* (London: Macmillan) (reprint of 2nd edition).

Carter, Anthony T. (1971). 'Household partition in rural Western Maharashtra', paper presented at the 1971 Annual Meeting of the American Anthropological Association, New York.

Catanach, I. J. (1970). *Rural Credit in Western India* (Berkeley: University of California Press).

Coats, Thomas (1823). 'Account of the present state of the township of Lony', *Transactions of the Literary Society of Bombay* 3:172–280.

Colson, E. (1962). 'Social control and vengeance', in *The Plateau Tonga of Northern Rhodesia* (E. Colson) (Manchester: Manchester University Press).

Dandekar, V. M. and G. J. Khudanpur (1957). *Working of Bombay Tenancy Act, 1948: Report of Investigation* (Poona: Gokhale Institute of Politics and Economics, Publication No. 35).

Deleury, G. A. (1960). *The Cult of Vithoba* (Poona: Deccan College Postgraduate and Research Institute).

Derrett, J. D. M. (1963). *Introduction to Modern Hindu Law* (Bombay: Oxford University Press).

Dhillon, Harvant Singh (1955). *Leadership and Groups in a South India Village* (New Delhi: Government of India Press; Planning Commission, Program Evaluation Organization).

Dobbin, Christine (1970). 'Competing elites in Bombay city politics in the mid-nineteenth century (1852–83)', in *Elites in South Asia* (E. R. Leach and S. N. Mukherjee, eds) (Cambridge: Cambridge University Press).

Dube, S. C. (1968). 'Caste dominance and factionalism', *Contributions to Indian Sociology* 2 (NS):58–81.

Dumont, Louis (1950). 'Kinship and alliance among the Pramalai Kallar', *Eastern Anthropologist* 4:3–26.

References

(1953). 'The Dravidian kinship terminology as an expression of marriage', *Man* 53: Art. 54.

(1957). *Hierarchy and Marriage Alliance in South Indian Kinship* (London: Royal Anthropological Institute Occasional Paper No. 12).

(1961). 'Marriage in India, the present state of the question, part I', *Contributions to Indian Sociology* 5:75–95.

(1962). 'The concept of kingship in ancient India', *Contributions to Indian Sociology* 6:48–77.

(1970). *Homo Hierarchicus: An Essay on the Caste System* (trans. by Mark Sainsbury) (Chicago: University of Chicago Press).

Dyson-Hudson, Neville (1966). *Karimojong Politics* (Oxford: Clarendon Press).

Elphinstone, Mountstuart (1821). *Report on the Territory Conquered from the Paishwa* (Calcutta: Government Gazette Press).

Enthoven, R. E. (1920). *The Tribes and Castes of Bombay*, Volume I (Bombay: Government Central Press).

(1922a). *The Tribes and Castes of Bombay*, Volume II (Bombay: Government Central Press).

(1922b). *The Tribes and Castes of Bombay*, Volume III (Bombay Government Central Press).

Firth, Raymond (1954). 'Social organization and social change', *Journal of the Royal Anthropological Institute* 84:1–20.

(1955). 'Some principles of social organization', *Journal of the Royal Anthropological Institute* 85:1–18.

(1957). Introduction to 'Factions in Indian and overseas Indian communities', *British Journal of Sociology* 8:291–5.

(1961). *Elements of Social Organization* (3rd ed.) (London: Watts).

(1964). 'Comments on "dynamic theory" in social anthropology', in *Essays on Social Organization and Values* (R. Firth) (London: The Athlone Press).

Fortes, Meyer (1945). *The Dynamics of Clanship among the Tallensi* (London: Oxford University Press).

(1949a). *The Web of Kinship among the Tallensi* (London: Oxford University Press).

(1949b). 'Time and social structure: an Ashanti case study', in *Social Structure: Studies Presented to A. R. Radcliffe-Brown* (M. Fortes, ed.) (Oxford: Clarendon Press).

(1953a). 'The structure of unilineal descent groups', *American Anthropologist* 55:17–41.

(1953b). 'Analysis and description in social anthropology', *The Advancement of Science* 10:190–201.

(1969). *Kinship and the Social Order* (Chicago: Aldine Publishing Co.).

Frykenberg, R. E. (1965). *Guntur District 1788–1848* (Oxford: Clarendon Press).

Fürer-Haimendorf, C. von (1963). 'Caste and politics in South Asia', in *Politics and Society in India* (C. H. Philips, ed.) (London: George Allen and Unwin Ltd).

Gardner, Peter M. (1968). 'Dominance in India: a re-appraisal', *Contributions to Indian Sociology* 2 (NS):82–97.

Ghurye, G. S. (1960). *After a Century and a Quarter* (Bombay: Popular Book Depot).

Gluckman, Max (1963). 'The peace in the feud', in *Custom and Conflict in Africa* (M. Gluckman) (Oxford: Basil Blackwell).

Gooddine, R. N. (1852). *Reports on the Village Communities of the Deccan* (Bombay: Selections from the Records of the Bombay Government, 4).

References

Gordon, R. G. (1959). *The Bombay Survey and Settlement Manual* (2nd ed.) (Nagpur: Government Press).

Gough, E. Kathleen (1960). 'Caste in a Tanjore Village', in *Aspects of Caste in South India, Ceylon and North-west Pakistan* (E. R. Leach, ed.) (Cambridge: Cambridge Papers in Social Anthropology No. 2).

Government of Bombay (1890). 'Papers Relating to the Revision Survey Settlement of 72 Government Villages of the Man Taluka of the Satara Collectorate', *Selections from the Records of the Bombay Government*, No. CCXL (NS) (Bombay: Government Central Press).

Government of India (1957). *Report of the Study Team on Community Development (Balwantray Mehta Committee)* (New Delhi: Committee on Plan Projects).

Government of Maharashtra (1961). *Report of the Committee on Democratic Decentralisation* (Bombay: Government Central Press).

(1963). *Satara District Census Handbook, 1961* (Bombay: Government Press).

Gray, Hugh (1962). 'The 1962 general election in a rural district of Andhra', *Asian Survey* 2:25–35.

(1963). 'The 1962 Indian general election in a communist stronghold of Andhra Pradesh', *Journal of Commonwealth Political Studies* 1:296–311.

(1970). 'The landed gentry of the Telengana, Andhra Pradesh', in *Elites in South Asia* (E. R. Leach and S. N. Mukherjee, eds) (Cambridge: Cambridge University Press).

Hardgrave, R. (1969). *The Nadars of Tamilnad: the Political Culture of a Community in Change* (Berkeley: University of California Press).

Harper, E. B. (1964). 'Ritual pollution as an integrator of caste and religion', *The Journal of Asian Studies* 23:151–96.

Harrison, Selig (1956). 'Caste and the Andhra Communists', *American Political Science Review* 50:378–404.

(1960). *India: the Most Dangerous Decades* (Princeton: Princeton University Press).

Hocart, A. M. (1950). *Caste: a Comparative Study* (London: Methuen).

Holmström, Mark (1969). 'Action-sets and ideology: a municipal election in South India', *Contributions to Indian Sociology* 3 (NS):76–93.

Homans, George C. (1951). *The Human Group* (London: Routledge and Kegan Paul).

Johnson, Gordon (1970). 'Chitpavan Brahmins and Politics in Western India in the late nineteeth and early twentieth centuries,' in *Elites in South Asia* (E. R. Leach and S. N. Mukherjee, eds) (Cambridge: Cambridge University Press).

Karve, I. (1961). *Hindu Society: an Interpretation* (Poona: Deccan College Postgraduate and Research Institute).

(1965). *Kinship Organization in India* (2nd ed.) (Bombay: Asia Publishing House).

Karve, I. and J. S. Ranadive (1965). *The Social Dynamics of a Growing Town and its Surrounding Area* (Poona: Deccan College Postgraduate and Research Institute).

Khera, S. S. (1964). *District Administration in India* (Bombay: Asia Publishing House).

Kothari, Rajni (ed.) (1970). *Caste in Indian Politics* (New Delhi: Orient Longmans).

Kothari, Rajni and Rushikesh Maru (1965). 'Caste and secularism in India', *Journal of Asian Studies* 24:33–50.

(1970). 'Federating for political interests: the Kshatriyas of Gujarat', in *Caste in Indian Politics* (R. Kothari, ed.) (New Delhi: Orient Longmans).

References

Kumar, Pavinder (1968). *Western India in the Nineteenth Century* (London: Routledge and Kegan Paul).

Lasswell, Harold D. (1931). 'Faction', in *Encyclopedia of Social Science* 3:49.

Latthe, A. B. (1924). *Memoirs of His Highness Shri Shahu Chhatrapati, Maharaja of Kolhapur* (Bombay: Times Press).

Leach, E. R. (1954). *Political Systems of Highland Burma* (London: G. Bell and Sons).

(1960). 'Introduction: what should we mean by caste?' in *Aspects of Caste in South India, Ceylon and North-west Pakistan* (E. R. Leach, ed.) (Cambridge: Cambridge Papers in Social Anthropology, No. 2).

(1961). *Pul Eliya, a Village in Ceylon* (Cambridge: Cambridge University Press).

Leach, E. R. and S. N. Mukherjee (eds) (1970). *Elites in South Asia* (Cambridge: Cambridge University Press).

Levi, Edward H. (1949). *An Introduction to Legal Reasoning* (Chicago: University of Chicago Press).

Lewis, Oscar (1954). 'Group dynamics in a North Indian village', *The Economic Weekly* 6:423–5, 445–51, 477–82, 501–6.

(1955). 'Peasant culture in India and Mexico: a comparative analysis', in *Village India* (McKim Marriott, ed.) (Chicago: University of Chicago Press).

(1958). *Village Life in Northern India* (Urbana: University of Illinois Press).

Lijphart, Arend (1969). *The Politics of Accommodation: Pluralism and Democracy in the Netherlands* (Berkeley: University of California Press).

Mayer, Adrian C. (1957). 'Factions in Fiji Indian rural settlements', *British Journal of Sociology* 8:317–28.

(1958a). 'The dominant caste in a region of Central India', *Southwestern Journal of Anthropology* 14:407–27.

(1958b). 'Local government elections in a Malwa village', *Eastern Anthropologist* 11:97–108.

(1960). *Caste and Kinship in Central India* (London: Routledge and Kegan Paul).

(1962). 'System and network: an approach to the study of politics in Dewas', in *Indian Anthropology* (T. N. Madan and G. Sarana, eds) (London: Asia Publishing House).

(1963a). 'Some political implications of community development in India', *Archives of European Sociology* 4:86–106.

(1963b). 'Municipal elections: a Central India case study', in *Politics and Society in India* (C. H. Philips, ed.) (London: George Allen & Unwin Ltd).

(1966). 'The significance of quasi-groups in the study of complex societies', in *The Social Anthropology of Complex Societies*. A.S.A. Monograph 4 (London: Tavistock Publications).

(1967a). 'Caste and local politics in India', in *India and Ceylon: Unity and Diversity* (Philip Mason, ed.) (London: Oxford University Press).

(1967b). 'Patrons and brokers: rural leadership in four overseas Indian communities', in *Social Organization: Essays Presented to Raymond Firth* (Maurice Freedman, ed.) (London: Frank Cass and Co. Ltd).

Menon, V. P. (1961). *The Story of the Integration of the Indian States* (Bombay: Orient Longmans) (first published in 1956).

Mills, C. Wright (1959). *The Power Elite* (New York: Galaxy Books) (first published in 1956).

Miller, D. F. (1965). 'Factions in Indian village politics', *Pacific Affairs* 38:17–31.

Molesworth, J. T., George Candy and Thomas Candy (1857). *A Dictionary, Marathi and English* (2nd ed.) (Bombay: Bombay Education Society Press).

References

Morris, H. S. (1957). 'Communal rivalry among Indians in Uganda', *British Journal of Sociology* 8:306–17.

Morris-Jones, W. H. (1960). 'The unhappy utopia – JP in wonderland', *The Economic Weekly* 12:1027–31.

Mosca, Gaetano (1939). *The Ruling Class* (trans. by Hannah D. Kahn) (New York: McGraw-Hill).

Mukherjee, S. N. (1970). 'Class, caste and politics in Calcutta, 1815–38', in *Elites in South Asia* (E. R. Leach and S. N. Mukherjee, eds) (Cambridge: Cambridge University Press).

Namier, Sir Lewis (1957). *The Structure of Politics at the Accession of George III* (2nd ed.) (London: Macmillan).

(1961). *England in the Age of the American Revolution* (2nd ed.) (London: Macmillan).

Nayar, Baldev Raj (1966). *Minority Politics in the Punjab* (Princeton: Princeton University Press).

Neale, Walter C. (1969). 'Land is to rule', in *Land Control and Social Structure in Indian History* (Robert E. Frykenberg, ed.) (Madison: University of Wisconsin Press).

Nicholas, Ralph W. (1965). 'Factions: a comparative analysis', in *Political Systems and the Distribution of Power*, A.S.A. Monograph 2 (London: Tavistock Publications).

Orenstein, Henry (1965). *Gaon* (Princeton: Princeton University Press).

Parry, J. P. (1970). 'The Koli dilemma', *Contributions to Indian Sociology* 4 (N.S.):84–104.

Pocock, David F. (1957). 'The bases of faction in Gujarat', *British Journal of Sociology* 8:269–306.

Potter, David C. (1964). *Government in Rural India* (London: London School of Economics and Political Science).

Radcliffe-Brown, A. R. (1953). 'Dravidian kinship terminology', *Man* 53: Art. 169.

Riker, William (1962). *The Theory of Political Coalitions* (New Haven: Yale University Press).

Rivers, W. H. R. (1968). *Kinship and Social Organization* (London: The Athlone Press) (first published 1914).

Rosenthal, Donald B. (1970). *The Limited Elite: Politics and Government in Two Indian Cities* (Chicago: University of Chicago Press).

Rowe, William L. (1968). *The new Cauhans: a caste mobility movement in North India*, in *Social Mobility in the Caste System in India* (J. Silverberg, ed.) (The Hague: Mouton, Comparative Studies in Society and History, Supplement III).

Rudolph, L. S. (1965). 'The modernity of tradition: the democratic incarnation of caste', *American Political Science Review* 59:975–89.

Rudolph, L. S. and S. H. Rudolph (1960). 'The political role of India's caste associations', *Pacific Affairs* 33:5–22.

(1967). *The Modernity of Tradition* (Chicago: University of Chicago Press).

Scheffler, Harold W. (1971). 'Dravidian-Iroquois: the Melanesian evidence', in *Anthropology in Oceania* (L. R. Hiatt and C. Jayawardena, eds) (Sydney: Angus Robertson).

Seal, Anil (1968). *The Emergence of Indian Nationalism* (Cambridge: Cambridge University Press).

Sirsikar, V. M. (1970). *The Rural Elite in a Developing Society* (New Delhi: Orient Longmans Ltd).

References

Srinivas, M. N. (1952). *Religion and Society among the Coorgs of South India* (Bombay: Asia Publishing House).

(1955). 'The social structure of a Mysore Village,' in *Village India* (McKim Marriott ed.) (Chicago: University of Chicago Press).

(1959). 'The dominant caste in Rampura', *American Anthropologist* 61:1–16.

Srinivas, M. N. and André Béteille (1964). 'Network in Indian social structure', *Man* 64:165–8.

Steele, Arthur (1868). *The Law and Customs of Hindoo Castes within the Dekhun Provinces Subject to the Presidency of Bombay* (London: W. H. Allen and Co.).

Stein, Burton (1968). 'Social mobility and medieval South Indian Hindu sects', in *Social Mobility in the Caste System in India* (J. Silverberg, ed.) (The Hague: Mouton, Comparative Studies in Society and History, Supplement III).

Stokes, Eric (1970). 'Traditional elites in the Great Rebellion of 1857: some aspects of rural revolt in the Upper and Central Doab', in *Elites in South Asia* (E. R. Leach and S. N. Mukherjee, eds) (Cambridge: Cambridge University Press).

Valunjkar, T. N. (1966). *Social Organization, Migration and Change in a Village Community* (Poona: Deccan College Postgraduate and Research Institute, Deccan College Dissertation Series No. 28).

Weiner, Myron (1957). *Party Politics in India* (Princeton: Princeton University Press).

(1967). *Party Building in a New Nation: the Indian National Congress* (Chicago: University of Chicago Press).

Whyte, William F. (1955). *Street Corner Society* (2nd ed.) (Chicago: University of Chicago Press).

Wilson, James Q. (1961). 'The economy of patronage', *Journal of Political Economy* 69:369–80.

Windmiller, Marshall (1956). 'The politics of states reorganization in India: the case of Bombay', *Far Eastern Survey* 25:129–43.

Wiser, W. H. (1936). *The Hindu Jajmani System* (Lucknow: Lucknow Publishing House).

Yalman, Nur (1967). *Under the Bo Tree* (Berkeley: University of California Press).

Zelliott, E. (1966). 'Buddhism and politics in Maharashtra', in *South Asian Politics and Religion* (Donald Smith, ed.) (Princeton: Princeton University Press).

General Index

(An Index of Persons follows)

action-set, 9, 106–7, 172–3
alliances, horizontal, 7–8, 101, 107, 112–16, 118–21, 153, 158–61, 163–4, 174–8; and arenas, 127, 138; and caste, 127, 138, 142–4; and kinship, 127, 138–42; and occasions, 127, 144–6; in General Election (1967), 110–21; in Girvi politics, 127–38; in Phaltan Municipal politics, 144–6; in Phaltan Taluka politics, 138–44
alliances, instability of horizontal, 5–8, 142, 147–9, 174; and consensus decision-making, 153–8; and indirect elections, 151–3; and structural frameworks, 149–160; as index of political stratification, 150–60
alliances, vertical, 7–8, 101, 107, 112, 114–16, 149–50, 158–61, 163, 174–8; and arenas, 114–21; and economic patronage, 121–2, 125–6; and kinship and affinity, 122–4; and occasions, 107, 114, 144; and ritual caste status, 121–4; in General Election (1967), 112, 115–21; in Girvi Panchayat election, 122–6, 130
Ambedkar, Babasaheb, 178
arenas, 8, 12, 48, 138–9, 141–2, 156, 160, 162, 164, 168, 175–7
Andhra, 169–70, 174–5

Bagri, 173
baluta/balutedar, 17, 22–3, 30, 62, 188
Bariya, 172–3
Baroda District, 172–3
Beldar, 47, 148
Bendur, 17, 25, 30, 54, 87, 127
Bhairavnath fair, 17, 31, 127–30, 188
bhakti, 19, 20, 55
Bhatake, 56
bhaubund, see under lineage
bhauki, see under kinship, categories of
Bhil, 172–3
binvirodh, 108, 112, 136, 145, 151, 153, 155–6
Bodkevadi, 15–17, 84–6, 88, 96, 117, 122, 125, 188
Brahmin, 16–17, 22–3, 38, 47–9, 51–6, 69–70, 74–5, 109, 117, 121–2, 127–9, 142–6, 149, 156, 162–3, 174, 176

caste, 22–3, 30, 61, 138, 167; and dominance, 5, 29, 49–51; hierarchy in Girvi, 54; in relation to credit, 74–5, 129; in relation to labor, 71–3; in relation to land, 67–71; in relation to office, 4–5, 46–8; in relation to political alliances, 121–4, 126–7, 138, 142–4, 149–51, 159, 167–74; numerical distribution, 51–7; principle of hierarchy, 49–51, 171–2; *see also under individual castes*
caste associations, 168–9, 172–4
Chambhar, 16, 22, 38, 47, 51–2, 54, 56, 68, 70, 74–5
Chauhan, 173
choice, *see under* social organization
clan, 79, 96–7, 120, 128, 138–9; and marriage rules, 92; Maratha clans in Girvi, 17
Coats, Thomas, 22–3
conflict, 102–4
consensus decision-making, 153–8
co-operative societies, 39–44; *see also under individual institutions*
credit, 59, 73–6, 125–6, 129
cross-cutting ties, 104

Dassara, 87
decision-making, *see under* social organization
descent, 79–92, 165–7
Dewas, Madhya Pradesh, 49–50, 170, 173
Dhangar, 16, 23, 38, 47–8, 51–2, 54–7, 70, 72–5, 118, 121, 142–4, 147–8, 154–5
Dhumalvadi, 15–17, 60, 84–5, 96, 118, 122, 188
domain theory, 10–11, 50–1
dominance, 29, 49–50, 59, 76, 127, 130, 162; in relation to caste, 49–51; levels of, 49

elections, general: **1952**, 109–10, 116; **1957**, 6, 115–16; **1962**, 109–10; **1967**, 101, 108, 111–21, 140, (results in Girvi), 117–18, (results in Phaltan–Khandala), 118–21, 185–7
elections, indirect, 114, 151–3
elections, local, 101, 144, 151; Girvi Multi-Purpose Credit Society (1966), 101, 135–7; Girvi Panchayat (1966), 101, 122–6, 130–5
Elphinstone, Mountstuart, 3, 22, 24–5

faction, 6, 7, 102–7, 191

Gadshi, 16, 38, 68, 70, 73–4

203

General Index

game theory, 10
generative models, 8–11
Girvi, 15–18, 20, 30–1, 54, 57, 60–1, 117–18, 122–38, 140–1, 150, 165–7; caste hierarchy in, 57; distribution of land in, 67–71; distribution of office in, 3–5; lineages in, 86–9; map of, 179; Maratha household composition in, 90–1; marriage networks in, 93–6; political alliances in, 117–18, 121–6, 127–38
Girvi Lift-Irrigation Society, 4, 40, 43, 75–6, 118
Girvi Multi-Purpose Credit Society, 4–5, 40–1, 73–6, 118, 125–6, 131, 135–8
Girvi Panchayat, 4–5, 37–8, 118, 154–5, 160, 167; election (1966), 122–6, 130–5; wards, 5, 37–8, (map of), 179–83
Guntur District, 49, 170, 174–5
Gurav, 22, 52

Holar, 73
household, Maratha, composition of in Girvi, 90–1; partition, 91, 165–7

inam, see under vətən and vətəndar
inheritance, 165–7
interest groups, 7, 150
issues, 116–17

Jadhavvada, 15–17, 31, 84, 86, 96, 122
Jain Gujars, 22, 30, 47–8, 52, 54–6, 73, 121–2, 127, 142–7, 149, 156, 162–3
Jan Sangh, 111

Kaira District, 170, 172
Kammas, 169–70, 174
Karan, 176
Kasar, 47
Khatav Taluka, 2, 18, 20
Khandala Mahal, 2, 20, 41, 108, 112–14, 118–19
kinship: as structural framework, 163, 165–7; categories of, 77–9, 91–2; in relation to political alliances, 102, 105–6, 139–42, 150–1, 159; in relation to political stratification, 77, 97; terminology, 77–8, 165
Koshti, 47, 52, 55–6, 142–4
kul, see under clan
kulkarni, 22–4, 31, 51, 62
Kumbhar, 16, 17, 22, 38, 51–2, 54–6, 68, 70, 74–5, 118, 124
kutumb, see under household

labor, agricultural, 59, 71–3, 76, 116–17, 125; Sugar Factory, 115–16; unions, 45–8, 109, 113, 115, 117
land, categories of, 60–1, 67–71; rights, distribution of in Girvi, 61, 67–71; rights, kinds of, 17–18, 22–5, 61–7, 88, 138, 190–1

Legislative Assembly Constituencies: Phaltan, 45; Phaltan–Khandala, 6, 45, 108–9, (results of 1967 General Election in), 118–21, 185–7; Phaltan–Man, 45, 111–112, 118; Phaltan–Man–Khandala, 45
lineage, 79–92; in relation to office, 23, 31, 86–9, 128; internal structure, 89–91, 133–5; of Marathas in Girvi, 16–18, 80–9, 123–4; proper and attached members, 16, 81–4, 87–9, 123–4, 192; ritual aspects, 86–8; role in Girvi political alliances, 123–4, 128–32
Lohar, 16, 22, 38, 52, 55–6, 69–70, 72, 74–5
Lonand, 21, 41, 42, 108

Mahar, 16, 17, 22, 38, 47, 51–7, 69–75, 111–12, 118, 124–6, 136, 138, 142–6, 149, 178, 188
Maharashtra, 2–3, 5–6, 18–26, 36, 42, 60–7, 116, 188
Maharashtra Apex Marketing Society, 40, 47, 111, 152
Maharashtra Pradesh Congress Committee, 109, 111, 113
Maharashtra State Farm Corporation, 116–17, 120
Mali, 16, 23, 38, 47–8, 51–2, 54–7, 68–70, 73–5, 110, 118, 121, 124–6, 147, 188
Malwa, 171
Man Taluka, 2, 17, 18, 20
Mang, 16, 17, 22, 38, 51–2, 54, 56–7, 70, 72–3
Maratha, 5, 17, 23, 38, 51–7, 142–9, 188; *vətəndar*, 4–5, 16, 38, 46–8, 50, 53, 55, 59, 68–77, 108–15, 117–30, 135, 137–42, 144, 147–9, 154, 157, 162–3, 166, 173–4; non-*vətəndar* (Kunbi), 4–5, 16, 23, 25, 38, 46–8, 50–3, 55, 59, 68–77, 117–18, 121–7, 129, 163, 173–4
marriage(s), geographical distribution of, 93–6; hypergamy, 96–7; in relation to political alliances, 91–2, 122, 135, 138–42; in relation to political stratification, 77, 97, 163; rules of, 92–3
Marvari, 22, 30
mauja, 22, 30, 32
meerasdar, see under land, kinds of rights in
mobilization, horizontal, 169, 174; vertical, 170, 174
mukəddəm, 86–7, 125, 133–5, 167
Muslim, 16, 22–3, 38, 47, 52, 54, 56, 70, 72–5, 118

Nadar, 169
Narayan, Jayaprakash, 6
natevaik, see under kinship, categories of
network, 106–7, 191
Nhavi, 16–17, 22, 38, 51–2, 54–6, 70, 74–5, 118
Nimbalak, 18, 20, 42
Nira Right Bank Canal, 116–17
Nirgudi, 15, 20, 43, 76, 86
Noniya, 173

General Index

office, distribution of: in Girvi, 4–5; in Phaltan Taluka, 46–8
oopree, see under land, kinds of rights in Orissa, 176

panchayati raj, 32–8, 189–90; *see also under individual institutions*
Parit, 16, 22, 38, 52, 70
Patidar, 170, 173
patil, 17–18, 22–5, 31, 53, 62, 86–8, 143–4; Girvi Police, 4, 88–90, 128, 138; Girvi Revenue, 88, 128, 138
patronage, 7, 37, 116, 120, 122, 125–7, 129, 146, 158–9, 162–3, 170
Patrut, 16, 38, 70
Phaltan Cotton Ginning and Pressing Society, 42, 47, 111, 152
Phaltan Education Society, 44–5, 47–8, 109, 119
Phaltan–Lonand Agricultural Produce Market Committee, 41–4, 112
Phaltan Municipality, 38–9, 46–8, 109, 142–6, 149–50, 156–7, 160–1
Phaltan Panchayat Samiti, 37–8, 46–7, 108–10, 113, 119–20, 133, 153–5, 157, 160, 164, 176
Phaltan Taluka, 2, 3, 15, 30, 138–44, 151
Phaltan Taluka Congress Committee, 109, 112
Phaltan Taluka Co-operative Supervising Union, 44, 47, 139
Phaltan Taluka Purchase and Sale Union, 40–1, 47, 109, 113, 139
Phaltan town, 3, 15, 18, 21, 41, 42, 55–6, 115, 119, 125–6
Phaltan Urban Co-operative Bank, 40–1, 47–8, 109, 119, 164
political class, 5, 7–8, 29–30, 46–8, 50, 59, 101, 138–9, 143, 150–1, 156–62, 170–1, 174–8
political elite, 5, 7–8, 29–30, 46–8, 138–9, 156–8
political interests, common, 164–7, 193; mutual, 164–7, 171–2, 193
political strategy, 159–61, 162–4
political stratification, 3–5, 29–30, 46–8, 174–8; and agricultural labor, 73; and alliances, 7–8, 101–2; and caste, 5, 46–8; and credit, 73–5; and kinship, 77, 97; and land, 59, 71; in relation to rural and urban arenas, 46–8
Poona, 2, 19, 21, 30
Pul Eliya, 165–6

quasi-groups, 9, 106–7

Rajputs, 56–7, 170, 172–3
Ramkheri, 166
Ramoshi, 16, 22–3, 38, 47, 52–6, 68–75, 117–18, 124–6, 129, 138, 142–4, 188
Rampur, 165–6
Reddi, 169–70, 174

ritual status, 59, 162–3; as element of political alliances, 51, 58, 121–4, 171–4; derived from principle of hierarchy, 49; in relation to dominance, 49–51

Sakharvadi, 114, 116–17, 120, 140
Sampoorna Maharashtra Samiti, 6, 111, 119
Samyukta Maharashtra Samiti, 6, 116
Satara District, 2, 3, 15, 21–2, 30, 51–2, 65, 110–11, 116, 160
Satara District Central Co-operative Bank, 40, 43, 47, 73–5, 110–11, 140, 152–3, 155
Satara District Congress Committee, 108–9, 110–11
Satara District Land Development Bank, 39–40, 47, 73–5
Satara District Purchase and Sale Union, 40, 47, 152
Satara Zilla Parishad, 38, 46, 47, 109–10, 113, 117, 120, 140, 152–4, 157, 164, 176
Scheduled Castes, 5, 17, 32–4, 38, 51, 122, 124, 130, 178
Shimpi, 16, 38, 47, 52, 54–6, 70, 110, 142–4, 156
Shivaji, 19, 97, 113
Shriram Co-operative Sugar Factory, 4, 41–3, 47, 75–6, 108–9, 111–12, 114–16, 119, 125–6, 139–41, 146–50, 160, 164
Shriram Education Society, 44–5, 47, 109–10, 112, 139, 141, 146, 164
social organization, 8–12, 104–7, 162
Sonar, 16, 22, 38, 52, 55–6, 69, 74
soyre, see under kinship, categories of
structural frameworks, 8–10, 12–14, 59, 101, 162
sutak, 87–8
Sutar, 16–17, 22, 38, 51–2, 54–6, 69–70, 74–5, 188

talathi, 4, 31, 51, 59, 61–2
Teli, 52, 55–6
transaction, 10, 107, 149, 162–4, 172–4
tulkaree, see under land, kinds of rights in

Vani Lingayat, 16, 30, 38, 47, 52, 54–6, 70, 142–4, 156
vatan, 17–18, 22–5, 88, 138, 190–1
vatandar/non-*vatandar* distinction among Marathas, and the political class, 4–5, 25, 46–8, 50, 101; as element of political alliances 123–4, 192; control of land, 62–4, 69; Kunbi caste status, 23, 25, 52–3; lineage structure, 77, 81–4, 88–9; marriage networks, 77, 93–7; traditional administrative system, 17–18, 22–5, 31, 62–4, 88–9
Vithoba, cult of, 19–22, 55

Wadar, 56
women, 32–4, 37–8, 122, 124, 131–5, 144–6, 151

Index of Persons

(Participants in Girvi, Phaltan, and Satara Politics)

Adsul, K. B. (Babanrao) (Mali, Taradgaon), 110–11, 113–14, 120, 141, 147, 193
Ahivale, T. B. (Mahar, Phaltan), 144–5
Anpat, Jayvantrao (vətəndar Maratha, Saswad), 112–13, 120

Bedke, Dattaji (BS of M. B. Bedke), 111, 113, 140, 148
Bedke, M. B. (Maratha, Phaltan), 147–8
Beldar, D. K. (Beldar, Andrud), 139, 148
Bhagat, R. B. (vətəndar Maratha, Pimparad), 108, 115
Bhandvalkar, J. B. (Maratha, Girvi), 124, 132
Bhandvalkar, R. R. (Ramoshi, Phaltan), 144–5
Bhilare, B. D., 110
Bhise, M., (Brahmin, Sakharvadi), 117, 120
Bhoite, J. M. (vətəndar Maratha, Hingangaon), 120
Bhoite, Krishnachandra Raghunathrao (vətəndar Maratha, Aradgaon), 6, 108–14, 117–20, 140–1, 152, 155, 160, 192
Bhoite M. R. (Maratha, Phaltan), 109, 111, 113, 148, 152
Bhosle, M. B. (vətəndar Maratha, Hol-Sakharvadi), 113, 117, 120, 148
Bhosle, S. R. (vətəndar Maratha, Phaltan), 109, 113, 140–1, 143–5, 147–50, 192–3
Bhosle, Sahebrao (vətəndar Maratha, Hol-Sakharvadi), 147
Bodre, S. D. (Ramoshi, Girvi), 124, 132
Borawake, K. K. (Mali, Phaltan), 147–9

Chamche, Mrs A. (Brahmin, Phaltan), 144–6
Chavan, Y. B., 109–14, 119, 140–1, 146, 151, 155, 160
Choramle, M. B. (Dhangar, Phaltan), 144–5

Date, M. G. (Brahmin, Phaltan), 109, 113, 144–5, 147–9, 160, 192
Desai, D. S. (Balasaheb), 110–11, 113, 155
Desai, Morarji, 110, 160
Dhembre, M. A. (Maratha, Girvi), 124–5
Dhumal, B. S. (Maratha, Girvi), 124, 132
Dhumal, Bhuvasaheb (vətəndar Maratha, Adarki Bk.), 113
Dhumal, M. T. (Maratha, Girvi), 124, 132
Doshi, D. R. (Jain Gujar, Phaltan), 139
Doshi, M. N. (Jain Gujar, Phaltan), 147

Gandhi, Indira, 110
Gaund, D. V. (vətəndar Dhangar, Gunavare), 147
Gawade, R. M. (vətəndar Dhangar, Gokhali), 147–8
Ghorpode, Baburao, 110

Hendre, N. S. (Shimpi, Phaltan), 144–5, 156

Jadhav, Namdev (Maratha, Phaltan), 112–13, 120, 139–41, 148–9, 192
Jadhav, S. G. (Mali, Girvi), 124, 131
Janavale, Vasantrao (Dhungur, Girvi), 154–5, 192

Kadam, Amrutrao Bapusaheb (Genealogy 1a, K25), 131, 136–7, 190, 192
Kadam, Babanrao Ganpatrao (Genealogy 1a, J17), 124, 128, 131–2
Kadam, Baburao Sitaram (Genealogy 2f, 112), 124, 128, 131–2, 137
Kadam, Balvantrao Kedari (Genealogy 2a, I11), 124, 131–2
Kadam, Bhagvantrao Gulabrao (Genealogy 1a, M6), 88, 128–9
Kadam, Bhujangrao Govindrao (Genealogy 1a, L20), 124, 131, 133
Kadam, Dattaji Govindrao (Genealogy 1a, L21), 136–7
Kadam, Dattatrya Dhondiram (Genealogy 2d, 18), 124, 131–5, 141, 160, 192
Kadam, Devrao Appasaheb (Genealogy 1a, L30), 125, 136–7, 192
Kadam, Eknath Sahebrao (Genealogy 2c, I11), 88
Kadam, Ganpatrao Eknath (Genealogy 2c, J4), 128, 131, 136
Kadam, Govindrao Madhavrao (Genealogy 1a, K13), 73, 136, 190
Kadam, H. J. (vətəndar Maratha, Kalaj), 119–20
Kadam, Hanmantrao Dolatrao (Genealogy 2a, I4), 124, 131–2
Kadam, Kashaba Anandrao (Genealogy 1d, E1), 136–7
Kadam, Keshavrao Appasaheb (Genealogy 1a, L25), 125–6, 140–1, 160, 192
Kadam, Khanderao Bajirao (Genealogy 2f, I13), 136
Kadam, Lakshman Maruti (Genealogy 2a, H3), 136

Index of Persons

Kadam, Mugatrao Appasaheb (Genealogy 1a, L29), 124–5, 131–5, 192
Kadam, Rajaram Baburao (Genealogy 1b, E5), 128, 136–7, 160
Kadam, Ramchandra Madhavrao (Genealogy 2b, J1), 136
Kadam, Ramkrishna Gulabrao (Genealogy 1a, M7), 72
Kadam, Ramrao Bapusaheb (Genealogy 1a, K27), 73, 124, 128, 131–3, 137, 190
Kadam, Sarjerao Sahebrao (Genealogy 2d, J10), 72, 128, 136–7
Kadam, Shamrao Govindrao (Genealogy 1a, L19), 136
Kadam, Shankar Appasaheb (Genealogy 2a, H1), 89, 124, 128, 131–2
Kadam, Sulochana Ganpatrao (Genealogy 2c, J4), 124, 131–2
Kadam, Suryajirao (Chimanrao) (Genealogy 1a, M4), 131, 133, 135, 140–1, 159–60, 192
Kadam, Vijaymala M. (Genealogy 1a, M2), 124, 131–5, 160, 192
Kadam, Vitthalrao Yeshvantrao (Genealogy 1a, L15), 72
Khalate, M. R. (*vətəndar* Maratha, Khunte), 113
Kumbhar, R. M. (Kumbhar, Girvi), 124, 132–3

Mahagaonkar, Dr V. V. (Brahmin, Phaltan), 144–6
Mandre, N. S. (Maratha, Phaltan), 144–5
Mane, G. B. (Buddhist Mahar, Phaltan), 111–12, 118, 142–6, 148, 156, 160, 192
Mane, Sahebrao (*vətəndar* Maratha, Asu), 139, 141, 148, 150
More, B. R. (*vətəndar* Maratha, Phaltan), 109, 140–1, 144–6, 148–9, 156, 161, 192

Naik, V. P., 113
Naik Nimbalkar, B. S. (*vətəndar* Maratha, Vathar), 139
Naik Nimbalkar, Bapusaheb Malojirao (S of Malojirao Naik Nimbalkar), 148
Naik Nimbalkar, Bhausaheb, 148–50
Naik Nimbalkar, Malojirao M. (Raja of Phaltan), 6, 18, 44, 61, 108–17, 125–6, 139–52, 156–7, 160, 163–4, 190, 192
Naik Nimbalkar, V. R. (*vətəndar* Maratha, Nimbalak), 139, 148–50

Naik Nimbalkar, Vijaysingh Malojirao (S of Malojirao Naik Nimbalkar), 6, 61, 111, 114–20, 139, 147–8, 190, 192
Nalavade, B. B. (*vətəndar* Maratha, Aljapur), 113, 120
Nikalje, B. R. (Mahar, Girvi), 124, 132
Nikalje, Sarjerao Shankarrao (Mahar, Girvi), 136–7
Nimbalkar, Bapusaheb (*vətəndar* Maratha, Nimbalak), 147–9
Nimbalkar, Haribhau (Maratha, Phaltan), 6, 113, 117, 120, 192
Nimbalkar, N. B. (Maratha, Phaltan), 144
Nimbkar, B. V. (Brahmin, Phaltan), 144–6

Parkale, Sakharam G. (*vətəndar* Maratha, Asu), 147–8
Parlekar, Yeshvantrao, 110
Patil, R. D., 110–11, 155
Patil, Vinaikrao, 113
Pawar, D. G. (*vətəndar* Maratha, Asu), 140–1, 147–50
Pawar, M. S. (Maratha, Phaltan), 144–6
Phadtare, D. A. (Maratha, Girvi), 124
Phadtare, R. N. (*vətəndar* Maratha, Hol-Sakharvadi), 113, 117, 120
Phanse, K. V. (Vani Lingayat, Phaltan), 144–5, 156–7

Rajvaidya, Dr P. J. (Jain Gujar, Phaltan), 144–5
Ranavare, Kondiram J. (*vətəndar* Maratha, Jinti), 147
Ranavare, Vishvasrao (*vətəndar* Maratha, Jinti), 139–40, 147–8, 150
Ranavare, Yeshvantrao (*vətəndar* Maratha, Jinti), 148–9

Saste, N. M. (*vətəndar* Maratha, Nirgudi), 111, 113
Shah, R. T. (Jain Gujar, Phaltan), 147
Shah, Mrs S. S. (Jain Gujar, Phaltan), 144–6
Shinde, T. R. (*vətəndar* Maratha, Shindevadi), 112, 120, 147–8
Sonavane, Dr Prabavathi, 118

Unavane, V. P. (Koshti, Phaltan), 144–5

Veer, Kisan, 110–11, 155, 160

207